"Organ Donation is simply the greate~ ~ift one human
bestow on another. The compilation of s ~
Organ Donation compiled by Brenda ~
and spirit of humanity on full display. T ~ ~ ~ ~ ~
the organ donors and their families cou~~~u with the immense
gratitude of the recipients proves to be a powerful read.
If you are looking to be inspired…look no further."

Simon Keith
Author, *Heart For the Game*
2x heart recipient, 1 x kidney recipient
First heart transplant recipient to play a professional sport
www.simonkeith.com

"Mom was a librarian so I know children's books and can relate to
Brenda's blend of soothing edutainment for kids to read and understand.
Because of Organ Donation is another success for its collaborative
collective storytelling that is amazingly innovative and awe inspiring."

Joe Lafferty
Author, *Justin Time: A Memoir of Faith and the Fight For Life*
Speaker, Organ Donation Advocate, Kidney and Pancreas Recipient

"Organ donation is the space where grief and gratefulness intersect. The
generous heroes and their families who say "yes" to donation give hope
to thousands like those in this book. You will be inspired by the lives and
stories impacted by donation that Brenda put together here."

Patti Niles
President/CEO, Southwest Transplant Alliance

"The collective voices of the heroes and heroines of the transplant
community are the lynchpin of the organ donation movement.
Whether recipients or donors and donor families, these stories reflect
the best of the human spirit—generosity, unconditional love, and
a deep respect and appreciation for life. Brenda Cortez and her fellow
writers skillfully use the power of storytelling to change hearts
and minds to save lives through organ donation."

Isabel Stenzel Byrnes
Author, Public Speaker, Social Worker

Because of Organ Donation
A Collection of Inspiring Stories Celebrating the Gift of Life

Foreword: Bill Ryan
Contributing Editor: Brenda E. Cortez
Contributing Editor/Proofreader: Lyda Rose Haerle
Associate Editors: Griffin Mill, Jean Sime
Contributing Authors: Brenda E. Cortez, Joey Gase, Jean Sime, Melissa McQueen, Jen Benson, Dawn Lyons-Wood, Kate Griggs, George Franklin, Brandi Thornton, Ellen Tuech, Lisa Barker, Hailey Steimel, Maria Teresa "Terri" Pilawa, Jill Dillon, Sara Solinsky, Jessica Wickersheimer, Deb Kavanaugh, ShirLey Scott Brill, Paul Osterholm, James Myers, Tonya Gomez, Michelle Schuerman, Richard Hanusa, Sarah Weaver, Tony Schmalstig, Victoria Schmalstig, Trisha Phillips, Shannon Andreas.

Cover Design: Dindo Contento
Interior Layout: Michael Nicloy
Front Cover Photo: Paul Osterholm
All images have been provided by the individual contributors.

ISBN: 978-0999360194

Published by Nico 11 Publishing & Design, Mukwonago, WI
Quantity order requests may be emailed to the Publisher:
mike@nico11publishing.com
or may be made by phone: 217-779-9677

Because of Organ Donation
A Collection of Inspiring Stories
Celebrating the Gift of Life

ISBN: 978-0999360194

NICO 11 PUBLISHING & DESIGN
MUKWONAGO, WISCONSIN
www.nico11publishing.com

Be well read.

Printed in the United States of America

I dedicate this book to everyone affected by organ donation. To all the donors and their families who said "Yes" to donation. To my fellow living donors who felt the calling to help another person in need. To all the transplant recipients who wait patiently; some fighting tirelessly to be saved.

To all the medical professionals and caregivers who make organ donation and transplantation what it is today. Without the donor and the medical professionals, there would be no hope and no second chance at life.

To my fellow chapter authors who believed in my vision for this book and were brave enough to share their story to help and inspire others. To our wonderful publisher, Mike, who always believes in my ideas and helps bring them to life. I am thankful to your living kidney donor for giving you a life free of dialysis.

To my best friend Jean, I am so blessed our paths crossed because of organ donation. You make each day brighter with your love and kindness. Thank you for helping make my dreams come true.

To my Dad, my Angel in Heaven, who left us unexpectedly during the writing of this book. I miss you so much and will hold you forever in my heart. I feel you with me every day and I know you are guiding me from the other side.

"Be an Organ Donor and Help Others With Love"

Brenda E. Cortez

Table of Contents

Introduction

Every Ten Minutes Someone
Is Added to the Transplant List

Has your life been affected by organ donation or the lack of available lifesaving organs? Were you, or someone else, one of the 39,000 people in the United States who received an organ transplant in 2020? Or maybe you or your loved one is one of the 110,000 men, women, and children on the transplant waiting list. Did you know the majority of people listed are waiting for a kidney; or that almost 20 people die each day in the U.S. waiting for the gift of life?

These numbers are staggering, especially if you think about it visually. Close your eyes and picture your favorite football or baseball stadium with every seat full; so many people, but yet there wouldn't be enough seats for each person on the transplant list. In fact, depending on the stadium, you may even need two stadiums in order to have a seat for every person who is waiting for an organ to save their life.

An opportunity was presented to me to give that ultimate gift 16 years ago, before I even knew how great the need for organ donation really was. I heard that an acquaintance, another mom at my children's school who was also a member of our church, was searching for a living kidney donor. (The wait for a kidney from a deceased donor can be years, so finding a living donor can not only help you receive your transplant sooner, it also frees up a spot on the transplant list.) Intrigued about this type of donation I had never heard of, I asked her for more information. I was already a registered donor on my driver's license, and would gladly share any organ at the time of my passing, but to give one away while still alive was never a thought that crossed my mind. *I could save someone's life and still live a normal, healthy life? Alright, let's do this!*

As you'll read in this book, I was a match for that mom and I donated my kidney. I saved another person's life, and so have many others! Some of us are living, while others are no longer physically here, but are living on in others. In this book, you will also read about recipients who have been given a second chance at life because of organ donation.

I've invited 24 others to share their stories with you. These include donor families, recipients of donated organs, and living donors. While each story is inspiring and unique, and paints a picture of the need for more organ donors, I believe collecting all of these stories in one book has the power and magic to move mountains; the power to put you into their shoes and to feel the calling, the hope, or the desire to help others. Be prepared to shed a few tears as you feel a tug at your heart while reading this book.

Will you or your loved one be the next one added to the transplant list? Do you have what it takes to make a difference in someone's life, even if yours has been turned upside down? Organ donation can do all of these things. Because of organ donation, countless lives have been saved. Because of organ donation I have found my true purpose in life. Because of organ donation this book exists.

-Brenda E. Cortez

Foreword

By Bill Ryan

In the 21st century, we live in a world where superheroes are revered by young and old. We expect our heroes to have superpowers and be able to save lives and make the universe a better place because of their existence. Of course, we recognize these superheroes by their outfits, but are we aware of the heroes that dress just like you and me, and walk among us quietly in an everyday fashion?

It is likely that each of us has met someone who meets the requirement of a superhero. Saving lives and making the universe a better place is an occurrence that happens every day, in every city and state, across the country.

Brenda Cortez is one of these superheroes and her book, *Because of Organ Donation*, has done an incredible job of shining a light on the incredible medical miracle of transplantation. Over 35,000 lives are dramatically changed every year in the United States because as humans we have made the decision to share our organs and those of our loved ones in order to give the gift of life. Brenda shares her own personal journal with living donation and has brought together 24 other individuals whose stories elevate the beautiful, unselfish nature of the human spirit.

I have had the pleasure of working with and celebrating thousands of heroes in my role leading the Transplant Life Foundation, which many associate with our biennial Transplant Games of America. Each chapter of this book is authored by a superhero who brings the reader into their life and provides them with a deeper understanding of the world of donation and transplantation. While I know many of the contributing authors personally, I know most of them for their continuous efforts to bring awareness to the mission of reducing the number of individuals on the waiting list for an organ. Yes, there is a chronic shortage of organs with over [110,000] patients waiting for a transplant. On average, almost [20] people die each day because an organ was not available. In addition, there are hundreds of thousands of individuals undergoing dialysis who are waiting for a transplant or will eventually need one. These authors, through their stories, will ultimately save lives as their words create awareness among readers like yourself and ultimately encourage others to join the legion of superheroes.

Brenda herself is certainly no stranger to the cause. She tells her living donation story in this new book, but her series of books about "Howl the Owl", and her work in the community to promote donation and transplantation, put her in a very special category of people who have become someone's superhero.

My history with donation and transplantation began 35 years ago with the tragic loss of my daughter Michelle in an automobile accident. It was her decision to be an organ donor that started me on a path of promoting organ, eye, and tissue donation. With the support of family, Michelle's gifts directly benefited four patients, and her legacy led to hundreds of others to follow her lead in joining the donor registry. She is my personal superhero, and her memory and sacrifice motivate me every single day.

I hope this book will motivate you in many ways, and that these stories will encourage you to join the cause. While you may not be ready to donate a kidney to someone in need just yet, you will likely feel comfortable encouraging others to explore donation, either as a living donor, or at the very least, by joining the millions of others on the national and state donor registries. Anyone can be a superhero and save a life.

Bill Ryan

Bill Ryan is President & CEO of Transplant Life Foundation, the nation's leading advocacy nonprofit for the donation and transplant community. Transplant Life Foundation's two main initiatives, Transplant Games of America and TransplantNation magazine, help save lives while actively working to increase the number of individuals on the national and state donor registries.

Brenda E. Cortez

A Purpose Becomes a Passion

A CALLING

I was 33 years old and married with two children when an opportunity presented itself to me in 2005—an opportunity to save another mom's life. My heart-strings are easily tugged at, so when this mom told me how she was searching for a kidney, I knew I wanted to help. I immediately asked her what I needed to do to be a kidney donor, while in my mind I put myself in her shoes.

Blood type was the first requirement to be considered when donating a kidney at the time, and I was the blood type match she needed. I am O- blood type and she is O+, so she needed someone with O blood. I later learned that an O blood type person can only receive from an O blood type donor. This can make it more challenging to find a donor, since you can only receive from one blood type. The other blood types can receive from their blood type or O; this means O is the universal blood type of organ donation.

I offered to get tested, but it was at that moment a peaceful feeling came over me, and I knew I would be a match for this mom. Our daughters were in fifth grade together while our sons shared second grade. We were both moms who volunteered a lot at school, and we chatted occasionally, but other than that we didn't really know each other very well.

A couple months later, after several blood tests, it was confirmed I was indeed a match. My physical and mental health were both examined over the next two months in addition to another 12 vials of blood drawn, and then a surgery date was finally scheduled. "My purpose" was about to happen, although I didn't know it just then. I already thought I was living my purpose as a mother and a wife; little did I know the direction my life would take. I was truly doing for someone what I hoped someone would do for me if I was in need.

My kidney donation surgery took place Wednesday, March 23, 2005, and it was a successful transplant. My left kidney had a new home, and it functioned as it should. I was up walking a bit the next day, but still in pain. My family visited me at the hospital every day and offered their unconditional support. I was released four days later.

For the next six years, I spoke about organ donation and my decision to become a living kidney donor when presented with the opportunity. For many years, however, I didn't know anyone else who had donated an organ to save another life. Today there are Facebook and online support groups for those considering donating, those who have donated, and for recipients. None of this existed when I donated. My hospital did not even have a mentorship program in place. I don't really know why I felt different and isolated, but looking back I think I was bursting at the seams wanting to share my story to help others. The right opportunity just hadn't presented itself yet.

AN INSPIRATION

It turned out my daughter gave me the inspiration I had unknowingly been looking for. Six years after I donated my kidney, my daughter, Kailey, wrote an essay about my kidney donation for acceptance into college. She wrote how scary it was to see her mom in the hospital . . . she was 11 years old. She said I had inspired her to want to be a better person, to help others, and to pursue a career in the medical field. When I read the essay, I immediately knew what I needed to do. I would write about my kidney donation to help other kids understand what surgery and kidney donation is all about. I envisioned transplant centers using the book as a helpful tool and giving it to living donor families with younger kids. It took a few years for my children's book, *My Mom is Having Surgery—A Kidney Story,* to get published, but it was exciting, and I had a lot of support from family and friends. The transplant center where my surgery took place has purchased several books to give to future living donor families in addition to some other hospitals.

I decided partial proceeds from my new book would benefit Donate Life America, an organization supporting organ donation awareness. It was the perfect group for me to align with. Donate Life is a slogan and logo used and recognized in the transplant community. There are many groups and foundations dedicated to raising awareness for organ donation, but Donate Life America is all-encompassing, including all organs and tissue.

Did you know one person can save up to eight lives through organ donation, restore sight for two people with cornea donation, and heal the lives of 75 people with tissue donation?

Even with advances in medicine, the need for organ donors still greatly exceeds the actual number of donors. A kidney is by far the most needed organ, so thankfully a kidney can come from either a living or deceased donor, but realistically we need more donors. Hopefully, my story and the others in this book will inspire you to consider donation.

AN ACRONYM

People suggested I reach out to children's hospitals about using my first book, but I really didn't feel it was the right choice for kids in the hospital. I decided I should write something for a child who is going through a transplant, but I wanted a cute character a child could relate to. Around that time, the acronym YOLO (You Only Live Once) was all the rage, and while it's a good saying, it wasn't a call to action. I wanted a saying that would inspire people to be kind and help others. HOWL . . . *Help Others With Love*™ popped into my head. It was the perfect acronym! I kept thinking about that phrase and what I could do with it, when one day it just came to me. HOWL rhymes with owl and I love owls! My character should be Howl the Owl®! I researched a stuffed animal version of an owl and decided what he would look like. Who wouldn't want a snuggle buddy to cuddle with while reading a book, especially an adorable owl? Eventually, I found the perfect plush owl but wondered how would people know his name and the special meaning? The solution was perfect. Plush Howl the Owl® would wear a shirt bearing his name, *HOWL*™, and the words *Help Others With Love*™!

Now that I had my adorable character for kids to love and relate to, it was time to write a book to help children understand organ donation if they were going through it. I knew I would need more than just one book to accomplish my goal since there are so many facets around organ donation and transplantation; it can be a "heavy" topic for children to comprehend. *Howl the Owl*®, *the Organ Donation Series* seemed appropriate, and the first book would help those kids who were in the hospital waiting for a transplant or who had already had one. Since I had already written a book about kidney transplant, I wanted to choose a different organ. I thought back to a story a friend shared about her nephew and his heart transplant.

Around this time, some stories were circulating on social media about donor families meeting the heart recipient their loved one donated to, and they were able to listen to the heart beating inside that recipient. How amazing! I chose a heart transplant for Howl the Owl® and wanted to portray this profound, life-saving miracle for children and their families by incorporating a lifelike feeling of what really happens when a child is sick and waiting for a heart. I also wanted to show the excitement, yet nervousness, of receiving that new organ and getting back to a normal life, but still needing to take medication for life. I also incorporated that amazing moment the donor family meets the person their loved one saved; listening to the heart beating inside the recipient. I wrote the first draft of *Howl Gets a Heart* in an hour while I sat in a Wendy's restaurant eating a salad for lunch. The story just flowed onto paper, and it felt right. Even though I hadn't personally met a child who needed or had received a heart, I really felt the pain and urgency of needing that miracle and then the excitement of receiving it. My heart was filled, hoping this book would serve its purpose and *Help Others With Love*™. I wanted it to bring comfort and healing to those in need and also raise great awareness for organ donation. The book came to life with amazing illustrations of an adorable owl on his journey to receive a new heart that would save his life!

A TRAGEDY

While the heart book was in the illustration process, my next story in the series unraveled. I knew I wanted to write something to help children understand when a loved one who is an organ donor passes away. This would be a book with a very specific purpose to help children and their families in a time of grief and hopefully bring comfort, but I just didn't have the storyline quite figured out yet.

Let me circle back a couple months to June 2016; I attended my first ever Transplant Games of America in Cleveland, Ohio, as a Team Wisconsin supporter. I met many wonderful people at this spectacular gathering of transplant recipients, living donors, and donor families who met to compete in fun games, show their resilience and appreciation for a second chance at life, and honor those who gave that amazing gift.

One family, however, stood out to me—Jessica and her husband, Chris, and their little girl, Bella. They had recently moved to Wisconsin after the death of Jessica's mom, who was a donor. They were at the games in honor of her memory. We had a connection because they lived near our weekend cabin, and I really adored little Bella. Two months after the games, an email went out to Team Wisconsin that Chris had unexpectedly passed away, and he was a donor. My heart sank as I felt so much empathy for Bella and Jessica. She had just lost her mom six months ago, and now her husband. Poor Bella was only five and now without her daddy and grandma.

What could I do to help them? This could be the storyline I wanted to write about to help children when they lose a loved one. I didn't know any details of what happened to Chris other than he passed away at work. I didn't want to reach out to Jessica because her pain was too fresh, and I didn't feel it was appropriate to talk about a book. Instead, I went with what was in my head and wrote the first draft of *Howl Helps Bella*. I needed to address the sadness of losing a loved one, but redirect that sadness toward the joy of their loved one saving lives like a superhero while living on in others. I wanted to honor Chris, and all the superheroes and their families who truly *Help Others With Love*™ with the greatest gift of all.

After a few months, I finally reached out to Jessica to let her know I had written this story, but I could easily change it if she wasn't comfortable. I was grateful when she shared how honored she was to have a book like this written in Chris' memory, and what a wonderful gift it would be for Bella and other kids. I met with Jessica and Bella a couple months later to show her the story and make any adjustments according to what really happened.

Howl Helps Bella was published in November 2017 and has brought healing comfort for Jessica, Bella, and many more families alike who are donor families. It honored me when I was invited to have a booth and sell my books at the Transplant Games in August 2018 in Salt Lake City. Jessica and Bella were in the booth with me, and Bella was so proud to have a book about herself and Daddy! Bella even signed the books people bought like a true star. I am happy to say this book is serving its purpose and being used by some Organ Procurement Organizations (OPO's) in their aftercare program. The positive feedback from people at the Transplant Games was amazing. Many commented they wished these books would have existed years ago. My heart was full of joy knowing my passion for helping others and writing about organ donation was serving its purpose.

A PURPOSE

I realized my kidney donation was not just meant to save one life, but to lead me to this greater purpose of spreading awareness about organ donation, which means more lives saved. My purpose as a kidney donor has led to a passion for writing, helping others, and inspiring those to do the same. I'm also addressing difficult topics for children and families in a way they can relate to and understand.

My fourth book, titled, *Howl Helps Others*, focuses on kindness and helping others, while touching on transplants, autism, and bullying. This book reaches younger children and is great for preschool to third grade. The third book in the organ donation series (my fifth book) is titled, *Howl Learns about Kidneys and Dialysis*. This book circles back to kidney donation, but a bit differently. It teaches children about dialysis, and what it means to search and wait for a life-saving kidney. It addresses real-life scenarios using social media and vehicle advertising to find a donor match.

The *Howl the Owl*® book series currently has eight books. At the request of some children's hospitals, I wrote a liver book, *Howl Loves His New Liver*, which is similar to the heart book, and as requested, I am working on a kidney version. I partnered with a NASCAR® driver, Joey Gase, on a book titled *Howl Goes to the Races*. As the title suggests, it's about racing but also connects to organ donation. In the story, Howl was invited to the races for Organ Donation Awareness Day by race car driver, Joey Gase. Joey is a big supporter of organ donation since his mom was a donor and saved other lives. It thrilled Howl to be at the racetrack and learn the ins and outs of racing! Joey has done amazing work honoring his mother and using his race car as a platform to raise awareness for organ donation.

I collaborated with Edward Drake, also known as Mr. YNOTT, on an inspiring story based on his experience with kidney disease. Because of his illness he could not follow his dream of playing college football, but he ultimately found his purpose in life. This book is titled *Howl Inspires Mr. YNOTT*. I have also collaborated with the Transplant Games of America, now known as Transplant Life Foundation, on the book *Howl Competes at the Transplant Games*. In this book Howl meets up with his friends Blaze and Spark (they are the mascots for the transplant games) at the games, and they have a blast taking in all the excitement that the transplant games offer!

Because of organ donation, I am truly blessed to have found my purpose in life. I have received so much more than I gave! It has led me to a wonderful career as a children's book writer, advocate for organ donation, and now lead author in this book. I have met so many wonderful people on this journey including Mike Nicloy, the publisher of my *Howl the Owl®* books. Mike is a kidney recipient from a living donor, and I believe it is by no coincidence our paths have crossed. I have an awesome team of advocates supporting Howl and helping spread his message. I call these people my Howl Ambassadors and I also call them my friends!

With the help of living kidney donor, Kate Griggs, and many others, plush *Howl the Owl®* has traveled the world promoting kindness and organ donation awareness. We have documented his travels on the Facebook page, *Howl the Owl on the Prowl*. I also created a Facebook group called "Howl's Heroes" and this group page shared inspiring stories of everyday heroes. Once the COVID-19 pandemic hit, Howl's Heroes evolved, and we started honoring essential worker heroes. My friend Jean Sime lost her sister Vivian to the virus. Vivian was an essential worker at a hospital, so Jean had the idea to honor these people who were putting their lives on the line to help others with love. We decided each "Howl Hero" would receive a plush Howl the Owl and a certificate of recognition. The Howl Ambassadors joined our effort, bought a bunch of plush Howls, and nominated people they knew were essential workers. After that, we started a fundraiser to buy more plush Howl's and certificates, and we took nominations. Since April 2020, we have honored over 100 heroes! Please visit the Howl's Heroes page and check out all the wonderful heroes and their stories.

I honestly would have never imaged that donating a kidney would lead to all this. Because of organ donation, I am a better person. I am surrounded by like-minded people who share in my passion for helping others. I have found a best friend who has been the wind beneath my wings, supporting me every step of the way. In addition to my blessings, I've been able to educate others about organ donation and promote kindness with school presentations and community-based events. I am also blessed to be a living kidney donor mentor at the hospital where I donated.

In case you are wondering, my kidney recipient is doing well and "our" kidney is functioning as if it were her own native kidney. Life had a calling for me, and I am grateful I listened and followed the path that was set before me. It's been a gift to find my purpose and continue to help others with my written words. I hope the words of HOWL inspire you to be a better person, and I hope this book inspires you to appreciate life and second chances. If so, please register as an organ donor and consider living donation. Visit RegisterMe.org or DonateLife.net.

Be like Howl, be kind, be good. Rise above and Help Others With Love!

About Brenda

Brenda is a living kidney donor and author with a passion for helping others. She was inspired to write her first book after her daughter entered her college entrance essay about Brenda's kidney donation and the inspiration she felt from it. Brenda is now a powerful advocate for organ donation awareness.

Brenda and her husband Shawn, along with their dogs, live in Franklin, Wisconsin. They have two grown children, Kailey and Kyle. They enjoy spending time at their cabin near Wisconsin Dells, boating, and visiting the sunshine state as often as they can.

Besides writing, Brenda enjoys coaching new authors. For more information about Brenda and Howl the Owl®, please visit www.howltheowl.com. You can follow Howl on Facebook at the Howl the Owl page and Howl the Owl on the Prowl. Howl can also be found on Twitter and Instagram. Connect with Brenda E. Cortez on Facebook and LinkedIn, or you can email her at Brenda@howtheowl.com

BC BOOKS, LLC

Brenda and Joey Gase at a Hand Prints of Hope event before a NASCAR race.

Howl encouraging organ donation.

Brenda with Kate Griggs meeting new friends Pat Milford, Jean Sime and Trish Phillips the night before the organ donation awareness cruise.

Brenda and Kate Griggs spreading awareness in the Bahamas.

Mascot Howl with Honey Bee, the mascot for Donate Life Ohio preparing for the Mascot Dash.

Brenda with Mike Nicloy and Mary Markham at a book party.

Brenda and Mascot Howl spreading awareness and sharing Howl's message at a trunk-or-treat event.

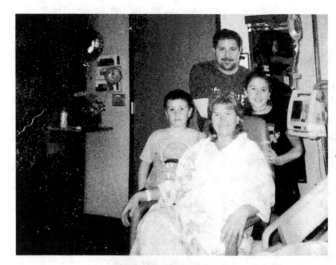

Brenda and her family a couple days after her kidney donation.

Brenda visiting her kidney recipient while in the hospital.

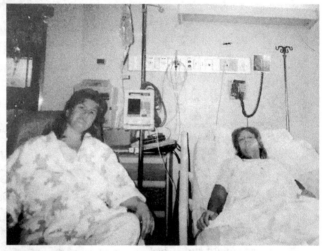

Brenda with Lance Allen after their interview for TMJ4 in Milwaukee.

Joey Gase

Hand Prints of Hope

In April 2011, I was 18 and thinking about senior prom, racing, and trying to figure out life. The last thing on my mind was losing my mom. One night in April, I was hanging with friends at my mom's house and getting ready to ask a girl to prom. Before we left the house, my mom complained about a small headache and asked if I could set up the PS3 so she could watch some movies that night. I set it up and told her I was leaving. As I headed out the door I told my mom I loved her. Little did I know that was the last time I would see her alive and well.

My friends and I left and headed for my potential prom date's house. When we arrived, I met her with flowers and asked her the question. Luckily she said yes! After this, my friends and I did what we normally did on a weekend night, which was drive around Cedar Rapids to bonfires and different friends' houses. When the night was coming to a close, I called my mom to see if I could have some friends spend the night, but there was no answer. I kept calling and calling, but still no answer. So, I called my mom's boyfriend Keith to see if he had heard from her. He said no. After a while, I started my way home, and on the drive home, Keith called. He sounded in a panic and told me not to bring any friends over. I felt this was kind of strange, but thought maybe they were just arguing or something. When I pulled into the driveway and opened the garage door, I heard Keith yelling in a panic. I walked into the living room, and the PlayStation and TV were on with a movie still playing. I looked down on the couch and saw the PlayStation remote and phone with vomit all over them. The phone was off the hook with the dial tone still going. I then looked in the bedroom, where I saw my mom on the floor and Keith on the phone with 911. She wasn't able to talk but continued to make very strange moaning sounds that I had never heard before.

A few years earlier, my mom suffered from stomach ulcers, and when the ulcers acted up she would vomit and was very weak. It took her doctors a long time to determine she had stomach ulcers. She went back to the doctor one time, and her blood pressure was dangerously low. This was due to her stomach bleeding so much internally, and she desperately needed blood. This was my first thought on what could be happening with my mom.

Keith told me to go open the front door and turn on all the lights at the front of the house, so when the first responders arrived they would know where to go. The police were the first ones to arrive, followed by the fire department and then the ambulance. They worked on her in the house for a few minutes and then transferred her to the ambulance where it felt like they sat for hours. The police asked us some questions and then asked where she kept her medication. After reviewing her medications, they didn't see anything that could have caused what was happening. They asked me to bring all the medication bottles to the hospital with us so the doctors would know everything she was taking. Eventually the ambulance left, and we followed it to the hospital. To make matters worse, the neighborhood we lived in was still building new houses, so there was a lot of road work. The first route the ambulance took went down to a dead end because of the road construction. When we finally arrived at the hospital, they had us wait in the hallway. My uncle was an emergency room doctor at the hospital, but he was not working this night. Another uncle was a police officer and rushed to the hospital. After stabilizing my mom with a breathing tube, which involved taking an X-ray to be sure the breathing tube was in the correct spot, the doctor came out and told us what he thought. He believed it was something cranial, meaning her head and brain, and they were going to transfer her to the University of Iowa Hospital, which was about 30 minutes away. Before they transferred her, they let me see her and hold her hand. The nurses were very nice, almost too nice, and told me I could say whatever I wanted to. This scared me more because I could tell how worried they were, and they wanted to make sure I could spend some time with her. After this, I rushed to pick up my sister Ashley, who was staying at a friend's house. Ashley is my younger sister and was in eighth grade. Of course, when I picked her up in the middle of the night, she was confused and scared.

When we arrived at the University of Iowa Hospital, the neurologist told us the brain scans revealed she suffered a sudden brain aneurysm, and it looked to be very severe. They asked me if they could take her to surgery to determine how much pressure was put on her brain and to ease the pressure. Since I just recently turned 18, and my mom and dad were divorced, I learned that I was her next of kin. Because of this, I was legally the one who had to sign all the paperwork for her surgery. I remember signing the papers and trying to keep my tears from ruining the paper. I also remember the neurologist examining my mom, and he kept calling out, "Mary, Mary, can you here me?" I wished more than anything she would respond and grab the breathing tube out. I was hopeful for a second because, as he was examining her, she would raise her feet and wiggle her toes. My uncle, who is the ER doctor, arrived and informed me that this, unfortunately, was only her reflexes and had little to do with brain activity.

While she was in surgery, they moved us up to the ICU waiting room and showed us where her room would be once the surgery was done. After what felt like many hours, the nurses asked our family to gather so the doctor could talk with us. My mom's side of the family is very big, so there were many of us anxiously waiting. When the doctor arrived, he shared the worst news anyone can ever be told. He informed us that the pressure on her brain, from the aneurysm, was way too much. Even though it looked like she was just sleeping, she was brain dead and would not recover. Shortly after, he asked if she would want to be an organ donor. This is by far the last thing anyone ever wanted to hear from a doctor. You always hope the doctor is going to tell you it's going to be okay, or give you some kind of hope. Thinking about organ donation was truly the hardest thing at that moment, especially when it looked like she was just in a deep sleep.

Two things made that moment a little easier. First, my uncle, the ER doctor, explained things to our family so we could comprehend what was really happening. And the second thing was that we knew, if she could no longer continue her life, she would want to do whatever she could to help others continue theirs. It would have been much easier if we would have had her driver's license with us, and also if we would have had a talk with my mom of her wishes if anything were to ever happen. Before this time, I had never really put much thought into organ donation, and I actually had to take out my own driver's license to see if I had designated that I would be an organ donor. I had a "yes" on my license, and when we eventually went home and found her license, she also had it marked that she was a registered organ donor. When we saw that, it made all the difference in the world knowing we made the right decision for what she had wanted.

The next step in the organ donation process was talking with Iowa Donor Network and the recovery team. There was a huge list of questions we had to answer in order for the potential recipients to have a successful transplant. The Iowa Donor Network team was very kind, but in my opinion this was the hardest part of the donation process because it is very long, and some questions they had to ask were very personal. One of the nice things is that you can designate which specific organs to donate, including eyes, tissues, and even specific bones. One thing that really surprised me is they were able to use my mom's corneas. She had very poor vision without her contacts or glasses, but I learned someone who is completely blind would be extremely thankful for the gift of eyesight. What surprised me the most about my mom's donation was we thought she might help five people or so, but to our amazement, she was able to help save and improve the lives of 66 different people!

I have been able to meet two of the people my mom saved with her gifts of organ donation. One being Jordan, her kidney recipient, and the other is Maggie, her liver recipient. When you think of donation, you think of the people who are receiving the organ and how thankful they must be, but what you don't realize is the ripple effect it has. Because of organ donation, each of those 66 people received a gift from my mom, and now they can make a difference in other people's lives! My family and I didn't realize this until we were able to meet Jordan and Maggie. It was amazing to not only meet these wonderful people, but to see how thankful they were to be alive because of my mom. It made you realize how big the ripple affect really is. You are not only helping one person, you are helping all of those people whose lives are connected to them as well. In fact, their entire families and friends were also extremely grateful. It was a weird feeling, but a good feeling, knowing my mom was living on through them. I can also say that organ donation helps not only the recipient and their family and friends, it helps the donor family as well. Knowing their loved one is still living on through other people and they could help others is very comforting.

For those that do not know, I am now a professional race car driver in the NASCAR Cup Series. Since my mom's passing, I have wanted to do whatever I can to raise awareness for organ, eye, and tissue donation, and also honor all of those affected by it. I want to help anyone who may be in the same situation as my family, and I want to encourage people to have a talk with their loved ones about their final wishes. It will make things much easier should the situation arise that they have to make a decision about donating a loved one's organs. I also want to do everything I can to raise awareness for how great the need is for organ donation. Right now, nationwide, there are over 110,000 people on the transplant waiting list, and I want to help change that. Finally, I want to let every donor family know their loved one will never be forgotten and we will always honor their gift. I do this using my NASCAR platform, including my race car. One of the most powerful things I do is to honor donors and their families by displaying a photo of the donor on the car and inviting their family to the racetrack as our special guest. The second thing is an event called Hand Prints of Hope. At this event, we take the actual car we race that weekend to a special location a few days before the race. If we have an honoree on the car, we like to tie in the location with something meaningful to that person, such as a high school or something in their community. Sometimes we will be at a location chosen by our sponsor for the week. During the event, we let anyone connected to donation physically paint their hand and place their hand print on the car. They can also write a small message if they would like. This can be a very emotional and healing time for those closely connected to a donor, recipient, or someone still on the wait list. At these events, we also get a lot of media attention. When we get to the racetrack, the fans and the media always want to know why we have someone's photo on the car and why we have hand prints all over the car. When this happens, we get to tell them about organ donation! We could have up to 300,000 people at our races and millions watching on TV because all of our races are broadcast live on FOX and NBC.

Although I would give anything to have my mom back, I am proud to say that she was a hero and saved and enhanced the lives of so many. I am honored to share her legacy, and the legacy of so many others with the world. I know my mom is proud of my accomplishments and all the work I do to raise awareness for organ donation.

Joey, Caitlin, and twins Jace and Carson.

Joey with his mom and sister Ashley.

Young Joey baking cookies with his mom.

Maggie, Mary's (Mom) liver recipient, with sister Ashley.

Jordan, one of Mary's (Mom) kidney recipients, with Joey and Ashley.

Hand Prints of Hope hoods.

Jace and Carson.

The Nevada Donor Network #15 car in action!

Hand Prints of Hope event.

About Joey

Joey Gase is married to Caitlin. Both are from Cedar Rapids, Iowa and attended Xavier High School. They have twin boys, Jace and Carson. They live in North Carolina but visit friends and family often in Iowa. Joey's dad, Bob, has always been a big part of his race team. Bob drives the RV and assists with many things, including entertaining team guests and sponsors at the track.

In addition to racing, Joey finds time to support numerous charities and non-profit organizations. He has a personal connection that links his desire to help those in need. At the young age of 18, Joey tragically lost his mother, Mary, to a sudden brain aneurysm. Faced with a difficult decision, Joey and his family decided to donate his mother's organs. Later, they learned that her gift helped to save and improve the lives of 66 people. Since then, Joey developed a desire and passion to educate others on the need and importance of organ, tissue, and eye donation, and honoring all affected by it. His hard work in the donation community has proven to be successful in his goals and he has received many honorable rewards, including the Inaugural COMCAST Community Outreach Award and AATB Communication and Education "The Groundbreaker Award".

Joey's car is regularly adorned with the face of his mother and others who have given the gift of life, making his one of the most unique cars in NASCAR.

At a young age of 8, Joey began his racing career with a desire to follow in his father's footsteps. He began his career when he won his very first race in the Jr 1 Go Karts at Hawkeye Downs Speedway in Iowa. Since then, Joey has worked up the ranks from modified cars when he was 14, to late models at 15, and his first NASCAR XFINITY Series start at 18. He made his first Daytona 500 start in 2017 at the age of 24.

In 2021, Joey Gase will continue driving in the NASCAR Cup Series for Rick Ware Racing.

Follow Joey: @JoeyGaseRacing on Facebook, Twitter, and Instagram

Jean Sime

Do you believe in miracles?
This is the story of PJ . . .

I never imagined being diagnosed with End Stage Renal Disease (ESRD) would lead me on a rewarding, life-changing journey—a journey full of amazing and inspiring people who have become not only my friends but my family. My journey has made me the person I am today. I hope my story inspires you! I dedicate this chapter to my sister Vivian, who passed away on 4/16/2020 from COVID-19 complications. She was my number one supporter through all my health complications and my kidney transplant journey. My family and I used to tease her all the time because she would constantly ask questions. Jokingly, we would ask her, "Are you still writing that book?" Unfortunately, she never wrote that book, and I never thought someone would ask me to share my story with the world. This one is for you, Viv, my amazing sister. I hope I make you proud . . . always in my heart, forever my sister ♥.

When asked to share my journey in this book, I immediately responded with a loud YES! I hope this chapter will inspire you to never give up faith, always believe in miracles, and that, no matter how bad things get or feel out of control, you have permission to have your pity party! It's ok to cry, scream, and be mad at the world. And when you are ready, you move on. Find your purpose in life. Find the bright side of the darkness, even if it is only a pinhole of light coming through. Accept your situation, even though you may not be happy with it, and make the best of it. Being miserable will not make the situation any better. But only when you are ready . . . then accept it. When you least expect it, miracles happen. I am living proof!

My kidney journey began in September 2013, when my lower torso started swelling from my waist to my feet for about a month. I tried hiding it from my family. It was hard to catch my breath, and I had to take a break from walking every five to ten minutes. The weight of my legs was so heavy it felt like I was dragging two tree trunks, and my feet felt like balloons. Pain pierced my feet any time I wore shoes due to the swelling. I thought to myself, *something is really wrong.* I needed to see a doctor; so, the next day I took myself to Urgent Care. The doctor examined me and immediately referred me to the hospital for the swelling and shortness of breath. My glucose levels and blood pressure readings taken at the clinic were high, and they were certain it could be my heart or my kidneys. Scared and confused, I proceeded home to tell my husband Eric I needed to get to the hospital right away. I had never volunteered to go to the hospital ever before, but I knew I had no choice. I needed help and feared for my life.

Upon arrival at the emergency department, my numbers were off the chart. After being admitted to the hospital, I lay in my bed, petrified, thinking I was going to die. But with my family by my side, supporting and encouraging me, I knew I wasn't alone. When my mom was alive, she was a diabetic and did in-center hemodialysis.

So, imagine my joy when the doctors checked my creatinine level at the hospital and it was normal. Although my glucose numbers and A1C numbers were elevated, my kidneys at that point were functioning normally. Doctors then thought it must be my heart. After many tests and hours of acute anxiety, it turned out I did in fact have a blockage in my heart that required a stent. The hospital I was at didn't perform heart stent surgery, so they transported me to a larger hospital specializing in heart surgeries. After I received my heart stent, I turned pink and then alarmingly red. They discovered I was allergic to the contrast dye. This required a lot of Benadryl and an extended stay in the hospital. They pump a lot of dye into your veins during testing for heart issues, and sometimes the excessive dye used can cause issues with your kidney function. In my case, each time I had testing done requiring contrast dye, my creatinine level would rise. They then referred me to the hospital's top nephrologist. He was a little perplexed since my kidney function was normal when I entered the emergency department. The combination of the dye, plus my high blood pressure and uncontrolled diabetes, made for a typical renal failure scenario.

Throughout the next year, my nephrologist monitored my kidney function. On one visit he had no choice but to say the dreaded three words, "You need dialysis." I couldn't believe it was happening. My worst fear was coming true. In March 2015, the doctor ordered for me to get a fistula. My mom used a catheter in her chest for her treatments, and I saw how she suffered and couldn't shower. To avoid this suffering, I agreed to get a fistula constructed in my upper arm, where they connect the artery and the vein in your arm. It became my lifeline. A fistula is where the techs and nurses insert two needles during each dialysis session. My fistula took seven months to mature before I could start using it.

My dialysis experience was frightening. I never imagined that one day I could go from my normal life to being hooked up to a life-support machine. I started my first round of treatments in the hospital so my nephrologist could monitor any issues. In the beginning, it wasn't bad except for the pain of the needles. I was in a dark place, however, and feeling sorry for myself. I often asked God, *What have I done to suffer the rest of my life like this?* How am I going to go to treatments three times a week and still hold down my full-time job? How will I afford the medical bills, and what if I have to stop working? So many emotions ran through my head, including confusion, sadness, anxiety, and depression. Yes, I was having a pity party, and it lasted for six months until I started at my dialysis center in November 2015. I was ashamed to tell my friends and coworkers that I had to go on dialysis or I would die. Three and a half hours plugged into a machine, three times a week, is a very long time to think and reflect. Imagine not being able to get up or move your arms for that duration. That was a lot of time to feel sorry for myself. Only after I accepted that the machine was saving my life, along with the techs and nurses, and after I thought about the 17 other people in my center were going through the same thing, was I able to end my pity party. I thought, I can make this a miserable journey for myself, or I can change my attitude and make the best of an unpleasant situation.

Preparing to get on the transplant list is not a simple task. You need to have consistent bloodwork numbers; be in a healthy state, both physically and mentally; and be infection free, including your teeth and gums. After a transplant, you are on immunosuppressant medications for the rest of your life, and it increases your chances of getting an infection. In New Jersey, the transplant wait list is an average of five to seven years. I needed to correct some issues before they could clear me for the transplant list, including dental work; I had 15 teeth extracted. I had several foot infections that lead to my big toe being amputated, and then a trans-metatarsal amputation of the same foot. All infections had to be clear, and they required many other tests, including a colonoscopy, mammogram, and a stress test for the heart. I asked myself often if it is all worth it; was I worth it?

Once I stopped feeling sorry for myself, I embraced my life!

After weighing myself each time I entered the dialysis center, I would walk around the room and say hello to every single patient. Many of the patients lived in a nursing home, and others lived by themselves. Some never received visitors, which made me sad, so I thought maybe I could bring a smile to their faces just by saying hello; I believe it worked.

I became close friends with many of my dialysis kidney warriors at the center. The staff referred to me as their ambassador or "the welcome wagon." They would often sit the new patients next to me so I could answer their questions and concerns and reassure them everything was going to be ok. Sadly, I lost many of these friends to kidney disease and its side effects. It was heartbreaking, but it reminded me to thank God for blessing me with another day.

After embracing my situation, my dialysis team started talking to me about transplant. I had no clue what options were available, I only knew I needed to be healthy enough to get on the active list. They mentioned a living kidney donor. I contemplated who could be my living donor but, in my heart, I felt I couldn't ask any of my immediate family. I feared they would die during the surgery and I would survive. If that happened, I could not live with myself. My sister Vivian told me several times she wanted to get tested to donate to me. I was appreciative but, in my heart, I could not accept her offer. If I continued to get healthier, I could get on the active list and wait for my miracle to happen.

On a chilly day in February 2017, I had to get bloodwork drawn, at my local hospital, to stay on the active list. That day, my blood was drawn by Bev, the phlebotomist who had been drawing my blood since I started dialysis. She had become very familiar with my kidney issues and my need for a transplant. Little did I know this visit would change my life!! After I left, Bev ran into a nurse friend, who had been a coworker of hers for many years, named Patricia Milford (aka Pat). Pat had considered donating to one of her patients many years ago, but due to her own family members' illness, the testing process was postponed. After some time, her patient received a kidney from a deceased donor. Pat thought again about donating when she saw a little boy on the news pleading for a life-saving kidney for his dad. She started testing for the little boy's dad, but then received a call to thank her and to let her know they found a few matches. Pat shared this with Bev when they ran into each other after my bloodwork visit. Bev's eyes lit up, and she immediately told Pat that one of her patients needed a kidney. She explained my need and asked Pat if she would consider donating her kidney to me. Pat replied without hesitation, "why not"?   Pat then asked Bev to have me reach out to her so we could discuss it. Later that day I received a voicemail message—a message I will never forget.

"Hi, Jean! It's Bev. You will not believe this! After you left the hospital, I ran into my nurse friend Pat. I told her about you and your need for a kidney transplant. She is considering donating to you. Here is her number. Please call her!"

In disbelief of what I just heard, I replayed the message so my sister could hear it. After listening, she turned to me and exclaimed, "You have to call her right now. This is wonderful news. I can't believe this!"

I looked at my sister and told her to calm down. I was not planning to get a living donor because of my fear of their passing away during the surgery. I needed to think about it and get my thoughts together before I called Pat.

Three days later, while getting my dialysis treatment, I was finally brave enough to call Pat. My hands were trembling, and I didn't know what I was going to say to her. She was sweet and tried to calm me down and get me to relax. After hearing her voice, I knew she was the miracle I was praying for. She answered all the random questions I fired at her, and then I had one last question for her. Why would you donate your kidney to me, a total stranger? I just needed to know why.

In her sweet voice, she replied she had been a nurse for 40 years and of all the things she had seen patients endure, watching someone hooked up to a machine to stay alive was the most heartbreaking. She wanted to give back.

It shocked me; I didn't know what to say to except "thank you," and it would be an honor to have her kidney. My miracle was going to happen. Once again, many emotions came across me. Why did God choose to save me? Why did he send this person to me to save my life?

Pat began the testing process as I continued mine. I wanted to meet, but also wanted to look my best for her. Since I was having issues with my foot and needed surgery, I waited a few months before asking to meet her. Should I ask her to meet me for a cup of coffee? What should I say to this angel who will save my life? We met one afternoon in the hospital after one of my doctor visits, and it was a beautiful moment I will never forget. As we embraced, I could feel our immediate connection. We even looked like we could be sisters! We were the same height, with short hair, glasses, and wearing hoop earrings. She was the one—I just knew it! Within a few months, we found out she was a match! What are the odds a total stranger would want to donate to me and be a perfect match for me?

Through the first year of testing, we both had medical issues pop up. It was a rollercoaster ride, but we stuck together through it all. We supported each other and shared tears of joy and disappointment. Both of us had to be physically and mentally strong for the transplant surgery! Finally, in May 2019, we got the green light for surgery. I remember pulling into my work parking lot when Pat called to tell me they scheduled us for surgery in early June. I was speechless! My heart raced, and I had so many emotions running through my mind. I was finally getting a kidney after three and a half years, 546 dialysis treatments, and at least 1100 needles stuck in my arm. Freedom was not far off!

The roller coaster ride wasn't over just yet. Pat had a cough and thought it was just allergies. At our final consultation and testing with the transplant team at the end of May, they detected pneumonia in her lungs. When Pat heard this news, disappointment and heartbreak overcame her. She wanted to tell me right away, because I had already arranged a leave of absence with my employer starting the upcoming Monday. Pat took a few minutes to get the courage to call me to let me know there was a delay in our surgery because of her illness. I had a gut feeling there was an issue as soon as I heard the phone ring. When I heard the tremble in her voice, my heart sank, and my worst fear flashed before me. What if they hadn't detected this in time? She might not have survived the surgery. How could I live without her? I assured her it was ok and not to worry about my disappointment. We needed her well, which was the primary focus. It thrilled both of us when they cleared her in a few weeks. I received my miracle on Tuesday, June 25, 2019! It was a day that changed my life, the day "PJ" was born! We named our kidney PJ—P for Patricia and J for Jean.

Pat and I felt at ease, and neither of us were nervous leading up to the big day. We agreed to meet at the hospital registration area at 8:00 am. The moment I saw her enter the room with her Vera Bradley overnight bag was THE MOMENT. That is when it finally hit me: this was happening! We both felt at peace and filled with happiness that the transplant was happening. My family joined us after registering, and it was surreal having them with me. My husband Eric, my sister Vivian, my brother-in-law Timmy, and my dad were there to support us both and cheer us on. It was one of my most proud moments. I felt so blessed to have them with us to witness the day of my miracle, the day my life was saved!

They rolled me into the operating room at 2:30 pm. As I entered, my first thought was, *Wow, this is a small room!* Then they asked me to move onto the table, which was a mere two feet wide. I voiced my concern, but thankfully I fit. As I was lying on the table getting prepped, I heard my surgeon and her team enter the room. They assured me I was in excellent hands. I felt calm and ready to receive my gift. I knew it was the perfect kidney for me, and I couldn't wait to wake up to a new life. As I was lying there, I noticed a shiny silver cooler filled with ice at the bottom of my feet. It looked like it was breathing! I asked the team about this fascinating contraption and learned it was to keep Pat's kidney cool prior to its final resting stop in my abdomen. I laughed as I asked if they could warm it up before putting it in me. That was the last thing I remember before waking up!

At 7:30 pm I woke in the recovery room. I knew I was in the hospital, but I didn't realize right away that I had my new kidney! I touched the area where they placed the kidney, and that was the moment I realized my miracle happened! I was overwhelmed with joy, wide awake, and had no pain. After realizing I had my new kidney, I immediately asked about Pat. I was so concerned about her that I forgot to ask if I was ok. Once I was assured she and I were doing well, I was ready to begin my new life. The hospital stay lasted four days. Fortunately, my recovery was smooth, except for the day the numbing shot wore off. I was able to eat foods I hadn't eaten in a long time because of my restricted renal diet. The first thing I ate was a banana! They are high in potassium, therefore not allowed for dialysis patients. The hardest part for me was all the fluids, especially water, I needed to drink. I went from a fluid restricted diet to an unlimited amount of water, which is challenging for me to this day, but, oh, so worth it. Recovery at home went well. I tried to limit my activities because of the stitches. Walking around my townhouse complex was a daily ritual, which I believe helped me get stronger and recover quicker, both physically and mentally.

I will always be grateful for Pat's selfless gift of life to me. Because of organ donation, I have my life back. Because of my donor, my life is back to normal. No more fluid restrictions; no more pain, nausea, restless nights, restricted renal diet; no more giant phosphorus binders or painful fistula grams; and no more high blood pressure medications! I got back 15 hours a week of priceless time with family and friends, and I can work and travel without the worry of scheduling dialysis. I enjoy the taste of food again and the freedom of not being hooked up to a machine. Because of my organ donor, my sister Vivian (she passed in April 2020) and my dad (he passed in August 2020) could witness my life-saving surgery. We had more time together as a family to create lasting memories. These memories help me cope with my grief for them.

Pat and I spent a lot of time together after our surgery. She and I vowed to give back by advocating for people to register as organ donors, and when possible, as living donors. We spoke to anyone who would listen about our surgery and we will continue. Our mission is to share how being a registered donor can save lives and how a living donor saved my life. We have offered to show our scars and, believe it or not, everyone has wanted to see them! We joined our Organ Procurement Organization (OPO) in New Jersey as certified volunteers. I speak with other patients when I go for my follow-up appointments at the hospital. The staff and many of the patients at my transplant center know me by name. Pat and I have joined many Facebook groups, some about transplant recipients and some about living donors. I also joined some kidney disease support groups on Facebook, and this is where I discovered my purpose in life and a way to give back. Here, I am able to educate people on dialysis and answer questions about having a kidney transplant. Through social media I have connected with some amazing people, both recipients, and donors, some of whom Pat and I met in person on an organ donation awareness cruise in February 2020. Not only did we advocate with the passengers on the ship, but also in the Bahamas. I've also revisited with my dialysis center Facility Administrator and head nephrologist, about speaking to the existing patients at the center about my transplant journey. I want to help the transplant community and my fellow kidney warriors waiting for their miracle.

Maybe my story will inspire them to search for a living donor. If I knew then what I know now, perhaps the duration of my dialysis could have been shorter.

Today, I network with others in the transplant community with the goal of making a difference in people's lives. I am a Howl Ambassador, spreading the word about kindness and organ donation awareness through Howl the Owl's book collection. Howl's creator, Brenda E. Cortez, and I have started Howl's Heroes, a project where we thank essential workers for their bravery and dedication during the coronavirus. The project honored the memory of my sister Vivian, who was also an essential worker during the pandemic, and who we sadly lost because of COVID-19. I became a mentor in a non-profit organization called The Transplant Journey, Inc., where I provide one-on-one support for others as they experience their journey from dialysis to transplant.

I have my life back, and I celebrate each day. Without the burden of dialysis, I can now focus on helping others and perhaps even inspire a few along the way. My miracle was my organ donor, a stranger who is now my friend. Instead of asking, "Why me?" I now ask, "Whose miracle can I be?" My mission is to inspire and help others with love, one person at a time. I do all of this because of my organ donor!

If my story has inspired you, please register as an organ donor at registerme.org, and if possible, consider living donation. I would not be here today without my living donor. Miracles DO happen every day! You just have to believe!

"Please don't take your organs with you; heaven knows we need them here on earth."

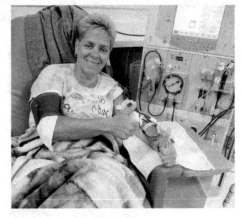

Jean's last day on dialysis: 6/24/2019.

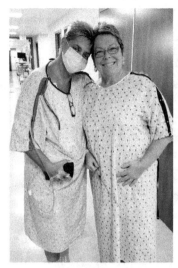

Jean with her dad, her brother Charlie and her sister Vivian.

Jean and Pat after surgery.

Jean showing PJ's new home.

Jean and Howl the Owl.

Jean and her husband Eric celebrating her transplant at Disneyworld.

Jean with her dad and sister celebrating his birthday in Atlantic City, NJ.

Jean with her sister Vivan, always having fun together.

One of Jean's favorite vacation memories with her family at Disneyland in California.

About Jean

Jean Sime has been married to her husband Eric for 27 years, and they live in New Jersey. Jean is the youngest of three children and spent her childhood growing up in Newark, New Jersey. She graduated from Rutgers University with a BS degree in Business Management with a concentration in Finance. She enjoyed 31 years working in the retail banking industry, and during her career she mentored and coached hundreds of employees and colleagues. Jean is extremely close to her family as they mean the world to her! Sadly, Jean lost her two best friends, her sister Vivian in April 2020 to COVID-19, and her dad Kazimierz passed in August 2020. She is heartbroken but is blessed that her sister and dad were here to witness her life-saving surgery and how her living donor gave her life again.

Jean began kidney dialysis treatments October 2015, and through its darkness she has found life. She received her gift of life from her living donor Patricia Milford on June 25, 2019. Since then, Jean has become a strong organ donation awareness advocate. She truly enjoys helping others.

Since her kidney transplant, Jean has connected with many living donors and recipients across the country. In February 2020, she had the honor of meeting many of them on an organ donation awareness cruise to the Bahamas. It was one of the best experiences of her life and was also life-changing! Meeting these amazing warriors and heroes inspired her to continue to help others with their transplant journeys. Jean now considers many of these friends her family.

Jean is a certified volunteer for her local Organ Procurement Organization, The New Jersey Sharing Network. She has been a virtual guest speaker and shares her story with high school students from around the world. Jean looks forward to more speaking engagements soon. She is also a member of the Morris County Donate Life Transplant Support Group. Jean is a Howl Ambassador for Howl the Owl, an organization that uses children's books to educate and spread awareness for organ donation, and encourages kindness and helping others. She is also a mentor for a non-profit organization, The Transplant Journey, Inc., where she mentors kidney patients, one-on-one, during their journey from dialysis to transplant. Jean is very active on social media and a member of many Facebook groups focused on transplant life and dialysis, and helping kidney warriors search for donors.

Jean is forever humbled, blessed and grateful for her gift of life! Stay tuned because Jean's story is to be continued…

You can connect with Jean Sime via Facebook or email at jeansime23@gmail.com.

About Patricia

Patricia Milford (aka Pat) lives in the state of NJ. She enjoyed her career as a nurse for 41 years. Pat retired shortly after her gift of life kidney donation. She now enjoys spending time with her family, reading, and doing crossword puzzles.

You can connect with Pat on Facebook or through her email address: PM78RN@AOL.COM

Jean and Pat celebrating their
1 month kidneyversary

Melissa McQueen

Little Miracles

It was 7:00 in the morning when contractions started. My husband and I were expecting our third child; a son whom we had waited to name until the last month because we had lost another baby before their time. We were excited, and I was absolutely finished with being pregnant. Our Ob/Gyn gave the clearance for me to come in a little after 9:00 a.m. When we arrived at the hospital just before 10:00 a.m., the nurses in labor and deliver got me settled into the room for the usual pre-delivery checks. I received my epidural, which only took on half of my body. It was weird to have complete labor pains on one side and nothing on the other. After injecting the second epidural, I felt I could finally relax. I however no longer had the use of one of my legs. They just flopped helplessly and were positioned by the nurse for the rest of the morning.

I figured myself a pro at this by now. This was my third baby in three years. After having trouble conceiving for the first three years, the proverbial floodgates had opened, and we were being blessed with children. This delivery seemed different somehow. There were two nurses in the room, and one was listening intently on my pregnant belly. She kept turning around to the other nurse and not speaking; then she would leave and come back to listen again. The third time she came back with what I like to call the baby taser. It was a little device that went on the belly and gave a little jolt. None of my other babies required this device, so I inquired about what was going on. Our nurse explained that the heartbeat was a little low and that sometimes this happens during the labor process. They were just giving a little jolt to give the baby a little extra energy to be born. I accepted this, being in somewhat of a haze from what was now a double epidural. Just carry on and carry forward; let's welcome our baby boy Dylan.

Meanwhile, our OB had another patient giving birth, at the same time who was having difficulty. I felt sorry for that other family, while the nurse's faces were growing more and more concerned in our own room. When our OB got to us, it took quite a bit of pushing, and when we finally got to see his sweet face, Dylan was one ounce short of 9 pounds, listless, and blue. The staff didn't bother to ask if my husband wanted to cut the cord this time. I got to hold him for a few seconds before they whisked him off to the ICU to "make sure he was ok." My doctor had a look of concern on his face and tears in his eyes. He told us he would be back later. My husband had been filming but quickly turned the camera off after our son was turning bluish. He feared the worst. He now had the job of distracting me.

An hour went by and then two and three. As patient as we were, while also trying to enjoy the quiet before the newborn, our concern was also growing. We would get quick updates about how he was just having a little trouble breathing. But then a pediatric cardiologist entered the room to speak with us. The cardiologist brought in a drawing of a heart. He explained that Dylan was born with a heart condition that they hoped could be corrected with surgery. But Dylan was very sick, and they feared they would lose him if he wasn't in a place equipped to deal with these kinds of issues. The doctors wanted to Life Flight him to Phoenix Children's Hospital to have their pediatric cardiology team observe him. They needed to send him right away. They brought my husband and me to a room outside of the helicopter launchpad to reach inside a travel incubator and wish our newborn son a safe trip. We could only hope that we would get to hold him again.

My husband asked should he stay or go with the baby. I told him to go and that I would be ok. I wasn't able to leave for at least 24 hours for observation. So, there I sat, in my hospital room with an empty bassinet, going between numbness and tears.

The next morning, I awoke hoping that the prior day had been a horrible dream. Like the result of watching too many Discovery Health documentaries on pregnancies gone wrong. Sadly, it wasn't; and there was more news to come. My husband came to get me to take me to the hospital so I could finally see my baby again. He warned me that Dylan was stable but could become critical at any moment and that it would be difficult to see him.

I had never been to a children's hospital before this very moment. We drove up to the colorful building. My husband escorted me carefully down the long corridors to the room. It was incredibly difficult to walk after a hard delivery. As we walked the halls, my husband brought me to the ICU area. There was another family standing near the entrance . . . a mother in tears. Nothing could prepare me for passing through those doors and into Dylan's room. There he was, sprawled out in an islet and connected to a bank of machines. He was bloated and his skin was purple. My legs started to give out from under me, and I gave an audible gasp as my husband caught me. It felt as if my soul came out of my body, if only for a moment, to rise above the room and take in the whole situation. Our ICU nurse immediately came over to tell me that my reaction was normal and that there was a team there to help Dylan. I had one of many doctors come and sit with me to tell me what was going on. We finally had a name for what we were facing with Dylan. That name, or diagnosis, was Dilated Cardiomyopathy, and it was inoperable. His heart muscle was stretched out and weak and therefore couldn't pump properly. Only one in a million are born with this condition, especially to this degree, and his condition was advanced. Statistics showed a third of babies get better, a third stay the same, and a third get worse. After he had coded the night before (after his Life Flight) and they revived him, his team felt encouraged that he could be stabilized and stay that way for 24 hours. My husband witnessed all of this and was there for our son. The medical team wanted to keep Dylan in a medical coma, hoping that, with some rest, his heart might get better. For now, that was the plan.

Two days later, Dylan was still in a medical coma, and they were monitoring his heart for signs of improvement. This is when a new nurse walked into the room. Her title was Transplant Coordinator, and when she introduced herself, I just wanted her to leave. I was so angry this was happening to our sweet little family. I didn't want to give up on his heart. Isn't a big a heart a good thing? I was just over it all. None of this was fair to Dylan or our family.

I have a feeling our transplant coordinator had walked into many a room like ours. She kindly introduced herself and asked how we were doing. She told us that Dylan was not doing well at all and that chances were high he would need a heart transplant to survive. We as a team (parents are included in the medical team) would need to come up with a plan for if, and when, things got worse. The medical team had already discussed Dylan's case, and they wanted to Life Flight him to a different hospital that had a pediatric heart transplant program. At the time, there was not a program in our area. They wanted to fly him to Loma Linda in California and have him listed for transplant there. She said they would give us 24 hours to consider these options.

We went home for the first time to get a good night's sleep. The ICU nurses gave us a phone number we could call anytime, and they would give us an update on Dylan. They could all see we were exhausted and had hit our limit, and we needed time for this major decision.

Upon walking into our house, my mom greeted us along with our two other children, and some other family. Alex, three, and Maddie, one, ran up to hug us. They were eager to see their parents again and hopeful to see their new brother. I almost burst into tears as I gave them a big bear hug. I was so happy to see my two younger kids, and it was a pleasant distraction to the current situation. After explaining Dylan's condition, one family member just looked at me trying their best to be comforting and said "sometimes babies just die." That night, my husband and I surrendered everything that we knew in prayer, together. We prayed as we had no idea what to do or what was to come next, but we gave everything to God in His time, will, and purpose. We did this knowing we would find comfort if we lost Dylan, but our hearts would soar if he miraculously got better and could stay with us.

Early the next morning, my husband and I were back at Dylan's bedside. When the team came in for rounds, they explained to us they had discussed Dylan's case and were fearful that he wouldn't survive the flight. They absolved us of a decision by deciding to keep Dylan in Phoenix until he got better. They then introduced us to ECMO (extracorporeal membrane oxygenation), which takes over for the heart and lungs so they can heal. It is a very large machine and the tubing that goes into the body is about as large as an adult finger. It was difficult to bear that this machine, the size of an end table, had large tubes that would go into our infant son to help him survive.

So now we wait, hour by hour, day by day, to see if Dylan would need ECMO or if he would somehow get better. The first day, his pressures improved, and by the end of the week, he had gotten to where they felt comfortable taking him out of a medicated coma. At the end of two weeks, he came out of sleep more and opened his eyes to greet us for the very first time. By the end of the third week, he reached for us, ever so gently, with his little hand, and we got to hold him. And at the end of week four, we hoped that, with medicinal therapy, we could bring him home to stay.

A discharge plan was written up with conditions. If one of his weekly clinic check-in appointments didn't look right, if his blood pressure was out of range, or if he looked more ill than normal, we would need to return to the hospital with Dylan as soon as possible. We brought him home, hopeful and energized. He was a sweet baby with a good temperament, and he slept often. He sweated excessively, but we didn't think too much of it because it was Phoenix in the summer. His appetite was low, and as hard as we tried to bottle feed, most of the time we had to give up and feed him through an NG-Tube to make sure he had his lower-level calorie requirements for the day. Some days he would seem like our other children when they were babies, and sometimes I wondered if we would make it through the night. He slept by my side in a bassinet with an alarm that would sound if he stopped moving or breathing in the night. When things got too scary, and he was sweating too much, or throwing up too much, we would call the cardiologist, which would result in another week of inpatient stay at the children's hospital. This kind of thing happened monthly. We always watched his ejection fraction (EF); this number measures the amount of blood pumped versus the amount of blood that remains in the chamber, or "the squeeze" of the heart. Normal range was between 50 and 70, but Dylan's highest was in the lower 30s. Medications kept it there for a few months. But when his EF dipped into the teens and below, our now beloved and trusted transplant coordinator sat us down for a tough discussion. It was the same discussion that we had when he was nearly three days old. She told us they had done everything they could do with medicines and that his numbers were slowly trending downwards. Even though they were working on having a pediatric heart transplant center in the Phoenix area, it wasn't quite ready for its first patient yet. She knew we had been scouring the internet, researching every potential treatment and hospital. She asked us to give her a transplant center of our choosing.

As great as the team was at preparing us for possibilities that lie in a situation like this, there is no better teacher than life experience. Just like when you're having a baby, no one can describe how it feels when someone is listed for and receives a life-saving organ transplant. On top of this, I had no choice but to move with Dylan to a different state with no specific time frame for when the transplant would even occur. This is because a heart transplant hinges on the enormous grace and giving of a family that loses their child.

Two days later, after calling the insurance company, we called to give our decision. We chose Children's Medical Center in Dallas because they had an impressive track record for pediatric transplants, and I have lots of family nearby who could help us. Our coordinator sent the paperwork in and, within a few days, their transplant coordinator called and welcomed us to come to their center for evaluation. They told us to pack for six days or six months. I booked an airplane ticket and packed some things for us, hopeful for anything better. In the meantime, I was leaving behind my two younger children and my husband.

When we got to Dallas, we discovered just how bad things were. His ejection fraction was six. His chest x-ray showed that his enlarged heart took up much of his chest cavity, forcing his lungs to the sides and his intestines downwards. It was clear why he was having issues breathing and eating. He was accepted as a candidate in an instant and, within a few days, admitted inpatient into the hospital for observation. Over the next three weeks we shifted between the ICU and the main hospital, never really leaving the hospital campus. This hospital became our village, and the medical practitioners within our extended family.

A week before Christmas we got a wonderful surprise, my stepmother, who had just retired from teaching had agreed to come up to Dallas and watch my two younger children while we waited for Dylan's heart. That way I wouldn't be away from my daughter as she learned to walk and talk, and away from my son who missed me dearly. We call Esmeralda our fairy stepmother, who saved the day. My husband continued in Arizona working and keeping our medical insurance intact.

When you are waiting for a life-saving organ transplant, all kinds of crazy thoughts go through your mind. How long will you wait? Will we make it in time for Dylan? How do I articulate the prayer asking for this gift? How do I pray for the donor family? Will this situation send us into bankruptcy? Is this going to destroy our children's self-esteem and healthy boundaries? Will my marriage survive this? How will I make it another day watching my child die slowly in front of me? You count days as they turn into weeks. Every holiday is a milestone, with hopes of that being "the day."

It was after New Year's, and snow was falling in Dallas. This was when I sat with our surgeon as she explained, in a distinct and approachable way, the next steps for Dylan; when we would get *the call*, what a suitable candidate would look like, and what happened if we didn't get the call in time. They described the actual surgery in terms I could understand. My being a software engineer by trade, our surgeon told me it was a plug and play type of operation, which is straightforward: disconnecting the heart from the major arteries and veins, and suturing the new heart in. If all went well, it would begin beating immediately and last Dylan a lifetime. A suitable candidate would be the same blood type as Dylan and a little older than Dylan. They needed a child who was slightly bigger because Dylan's current heart was so enlarged. If we didn't get the call in time, the team had ordered a Berlin heart on the basis of compassionate usage. This was a mechanical ventricular assist device that would act like a heart in the chance that Dylan's heart failed him before he got the call. The heart was already being constructed per specification and would arrive within another week.

The day that the Berlin heart was due to arrive, January 13th, we got a call in the dark hours of the morning. Our transplant coordinator's first words were, "Stay calm . . . we got the call. The heart is good and a perfect match for Dylan. Take your time, but slowly start making your way to the hospital to get Dylan prepped for pre-op." I took the quickest shower possible, told Esmeralda where I was going and to let the other kiddos know not to worry. Shaking with fear and possibility, I called my husband and told him to get the first flight out of Phoenix because we had just gotten the call. Could this really be it?

When I got to the hospital, Dylan was hopping in his bumbo seat like he knew something big was coming. When they rolled his hospital gurney through the ICU, he got a standing ovation from the entire staff. I was able to walk him to the operating room (OR) doors where I got to kiss his little head and squeeze his hand goodbye. I saw the OR doors swing shut, let out a big sigh, and headed to the waiting area, not knowing how long things would take or if he would survive. Luckily, my cousin and her husband were there to distract me with coffee and casual conversation over the next five hours. Serendipitously, my husband Brandon walked into the waiting room, suitcase in hand, just as they led us over to the operating room doors to see Dylan being wheeled back from his surgery. But this time, we saw him on a gurney connected to many wires. But this time was hopeful; we were hopeful it would be one of the last times he was critical.

Over the next few days, Dylan recovered in the ICU. He had a boost in energy, and for the first time, was constantly moving around in his seat. He had previously lacked the strength to develop any crawling or walking skills, so all he could do was move side to side in his seat and smile ear to ear. After two weeks, they discharged us to a local apartment we had. We were to stay for three months and come into the clinic weekly for follow up. It was hard to leave our hospital home and family, but we could still visit and we had a new crew of therapists that would visit our home for physical speech and eating, and occupational therapy for Dylan. The team was going to make up for lost time on milestones and get Dylan up to speed.

The next three months were a blur of therapy and clinic appointments. Sometimes I had all three kids in tow. We had a new enemy now, contagious disease and illness. Any number of illnesses could threaten Dylan's new heart considering his immune suppressed state. He was on a multitude of medications and formula feeds via pump around the clock. I felt like I had a newborn again, only sleeping a few hours at a time.

Before I knew it, it was spring again. Dylan was doing well, and we got the green light from our transplant team to go back home to Phoenix. We would have to fly out for regular monthly clinic appointments. We packed up our new life, which now filled up our minivan, and made our way on the two-day journey home. Our entire family was finally together.

Even though the operation was done, our hospital stay was over, and we were back at home, it was still challenging to find our new normal. We sold our home to cover extra expenses and to stay out of bankruptcy. As with most families in our position, we were thankfully approved for Medicaid to help with a flood of extra medical expenses and therapies. It took years to piece back time that we missed with our kids, to put our marriage back together, and to get Dylan where he was up to speed with his peers. By the time Dylan was starting Kindergarten, a gift we never dreamed possible, is when we finally found comfort with our new normal.

Because Dylan's gift was beyond comprehension in terms of grace and love, we felt that we needed to honor that gift. We were out every weekend showing Dylan new things and traveling. Still in that mode of not knowing when your last day will be, we were treating every day like a gift.

Over the years, the research I had compiled had been put into a website so I could share with others. After many years of feeling isolated, I finally met other parents like myself. In the early years, I was lucky to have two other transplant moms that helped guide my journey and give us great hope. We wanted that for every transplant parent, and many new transplant moms I was meeting agreed. Because there was no official support for pediatric transplant, we decided to take Transplant Families to the next level. Before, there was no official support group for pediatric transplant parents. If you were lucky, they might introduce you to another transplant parent that happened to be in the ICU at the same time. Most of the time you sat alone with no one to talk to for advice on this level. After many years operating unofficially, we became official in 2017. We have been able to grow a tremendous online presence of support that is available 24 hours a day, 7 days a week. Now, no parent has to worry alone.

I, as a mother, also saw how many people and organizations made the miracle of organ donation possible. On a hope, and a prayer, I submitted my application to serve with OPTN/UNOS. UNOS (United Network for Organ Sharing) is the listing organization that matches donors and recipients on the transplant list, and the OPTN (Organ Procurement and Transplant Network) sets policies around organ donation. To my utter surprise, they accepted me into the Pediatric Committee to help serve as the parent voice. Since then, I have been fortunate to serve on many other committees.

From service to the community and formation of the nonprofit, it was the perfect time and place to help grow the community. I was fortunate to help author "What Every Parent Needs to Know" guide. Transplant Families was one of the first organizations that helped pilot Donate Life's National Pediatric Transplant Week. In addition, I serve with medical Quality Improvement groups, ACTION and Starzl to help improve outcomes for all transplant children. We look forward to continued growth and excellence in our pediatric transplant community. With all the amazing stories of overcoming adversity, and the phenomenal medical community that strives for perfection, we are hopeful there will be an end to the waiting list for children.

And now, 12 years after our journey began, I have happily been interrupted about a dozen times while writing this chapter, to help Dylan with his middle school algebra homework. Even though we are amidst a pandemic, Dylan is longing to be with his friends again and play sports. He runs cross-country, plays football, and, two years ago, even won fifth place in the state for wrestling in his age and weight range. He has also won four medals in the first (and last) Transplant Games of America that he took part in. One of those medals he proudly sent to his donor family.

Our biggest thank you is to the Kittrell family. We learned their son Wyatt provided Dylan's hero heart. We met them online the last day of the Transplant Olympics and were fortunate enough to meet them in person a few months later. This was the same weekend as the 30th anniversary of the Children's Medical Center transplant team. That day, we also got to see Dylan's transplant team again. Without these clinicians and our donor families, these miracles wouldn't occur. Because of organ donation, we hope to continue to honor them with Dylan living a life well led.

The whole family, about to march with the Donate Life Arizona section at the Fiesta Bowl Parade.

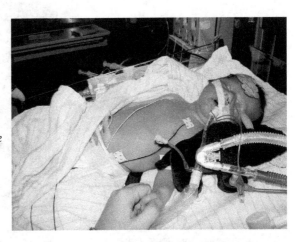

This photo was taken right after Dylan was born and about to be life-flighted to Phoenix Children's Hospital, where he was diagnosed with cardiomyopathy.

Dylan and Melissa at Children's Medical Center in Dallas for transplant evaluation.

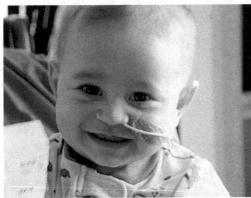

Dylan the day before his heart transplant.

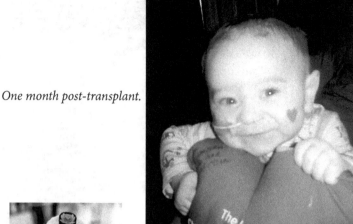

One month post-transplant.

Dyaln with his medals at the Utah Transplant Games of America in 2018.

Wyatt Kittrell , Dylan's donor of his hero heart.

*The Kittrell family Koy, Sarah, and their daughter Morgan,
with Melissa and Dylan at their first meeting.*

About Melissa

Melissa McQueen is the Executive Director of Transplant Families, a non-profit organization that works with parents and caregivers of children being listed for or who have already received a lifesaving organ transplant. This organization guides them to support, education, and assistance to help them through this very difficult time.

Melissa believes that education and support bring hope and healing for families. She is honored to volunteer with the OPTN/UNOS on their Pediatric Committee and their Data Advisory Committee, where she helped co-author, "What Every Parent Needs to Know," and she is now a part of OPTN/UNOS Board of Directors. Melissa has also been selected as leadership with Quality Improvement Collaboratives ACTION Learning Network (pediatric cardiac QI based out of Cincinnati Children's Hospital), and Starzl Learning Network (pediatric liver QI based out of the University of Pittsburgh Medical Center) to give input and help co-create materials for clinicians and families. She worked on the spearheading committee that helped Donate Life America create National Pediatric Transplant Week (every year on the last week of every April). She is the charter chair of the Heart Center Family Advisory Council and Alumni Family Advisory Council at Phoenix Children's Hospital. Melissa is a proud volunteer and editor of the newsletter for Transplant Community Alliance and a supporter of Team Transplant Arizona.

Melissa is a trained developer/engineer by trade who has worked at companies such as Honeywell - Aeronautics Division, APS, Wells Fargo, and Phoenix Children's Hospital. Most recently, she helped to develop "My journey with" applications covering patient education from diabetes to transplant for newly diagnosed families. Melissa holds a Bachelor's in Computer Information Systems from DeVry University.

When Melissa is not working, she loves hiking and traveling with her college sweetheart and husband, Brandon, and spending time with their three beautiful children: Alex, Maddie, and Dylan. Dylan received his gift of life (heart) at 8 months old and is now a healthy and happy 12-year-old.

Jen Benson

A Journey That Lead Me Where I Am Today

On the ill-fated day of October 15, 1990, my nightmare began when I was told, "You have diabetes!" I was eleven years old and I had no idea what diabetes was or what my future would hold. Perhaps if I had, I might not be here today to share my journey. It is this journey that has made me the person I am today.

I am a forty-one-year-old woman who battled twenty-six years of brittle diabetes, seven years of dialysis, and one eleven-hour surgery that ended my twenty-six-year nightmare. After that surgery, I had a new life, free of what had haunted me. Almost three decades of finger sticks and insulin shots, and seven years of being strapped to a machine three times a week, for four hours at a time. I no longer hold the title of Type 1 diabetic or dialysis patient. I have received a kidney and pancreas transplant and I am a transplant survivor!

A transplant warrior! A woman who is ready to conquer the world with my new title.

I would turn from a young child into a rebellious teenager, then into an adult woman with a strong will and determination to fight everything that was presented to me. From the original diagnosis of diabetes to, "You need dialysis and a transplant."—from one dependency to another, and not the typical dependency one is familiar with! Mine was a life-saving dependency, relying on insulin shots and the dialysis machines. I was a full-fledged addict to the medical community. New York-Presbyterian/ Columbia University Irving Medical Center, my selfless Donor, and his amazing family, ended my true life struggle on August 17, 2015, and for that I will forever be beholden.

There are no words that can begin to express my gratitude for being gifted another chance at life. These words seem like such a cliché, but that's how I felt after spending over six years in bed, in my early 30's, on oxygen, and unable to walk on my own. I was just married and watching the world pass me by. I wondered every night if I would wake to see the next morning. Those nights were lonely, long, and very dark. Yet somehow every morning came, and there I was struggling through the same routine which seemed never-ending.

My husband, my family, and I endured a total of 12 or 13 prospective offers of organs for a transplant—none of which panned out for various reasons. Each and every single one was a total roller coaster ride of emotions, not just for me, but for my entire family. After the first three or four offers, we stopped telling people to avoid crushing their hopes, and I think ours as well. It was easier this way and took less of a toll. The emotional aspect was just too severe. My family and I even relocated from Connecticut to Minnesota, at one point, to be closer to the transplant center at which I was listed for many years. While we lived there, my husband and my father worked remotely in the furnished apartment we rented. We literally left our lives behind to try and save mine. The waitlist is long in the Northeast where I grew up and where we lived. There was excellent healthcare and top notch hospitals, so how could this be happening? The average wait for a kidney in the New York area, then, was seven years. The wait currently in 2021 is many years for a deceased donor. Kidneys are the most sought after organ with almost 93,000 people on the transplant list needing this organ.

I was bedridden, and my days consisted of TV, which I lived vicariously through. Television actors and reality stars helped me escape my nightmare and my boredom. I watched them live their lives, their dramas, and their excitement. All I really had was monotonous doctor appointments, which were carefully scheduled around my life-saving dialysis. My treatments were usually three or four times a week at my clinic. When we lived in downtown Minneapolis, I would enjoy the sights and sounds of the city on my way to the clinic. It was an outing which always included my enormous wheelchair and my portable oxygen machine, with multiple batteries just in case. It was an exhausting ordeal not only for me, but for my husband and family as well. Besides the wheelchair and oxygen machine, there was a massive duffel bag which we lugged back and forth that supplied me with big fluffy warm blankets to wrap myself like a cocoon. Also a neck pillow and headphones for the TV set. Along with this camping bag was a basin for my nausea that was a constant from my raging high blood pressure levels. Thankfully the four hours of dialysis allowed me to nap for the entire time and to block out the obnoxious blood pressure cuff's consistent alarming every twenty minutes, and the continual beeping from my dialysis machine and the surrounding dialysis machines from other nearby kidney patients.

The other patients were also coping with struggles, issues, and hardships of their own. Every transplant patient has a very unique story to tell. They are all fighters and warriors in their own right.

My story begins with a kidney stone that became lodged in my urethra. It caused septic shock. My organs began shutting down, and my blood pressure dropped so severely that I temporarily lost my hearing for hours; I almost died. Over the next two days, I was given so much saline fluid that I gained 30 pounds in water weight. Ultimately it destroyed my kidneys. They were never able to recover from this trauma. Two weeks after returning from my honeymoon, I was told I would need to start dialysis which would hold me over until I received a life-saving transplant from a selfless hero. A nineteen-year-old young man would be my hero later on along my journey. My husband didn't even know what dialysis was or what it entailed. And so the horrendous adventure began as a married couple. The phrase "in sickness and in health" rang true in our case. For us it was the epitome of sickness.

It started with the nausea, pounding migraine-like headaches, uncomfortable swelling in my legs, abdomen, face, hands, feet, and toes that resembled little sausages. Constant itching that forced me to scratch so much I eventually bled all over my pajamas and sheets from random unexplainable bumps covering my body and scalp. I was constantly freezing and nothing kept me warm. My body was unable to regulate its own temperature. The effects of diabetes and kidney failure, combined with dialysis, were taking its toll on my body at this point, and I was just a young woman.

Here I was watching all my friends, before my very eyes, gain job promotions, get married, buy new homes, and have babies. All while I was lying in bed, going to dialysis treatments, and doctor appointments. Sure, they would call and check in to see how I was doing, but what was I supposed to tell them? Especially after several years, it had started to get old. There were no new updates. Nothing had changed in my life. I was still just sitting there; sitting and waiting for a selfless donor to save my life. How long would it take? Would I survive on dialysis? There was always the pressing question of when would I get to the top of the list? I loved hearing their updates, however, and I longed for the diversion and the visits. It was the getaway I needed from my daily torment. I was a prisoner in my own home and a convict to my own body.

I began my ordeal with in-center hemodialysis. I was the youngest patient there. The first day I walked in, the stares I received were feral. People were practically strapped into their respective chairs with tubes, wires, and cords; covered by blankets; some had pillows they had brought from home. The chairs do recline somewhat and elevate the legs, but they are by no means comfortable or cushy. This is especially true when you are unable to move for four hours. You are forced to remain still with your arm extended with a blood pressure cuff connected. Any movement causes the cuff to register a false reading which can be dangerous in the treatment. It also causes more frustrating beeping. Everyone had a TV in front of them. Most people were older and looked either completely bewildered or were asleep. Sleep was a godsend if you could get it while you were there. It made the time go by faster. The majority of patients had headphones or earbuds on. An hour into my first treatment, I learned that headphones or earbuds were the secret to surviving the four hours of anguish with the machines and the constant beeping of alarms. Nurses and dialysis technicians would scurry about the room taking vital signs and talking amongst themselves, either in dull whispers or loudly. I had a chest catheter placed on my right side. I was warned of all the risks for infection and told that this so-called life-line led directly into my heart. The exposure to infection was exceptionally high since the blood flowed directly into my heart immediately. I was also sharply instructed by the center that showers were a no-go from day one. It was sponge baths or trying to navigate a hand held shower and to avoid getting the site wet or sweaty. *Good luck*, I thought to myself. As time turned from days, to months, to years, I began to wash my hair in the kitchen sink with the help of my family. The fear of infection became too great, and I didn't want to risk becoming inactive on the transplant list. I had waited too long for my miracle donor to come along to lose that opportunity because of a shower or washing my hair. The kitchen sink was my new hair salon. The dialysis center was pushing me for a fistula in my arm, and they were pushing hard. They explained it would be safer, with less risk for infection. I was skeptical since all the fistulas I had seen were atrocities. They warned that there were also restrictions with a fistula, if I had one done. We met with a vascular surgeon and reviewed the facts. He recommended some precautionary measures to take if I continued with the chest catheter, those measures I followed to a T. To this day he still calls me a miracle patient.

My endocrinologist introduced the idea of a kidney and pancreas transplant to my family several months into my dialysis treatment. We were completely flabbergasted. We had never heard of such a thing. Why hadn't my nephrologist or my clinic brought this up? Did this really mean I could get rid of my diabetes while solving my kidney failure, all in one surgery? I had suffered so long with the diabetes, and now one operation could eradicate the insulin injections and finger sticks. Was I dreaming? It must be a fantasy. The dialysis clinic and my nephrologist had only talked about a kidney transplant. No one had brought up a dual transplant.

When we were discussing just the kidney transplant, I wasn't sure I was ready to ask family and friends, let alone strangers for a kidney. How does one go about doing that? I couldn't wrap my head around it. All I could imagine was that one day, down the road, I would land in an argument with the person who had saved my life, and it would be thrown in my face that they had saved my life. People can be vicious when pushed into a corner. That was my mentality. I had my mind made up. My thinking was firm and stubborn. I wasn't going to ask any family members or friends. Yet in actuality not a single friend or family member ever offered to be tested to see if they could even donate. The only people who ever offered were my parents, but since my mother was one of my primary caregivers she was turned down. My dad has some kidney issues so he too was declined. No one else came forward and offered to be tested or to donate a kidney. My parents did their best to try and cover for, or perhaps make up for, my family members' lack of offering by saying, "Maybe they didn't think they could donate since you are adopted."

It was more the idea of not even offering to get tested that spoke volumes to me. People have their reasons for their actions, some of which are understandable, and others of which I can and will never fully grasp. I strongly believe that there are many misconceptions surrounding organ donation. The one I still hear most frequently is, "If they see I'm a donor at the hospital, they won't try to save my life." Until people are put in a situation, or have been properly educated about organ donation, it's really not their fault. I can't blame people; because it wasn't until I walked in my own shoes that I learned all of the facts, myths, and realities regarding organ donation.

Years would go by, and several medical issues would come up, ranging from uncontrollable blood pressure that resulted in multiple mini strokes that resulted in several brain lesions; ongoing bouts of C-Diff, an intermittent stomach infection that would rear its ugly head every six weeks; one heart attack scare while in the ICU because of sky high blood pressure readings; a brain tumor; followed by "Well, it's not a brain tumor. So, the good news is it's multiple sclerosis." Shingles also made an appearance during this time. All of these health limits are what caused me to be on dialysis for seven years. I was continually inactive on the transplant list from these obstacles. Although I was accruing time on the list, I wouldn't be able to receive a transplant if an offer had come through. I'm not sure if any of my family, friends, or husband's work colleagues truly grasped this concept. I vividly remember, at some point in our challenge, my husband telling me how middle management had come to him and mentioned that our scenario had gotten old, "Blockbuster didn't close when someone got sick they continued to rent DVDs." His desk head had been someone that he looked up to as a father figure; throughout my illness the CEO was viewed as his guardian angel. Eventually my husband filed with his company for Family Medical Leave Act to help care for me. The decision to do so was not an easy one. There were several discussions of pros and cons to filing for FMLA.

It was around year four and a half when I switched to home hemodialysis. My husband worked from home while I underwent my grueling dialysis upstairs with my nurse. Going to in-center dialysis had truly drained me both physically and mentally. I just couldn't do it anymore. I was no longer healthy on either level. It was a change I needed for the soul and body. I honestly felt as though my brain was rotting and I was losing control of simple things with my body. I was completely bedridden and had been for years. That occurred within the first year of my kidney failure. My only walking was from the bed to the bathroom, and that was a total chore. When I did make that marathon walk, or what seemed like a 26-mile run, it was done on my tiptoes. Due to all my time in bed, my muscles had shortened and atrophied. While making these walks, I was followed by my oxygen tubing dragging behind me. I stopped urinating pretty early on in my struggle. That was something no one ever warned me would happen. My husband would joke that I was the best person to travel with on long car rides and plane trips, or how we saved a fortune on toilet paper. He tried to make light of the situation with humor. Some people understood, others thought it was cruel and heartless. I personally found it pretty funny and true. We all cope differently. On exceptionally good days, I would go downstairs to the family room and watch a movie. These were not the days of a treatment.

I had to go to the clinic to be trained in home hemo. Due to the complexities of the machine, a person is not allowed to perform the treatment alone. You must have a partner, and since my husband was working, we were forced to hire a nurse. Well, two nurses into the training, no one felt comfortable performing dialysis at home because my blood pressures were so erratic on the machine. We finally hired nurse number three, and she was fantastic, kind, warm, and eager to learn. She was also a paramedic, so her medical background was a huge help. Months went by, and slowly my blood started to resemble Hershey syrup in the lines. Clotting started to become a problem, and what used to be a four-hour treatment, three days a week, was turning into five or six hours. It finally became too dangerous when an air embolism in my lines went towards my heart, but thankfully didn't reach it due to the EMS team that was called by my nurse. A fourth nurse was hired for a short term, but the treatment was deemed too dangerous by my clinic, and I was forced to go back to in-center hemodialysis. She was by my side through it all and I am grateful. She continues to help many people to this day as a nurse practitioner. My spirit was completely devastated. My fury had reached a new level, and I didn't trust that this transplant was ever going to happen. I deeply believed that I would die on dialysis or while I waited for my prodigy organs.

My enchanted call came while I was in the middle of dialysis, and it didn't seem real. It was a coordinator from Columbia New York-Presbyterian/ Columbia University Irving Medical Center, explaining they had organs flying in from Vanderbilt University Medical Center in Nashville, Tennessee and could I make it in? I simply responded with an unruffled, "Yes, of course, I'm having dialysis." Her answer was to cut the treatment short, go home and shower, get in the car, and head to the ER of the hospital. I recall flagging my nurse down, relaying the message quite calmly, and then calling my husband. He didn't believe me at first, I don't think, because we had received so many calls in the past. He called my parents, and they immediately phoned me back, and I retold the scenario. We all met at the dialysis center. They were teary-eyed already, as we had been waiting for so long. That's when my stomach started to break-dance and it was becoming somewhat surreal. Could this offer be the actual one? The roller coaster ride we had been on was like a Six Flags Adventure Theme Park ride, and I wasn't sure I was ready to board that ride again.

We arrived at Columbia NYPH. The car ride was a complete blur of emotions. Once we got there, I was ushered to a back bay area and put in a gown, as they explained how the surgery would proceed. Some details of my donor were shared, and I was introduced to my amazingly young spunky surgeon, Dr Kasi McCune. She had "piano hands," as she described them. A phrase that is etched in my brain forever and, to this day, produces a smile on my face. I adored her from the minute I met her. I was comfortable at that moment and ready to move forward, although deep down I still didn't believe it was going to proceed. There had been so many obstacles that we faced prior to this day that I figured there was something we would have to hurdle yet again. She explained to us that if we didn't see her again it meant the organs were a go and that I'd be seeing her in the operating room. Well, about an hour and a half later I was being rolled towards the OR door with tears streaming down my cheeks thinking my life was about to drastically change for the better. I kissed my parents and husband goodbye, hoping to wake up from this surgery. I couldn't help but think, *holy shit, is this really happening? Wow, I have waited so long for this day that I cannot believe it is really here. I must be dreaming!* I actually did grab the top of my right hand and pinch the skin to make sure it was reality. The stretcher stopped in front of the metal doors and with a large white blanket wrapped around my shoulders and those gripper socks on my feet, I questioned the kind woman pushing the stretcher. I inquired if I had the help of two nurses on each side of me, could I walk my way into the OR. Dr. McCune stopped me on the way in and asked if I wanted to see my organs? There they sat, in a silver bowl on ice. My new little bean and pancreas. They were such beautiful and glorious life-saving organs. True miracles and all mine! It was like out of a sci-fi movie. Literally—that picture will be frozen in my brain forever!!!!

My surgery lasted 11 hours. I woke up in the ICU with tubes everywhere but I knew one thing, I was alive and I had survived. Now thanks to my donor, I was going to make every day count and live for him and his gracious family. I had been cut straight down the middle of my abdomen to just above my pubic bone, but I didn't really care. My scars tell an amazing story of survival. They are victorious. I spent eleven days in the hospital recovering and learning to walk again with physical therapy. Getting trained in immune-suppression medications and new lifestyle changes wasn't easy. Yet all of this I welcomed with broad open arms. I was gaining a new healthy life. One I hadn't seen in over 25 years, and I couldn't remember feeling this fantastic since I was almost ten years old.

Almost six months later, I returned back to my old stomping grounds so to speak. I wanted to thank all the nurses and techs at the dialysis center for taking care of me for the last seven years. I also wanted to offer to sit with some of the patients and share my story. I wanted to offer support, to let them see my scars, or just to let them ask whatever questions they may have had. When I walked into the center, I was met with gasps, shocked looks, and smiles. People were in total disbelief that it was me walking into the center. No one had expected me to make it off the operating table. I met with the head of the facility, and she mentioned to me that there was a gentleman who had just started an organization that I might be interested in. He was speaking at a local library. He had just donated one of his kidneys to a total stranger. His name was Ned, and I attended his speech. The attendance was minimal, but I was very moved by his story because of my own journey. I approached him at the end, and we exchanged numbers and agreed to meet for lunch a week later. Ned had the donor experience, and I had the patient perspective. Together we were a perfect pair. He had just formed an organization called Donor To Donor. He had donated at Weil-Cornell in New York City, and I at Columbia, also in New York City. At that point my volunteer experience with transplantation was in full bloom. A year later I also joined The Transplant Forum Executive Committee and Benefit Committee at Columbia University. My surgeon, Dr Kasi McCune, and I, along with Josh Morrison from Waitlist Zero, created a project at Columbia NYPH called Philter, to help patients find living donors, educate the public, and raise awareness about organ donation. In addition, I became a UNOS Ambassador and NKF Peer Mentor.

None of this would have been possible had it not been for my noble hero donor and his extraordinary family that I hope to meet someday. Because of organ donation, I am alive, and I will continue to live each day fully committed to helping people avoid what I endured. I know that I was only able to get through the journey because of my family, their steadfast support, and undying devoted love for me.

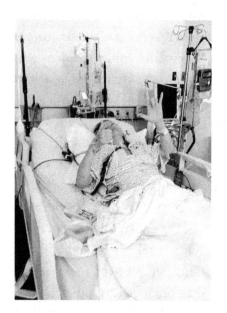

Love with all my Heart—
my support system to this day

About Jen

Jen graduated high school from Frankfurt International School in Germany and went on to Wheaton College in Norton, Massachusetts, where she obtained a B.A. degree in Philosophy. With an interest in both medicine and fashion she looked at both areas, and after an internship at a local hospital and working at a fashion company in Manhattan, New York, she had yet to find her life's passion. She found herself in retained Executive Search for many years. After she had been given the "Gift of Life," her dual transplant (pancreas/kidney) allowed her mind and body to strengthen and grow. From this strengthening the real purpose of her life emerged. Organ donation saved her, and the selfless act of her donor family changed her priorities.

Today, Jen is dedicating her life to assisting others in finding an easier path towards attaining a transplant. She hopes that their journey is met with less emotional stress, struggle, and turmoil, through her work. Jen promotes active support systems/networks and positive thinking being key factors in a successful transplant and a happy life. None of this would have been possible had it not been for her incredible parents by her side!

Jen currently resides in Connecticut and is the founder of The Transplant Journey, Inc. You can connect with her through the website www.transplantjourney.org.

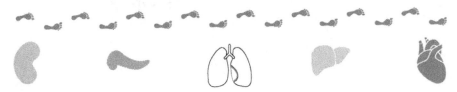

THE TRANSPLANT JOURNEY, INC.

Dawn Lyons-Wood

#Emstrong

During an interview, a couple years ago, I was asked how Organ Donation had changed my life. Typically, I am not at a loss for words; however, this question left me speechless. The only response I could think of was, "How has it *not* changed my life?"

My story started in October 1995 when I gave birth to my beautiful daughter, Emily Christine Lyons. Emily was born with her eyes wide open, and she never stopped her zest for learning about the world until the very last time she closed them. Life allowed me to be a stay-at-home mom for the early years. Emily and I were inseparable. We were blessed again, two years later, and we gave Emily her first best friend, her sister Sarah. Two years after that, we completed our family with the birth of her brother, Emmett Joseph.

Every day was better than the one before. I loved my children, and they loved each other as well. The girls were as tight as two sisters could be, and they doted on their little brother. We enjoyed life to the fullest and made the most of every day. These will forever be some of the best times of my life. Every day was an adventure. I will forever be grateful for being able to spend so much time with my children during these important years. I was able to get to know them as individuals and nurture them in their unique abilities and interests; and, I loved them to pieces.

As we all know, life moves too fast. The kids went to school, I got a job, and life got busier and busier. However, our bond and their sibling-love never changed. Their father was a superintendent at the local Country Club and the golf course became their evening playground. We did everything together. We raised the kids with a love for friends and family, care and concern for their fellow human beings, and a respect for nature. Emily was the natural leader. She led her sister and brother with her yearning to learn and teach. She was born an over-achiever, and we often joked that everything she touched was golden.

Case in point, Emily was a shy child, and I spent a lot of time being friendly or striking up conversations with strangers to guide her to become more outgoing. I was downright embarrassing and heard more than my fair share of, "Mom, please stop that." However, the summer that Emily was nine years old, everything changed. I thought it would be beneficial for her to audition for the local tell-a-tale community theater. The play was *Winnie the Pooh*, and who does not like Pooh? During the auditions, kids were singing "Twinkle Twinkle Little Star," "Happy Birthday," and other songs they knew the words to. My Emily got on stage and belted out Daniel Powter's "Bad Day." I was proud but had no idea what I was in for. She nailed the audition and got the lead. Emily was Pooh, and the best Winnie the Pooh I had ever seen or will ever see again. She sang, danced, and did not miss a mark. She loved it from beginning to end, and she blossomed! From those days on, we based every proud moment on the Pooh scale. In fact, my last words to Emily were how "Pooh proud" I was of her.

Emily continued to show her character and beautiful soul. She was always a giving and nurturing human, and that was apparent during her young years. I often had to remind her that her brother and sister already had parents. She would spend hours making craft projects to give people. We spent many hours and weekends taking part in charity walks. Emily was active in her church and the community. She loved her grandparents, aunts, uncles, and cousins, and was grateful for every moment with them. She was the first to give hugs when she walked in the door. Emily was the ideal student and student athlete. Her stepfather is a coach, and the term they use is "coachable." Emily was that. She was a people pleaser, a giver, a great friend, and a genuine, wonderful human being, with the most beautiful eyes and smile you have ever seen.

Her teenage years were not much different. Emily continued to blossom, and I could see what type of adult she was developing into. She was a straight-A student, tri-sport athlete, and everyone's friend. I know it sounds too good to be true, but that was Emily. She also had her downfalls. Emily was a perfectionist. Regarding her studies and sports, everything had to be perfect. She was harder on herself than her teachers, coaches, or we, as her parents, could be. She would spend hours checking her test scores and grades, and training to be the best she could be at whatever she was working on. Emily had very high expectations of herself, and it showed. However, she kept herself grounded by wearing her favorite purple shorts, a mismatched t-shirt, and crocs with socks. We always said she was the perfect package.

It was her senior year in high school that Emily really thrived and became the strong, confident young woman I will always remember and be proud of. She embraced every opportunity and made the most of every moment. That is a lesson she taught me, and one I will continue for the rest of my life. Her senior year was full of adventures. She was all-conference and team captain of the Girls Varsity Golf team. She was a lawyer on her Mock Trial team and took the Mock Trial team to the state competition in the morning, and attended a Miley Cyrus concert in the evening. She embraced the best of both worlds. Thinking back on her outfit changes that day will always make me smile. She took part in a class trip to Spain and made lifetime friends and memories. However, one of my favorite memories of Emily will be the day they crowned her Homecoming Queen. I guess I will admit, we were not surprised when she was nominated for court. After all, we knew Emmy was well-liked and involved in a lot of activities in high school, which are two of the major requirements to be nominated. As I sat there in the gymnasium with my parents, I was unprepared for the feeling I received when I saw the happiness on her face when they called her name as the queen. It seemed, almost for a moment, she felt as beautiful and amazing as everyone else viewed her as. She saw in herself what everyone else saw in her every day. She shined. She shined in the parade; she shined that night in a football jersey standing next to her boyfriend who was elected King, and she glowed the following day in her dress, sash, and crown. I will never forget standing with my parents on the streets of small-town, Beaver Dam, waiting for the convertible to turn the corner. I looked up and down the streets, packed with the community and students full of school spirit, and thought, *My daughter did it. She is the queen!* That moment impacted more people than I realized. Many people share that experience as their last memory of Emily.

Looking back, it was such a big moment for me as her mother, but it was only a steppingstone for Emily. She always looked ahead, knowing she was going to accomplish greater things, and every task or goal she completed only brought her to her next one. She was ready to grow. Emily was always strong, confident, smart, kind, and all the other characteristics to make her a success. However, she was now going to be a smaller fish in a much bigger pond. I was a little worried about her entering college and having to face that reality. My worries disappeared once she was comfortable. She loved college, she loved learning, and she loved her newfound freedom and independence. She used it wisely. In Emily's short time at college, she continued to flourish. She made friends, she made impressions on her professors, and she welcomed the opportunity to further her education in her desired field. She made a difference. One thing that I will always be thankful for is Emily's ability to embrace every situation, every adventure and experience, and everything that life offered her. However, I also fear that this determination brought her to that snowmobile on February 28, 2015.

While on a weekend getaway with her boyfriend and his family, Emily went on a morning snowmobile ride. Before the ride really got started, Emily hit a tree while traveling from one gas station to the next. We received a call that is by far every parent's worst nightmare. People use this expression, but it is far beyond a nightmare. There are no words to describe the next couple days. There were feelings of emptiness, disbelief, faith, anger, love, denial, and immense heartbreak. The events that were happening around us were surreal. I believe my brain protects me and stores some of those memories in parts that I never have to revisit. However, I can tell you what helped me survive. It was the moment we realized Emily signed up to be an organ and tissue donor. She even took the next step and signed the online donor registry. Emily's organ donation not only saved many others, I believe it even saved me.

After all the last tests were evaluated and they informed us that Emily's brain was not signaling her body, I tried to comprehend that I would not be bringing my daughter home. Again, my body and brain protected me, and I went into business mode. I knew that I needed to make sense of my family's tragedy. I needed to protect my other children and family members and take charge. I needed to focus elsewhere. I preferred to live in denial, and I could always grieve later. I worked with the organ donor liaison at the hospital, and I wrote a letter about Emily for the organ procurement team. We asked the team to find recipients as fast as they could to protect our other children and family members, and shorten time of the vigil at

Emily's bedside. It was almost like Emily decided, and it left me to carry out all her wishes. In her lifetime, Emily gave me many, many reasons to be proud. However, this moment was a different level of pride. My daughter was a hero, and she was going to perform her last unselfish act.

Emily's surgery was scheduled for March 2. The organ procurement team met us waiting outside her hospital room. We were all allowed to say our goodbyes separately and then walk with her to the last doors of the operating room. I recall feeling sorry for the nurse walking with us, having to witness such a heartbreaking moment. Months later, this nurse thanked me for allowing her to witness such a moment of pure love. It changed the way I viewed our goodbye. It was then that I learned to open my mind and embrace Emily's signs and my new direction in life.

My daughter Emily saved six people's lives, gave sight to two people, and improved the lives of over 60 people in 22 different states.

On our first morning of waking up in a house without Emily, I received a call from a social worker assigned to our case. Her name was Christine, and she worked with the University of Wisconsin Organ and Tissue Donation. That was the call and individual that changed my life. We clicked instantly. She listened with a loving ear, and her voice was soothing. She called Emily by her name and made me feel like I was not about to lose my mind. She shared the story of the mustard seed, which I have referred to often in the years since to give me strength and comfort. She gave me the opportunity to talk to someone outside of my tight circle of family and friends, who were also grieving. This, I found out, is a rare gift in this journey. Above all of that, she introduced me into the land of organ and tissue donation, and along with Emily's induction, she gave me purpose. I started to live the moment I realized my daughter would not.

Becoming an active member in this unknown world of organ and tissue donation came easy and fast to me. Emily was a doer, much more than I was. She would take the "bull by the horn" and get things done, and do it with kindness. Emily was no longer physically here. Instead of feeling the weight of the world on my shoulders, I was going to become a donor mom on a mission. I was going to make sure the world never forgot my daughter, help others with kindness, and, above all, spread awareness of organ and tissue donation everywhere I went. Every morning I had to decide to give in or give it my all. I was going to fulfill what Emily started and make her proud.

As I mentioned, Emily and I were a lot alike, but we were also very different. I often said that I was her mother, but I looked up to her. I marveled at her confidence and took pride because I helped create it. I was not at that level. However, I would have to quickly learn to get there.

A month after the accident, the high school was having an event in Emily's honor. Not only did we miss her, but the entire community was shocked and grieving as well. A local news channel heard of Emily's story and asked to interview us and promote the upcoming event. They arrived at my house, and, I must admit, I still did not quite understand what was happening. They interviewed me. It was a beautiful piece for the news, and it overwhelmed me with the results. More and more people would hear of my daughter, the hero, and sign up to be organ donors. UW Organ and Tissue Donation had a volunteer assigned to our event at the high school. She was giving information and talking to people about being donors, and people were signing up. Emily was still working her magic. I realized Emily was not done with her job here. She still had many things to accomplish and she would need a "wing woman." Enter Mom!

I became a certified volunteer with the UW Organ and Tissue Donation offices. I became immersed in learning all I could about the world of organ and tissue donation. I was quick to write letters to Emily's organ recipients. I wanted to know everything there was to learn. This is a slippery slope when you just lost your daughter, and, truth be told, there are some things I wish I had not learned right away. However, I referred to Emily's lessons of *knowledge is power*, and I learned to embrace everything my new world offered.

Not that I was ever shy, but I did not offer myself up to speak in public or draw attention to myself. However, I now found myself sharing Emily's story in front of church congregations, donor family events, and anywhere else someone asked me to speak. While this world was still very new to me, and I was continuing to comprehend living without my daughter, and caring for my other family members, I was asked to speak at the UW Health Transplant 50th celebration. I was there to share Emily's story and represent "Hope." I believe I was still operating on autopilot and had no idea of how big the transplant world, or this event, was. For the first time, I stood in front of almost 1,000 people and shared our story. I met recipient after recipient. People waited in line after the event and wanted to thank me. This was a very confusing moment for me. After all, I did nothing. All I did was share my story of my amazing daughter. She was the one they should thank. I met the most amazing people in the world. Every one of them had a story, and I wanted to hear each one. In fact, I made some lifelong friends that day. I realized that the support from the system that took care of my daughter and her organs will never leave me. I realized that even though there are other families that have lost their children and loved ones, we respect each other's feelings with sympathy and empathy. We are together yet still alone. Above all, I realized what an amazing hero my daughter was and what an incredible honor she gifted to me. She saved and improved the lives of others with her organ and tissue donations, and she saved my life by giving me something positive to focus on.

The day of her accident, Emily was to be inducted into the University of La Crosse Lions Club. She was studying biology and chemistry, with dreams of becoming an optometrist. Vision was always very important to her. One of my proudest moments will always be the day they inducted me into the Beaver Dam Lions Club.

I did it on her behalf and could not have been prouder. I had tears in my eyes as they read the statements and I agreed to uphold the duties. After this memorable evening, I received a call to be a cornea transporter. It was Valentine's Day, which is also National Donor Day. Again, I could not help but recognize the signs. My husband, son, and I transported the corneas that evening. It overwhelmed me with the realization that someone did the exact same thing for our Emily. To this day, every time I transport corneas, I am overwhelmed with emotion for the donor and the recipient. Being a transporter and donor mom introduced me to the Lions Eye Bank of Wisconsin.

The office staff at Lions Eye Bank of Wisconsin have become like family and have supported me and allowed me to grow. They have presented me with the Crystal Vision Award, and the Lions Legacy of Sight Award, for my work on raising awareness for organ and tissue donation. They trusted me to represent them in a commercial and share Emily's story. As I mentioned, my purpose is to finish what Emily started. This may not have originated as my path, but it ended as mine. Raising organ and tissue donation awareness, sharing Emily's story, and continuing her legacy is about as natural to me as breathing. I am so blessed to be surrounded and supported by amazing people, both professionally and personally, who recognize my passion and join me for the causes. I loved my life before. I did not ask for this new journey, and I was unprepared for it. No one can ever be prepared. However, I will survive with the support and love of many, and this is a true testament to Emily. I thank her every day for the people she places in my path.

Like I said, I started living after my daughter did not. She taught me many things and I continue to learn from her lessons. I understand the result from loving hard is also hurting hard. I would not change one day of those 19 years, four months, and 26 days I had with physical Emily. Emily was a gift from the beginning and that has never changed. She has opened my eyes and taught me so much. She continues to teach the people she knew and even people that never had the opportunity to know her. She is a beautiful and amazing spirit and her wingspan is immense.

We have coined the phrase #emstrong, and we use #emstrong to remind ourselves to be kinder, be nicer, be gentler, and to take care of our fellow human beings. We have also created Team #Emstrong. Team #Emstrong is a group of family and friends that volunteer for many events helping many causes. Together we raise money and awareness for the UW Organ and Tissue Donation Educational Fund, Lions Eye Bank of Wisconsin, Parkinson's disease, and the Emily C. Lyons Memorial Scholarship, which allows us to give financial assistance to two seniors with Emily's same characteristics during their freshman year at college. I am beyond proud whenever I see a #emstrong wristband, bumper sticker, or t-shirt; or when someone shares a story of how #emstrong helped get them through a moment or feeling.

So, how is my life different? Honestly, nothing is the same. I love harder because nothing is promised. I work harder because I now know I can give everything 100%. I appreciate everything more because I know it can be taken from me at a moment's notice. I even see colors brighter. I embrace every moment; I jump out of planes; I learned to ballroom dance; I transport corneas; I train nurses to get families to consent to organ donation; I teach driver's education students about organ and tissue donation; I have met Governors and have spoken at the Governor's mansion; I have had articles in magazines; I wear my donor family pin every day; and I don't stop talking, ever. I may not be an organ recipient, but organ donation and my beautiful daughter's decision saved my life.

I understand now that I will live the rest of my life grieving. I will grieve for my daughter and all her potential. I grieve for the children she will never have. I grieve for my other children growing older than their oldest sister. However, I will also live my life with a heart full of gratitude. Through time, I have learned that Emily's legacy was not just her organ donation—it was her ripple effect. Her wisdom, her giving, and her spirit continue to teach, and now I am so grateful to learn. I will live every day to the fullest and try to make a difference while I am here. Life is full of give and takes, and nothing defines that more than organ and tissue donation.

Here is to you, Emily Christine Lyons! I will forever be grateful God made me your mother, and I am forever Pooh proud!

"When we lose someone we love, we must learn not to live without them, but to live with the love they left behind."

– Unknown

Our hero.

Emily, Sarah, and Emmett—
the happy siblings.

Pooh Proud

Homecoming Queen Emily.

Golfing was her favorite.

Proud Mom.

Proud Dad.

Emily's loving family.

Cornea transport in honor of Emily

All the love #emstrong.

About Dawn

Dawn Lyons-Wood is a Customer Service Manager at a large printing company, but her passion is advocating for organ donation awareness. Dawn has made many personal appearances and given many radio, TV, and magazine interviews, all to promote organ donation and how the impacts of giving and kindness can change lives. She is a volunteer for UW Organ and Tissue Donation, Lions Eye Bank of Wisconsin, and a member of the Beaver Dam Lions Club (2020 Lion of the Year). Dawn is a recipient of the Legacy of Sight award, Crystal Vision award, and has even danced in the National Kidney Foundation's Spotlight on Life Gala. She also speaks to driver's education students, college students, nurses, and everyone else she can, to share the legacy of donation that her daughter Emily started when she donated her gifts to save six lives, to give sight to two others, and to help over 60 more people, after the effects of a tragic snowmobile accident. Dawn is a proud donor mother!

Dawn tirelessly organizes and promotes the annual Emily C. Lyons Memorial Golf outing to raise money for the Lions Eye Bank of Wisconsin, UW Organ and Tissue Donation Education Fund and the Emily C. Lyons Memorial Scholarship. One of Dawn's missions in life is to let people know about her beautiful, heroic daughter and to spread the word about giving and kindness. #emstrong

Dawn and her husband Michael live in Beaver Dam, Wisconsin, and have a large blended family of seven adult children. In Dawn's free time she enjoys movies, knitting, and taking walks while enjoying nature. She also enjoys music, dancing, and a good craft beer from time to time.

Dawn shares Emily's "ripple effect" on Facebook (Emstrong).

Kate Griggs

Kate's Journey to Donate a Kidney

I had living donation on my mind for years as a life goal. On March 3rd, 2016, around 3:00 a.m., I saw a story on Facebook of a young man in Kentucky who needed a kidney, and I sent a message to the contact person, his mother, telling her I would try to donate to him. The next morning, I told my husband as he was cooking brunch for us. He wasn't shocked at all as I had expected he would be. Instead, he was 100% on board and in for the journey that would define the rest of our lives.

I filled out the initial paperwork and faxed it to the transplant coordinator. My husband came up behind me for a hug as I sat at my office chair staring at my computer and he told me, "Only my Kate would do something like this."

At that moment, I knew I had his full support for the roller coaster ride we were both about to take. The journey brought us closer together in our marriage than ever before.

My 20-year-old son, Andrew, was nervous of my decision to donate, but after I was home and recovering we also became more close. He was a great help to me during my recovery, and the years after when I struggled with depression. It was the rest of the journey that was difficult.

The man from the story, to whom I had wanted to donate, also had someone else testing for him at the same time I was testing. That man was a better match, so I was no longer considered as his donor. My coordinator asked if I'd be willing to donate to a stranger and start a kidney chain, and of course, I said yes!

After 6 months of testing and delays, I donated my left kidney. I started what they call a kidney chain at the University of Kentucky in Lexington. A chain starts by a stranger who wants to donate to anyone in need. The original chain was 5 recipients long, but after several cancelations for various reasons, including the day prior to the first surgery date, it ended up being only 2 recipients who received their life-saving gift. My heart broke that the chain went from five, to four, to three, and then to just two. I was hoping to make a bigger impact with my kidney, affectionately named Grace after Grace Vanderwaal who auditioned and won America's Got Talent in 2016, but it wasn't meant to be. I was told that, in the original chain of five, two of the intended recipients were sick the day prior to surgery, and one donor changed his/her mind. Later, I was told that they had lost their chance for a transplant and wouldn't be added back to the transplant list. I often wonder about who those people were and if they are still being kept alive on dialysis machines.

In the beginning, I told only a few of my closest friends of my plan to donate, and it was those friends who would get me through some of the toughest days of my life. Eight years prior to my donation, my house had flooded, and during the year-long renovation, we bought another house in Bloomington, Indiana. I thought almost losing my house and many personal belongings was the worst thing that could happen to me. However, I came to realize that material things are replaceable, and don't matter at all compared to my relationships with family, friends, and community. Had my house not flooded, I would not have had any support with my donation journey other than my husband, because when I moved to my new house, I made several new friends who stuck with me through the roller coaster ride on my journey to donate a kidney. Bianca, Holly, Lindsey, and Tana were there before the donation, and they remain my closest friends today—four years later. They were the first to know, and although surprised, remained very supportive throughout my donation journey.

I was ostracized by some family, friends, and colleagues for donating my kidney to a stranger. They referred to me as mentally ill. My husband lost all of his closest friends because they also thought I was crazy. Many people questioned, "Why would you do something like that?" I came to expect the reaction and then stopped talking about my donation all together. It hurt so much to have people, who I considered my great friends, not talk to me for the entire time I was testing, donating, and recovering. Even years later, some relationships are just very awkward. I don't use the "D" word in front of them.

I own a forensics company, and my husband is the Chief Pathologist and Attorney for the company. For a decade we have traveled the states of Indiana and Illinois performing autopsies for 54 counties. We have also performed private autopsies for families and attorneys. Many of our forensics business clients turned on us because of my donation, and we lost almost all of our accounts because of my kidney donation. This was ironic because coroners deal with deceased donation regularly. Many of them consider donation a bother as it makes more work for them, and for the funeral directors as well. They couldn't understand why I would want to donate, but I'm sure if they, or a loved one, ever needed an organ, they would want someone to step up to save their life. They harassed my husband at several of the forensics offices he works in. Our largest account at the time became a hostile work environment.

My husband was becoming ill at the thought of going to that office to perform autopsies. No one would talk to him or look him in the eyes anymore. We had that account for twelve years, and because of my organ donation, we ended up losing it after I emailed the Coroner, telling her how we felt about how she and her employees were treating us.

I believe everything happens for a reason, and I can only believe that the way they treated us led me to create what I call my "happiness projects." On post-op day six, I was in more pain and started looking around at the little things that brought me comfort. A light bulb went off in my head, illuminating something positive that I could do to make future donors' recoveries more comfortable and rewarding than mine had been. I made a list of each item that brought me comfort as I sat on my front porch getting some fresh air and watching the golfers on hole number seven of the golf course across from our house. I was trying to come up with the name for my idea. As I sat there thinking, a man walked by on the fairway. He stopped and asked if I was Kate and if I had donated my kidney. I told him, "Yes," and he said, "That was a noble thing." *How did he know?* I wondered. I had forgotten, for a moment, that my friend, Holly, had decorated an enormous sheet with the words, *Kate Gave a Kidney to a Stranger*, and had hung it from my garage to welcome me home after my surgery and for passersby to see. It was such a surprise to come home to, and I'll always remember it as one of the kindest gestures anyone has ever done for me. With my newfound inspiration, on that day, I named my project "Kate Cares Kidney Donor Care Packages."

Shortly thereafter, I was choosing the recipients of these care packages from a support group for living donors that I am in. That group had supported me throughout my journey, and I wanted to give back to future donors. A few months later, I started another project of giving away kidney donor decals to living donors in the same support group. A fellow donor-sister, Lindsay, created the original design, and with her permission I started mass producing them to give away. This project has become known worldwide. With so much negativity in my life because of my donation, I needed some happiness to get me through the severe depression I went through post-donation. Losing friends and clients took its toll on my mental health for a while.

Today, I am so much better for what I went through, and know who my genuine friends are, and have made so many more than I ever would have, had I not donated my kidney. Everything happens for a reason. I am proud to say that 4½ years after my "happiness projects" began, there are over 9,000 decals of all sorts on every continent all over the world. I have expanded my project to include liver donors, and kidney, heart, and lung recipients, and a special decal with a butterfly on the green organ donation ribbon for donor families.

In January 2019, I added another project to include custom banners for living donors and recipients to take with them in their travels, to spread awareness for organ donation. I also donate my banners to as many of the National Kidney Foundation Kidney Walks around the country as possible, in order to spread awareness. My Donate Life Banner Ambassadors, made up of mostly living donors, have taken my banners to every continent on this great planet called Earth. This makes me very proud! Leah was the inspiration who made me decide to create traveling banners. I wanted my decals to reach every continent, but since there are no living donors in Antarctica, I needed a plan B. I knew Leah was planning a trip from her home country of New Zealand to Antarctica, so, I asked if she would take a banner with her. A picture of the kidney decal is on each banner, therefore, the decal made it to every continent!! She also took some decals with her that were on the outside of her laptop and water bottle.

I invite you to check out my Facebook page, Living Donor Kidney Decal, to see pictures of all the decals I've made and have given away. Shannon took a banner with her on a 6-week adventure through Southeast Asia visiting five countries including Singapore, Malaysia, Thailand, Vietnam and China. Later, she took another custom banner to Ireland. Jodi took her banner to climb the summit of Aconcagua–the highest mountain in South America! Sophan took her banner to Banff, Canada, which is on my bucket list! Dori took her banner to Israel and posed with it in the Dead Sea. Mary Frances took hers to Ecuador to visit her son. Brandy traveled with her banner to Yemen and Jordan, and Devon went on Safari with her banner in Africa.

Most recently, several donors and recipients carried banners on a cruise to the Bahamas that I organized in February 2020. We were one of the last cruise ships to return safely prior to the pandemic. I am so grateful we could take that trip as it cultivated the many friendships we all made through social media the past few years. It has helped us to get through the many months of uncertainty we have all faced in 2020. It's so fun to have a way to spread awareness for organ donation all over the world. I invite you to check out my Facebook page, Donate Life Banner Ambassadors, to see where they've all been around the world. I delight in living vicariously through these ambassadors for organ donation! There are now dozens of my banners all over the world.

Even though it was a rough road at first, the friends and connections I have made from my happiness projects more than make up for all the ones I've lost along my journey. I have found that being around like-minded donors is what I needed to combat my depression. In the beginning of my journey, I did research on living donation. My research led me to my very first donor friend, Laurie. She has a blog called Spare Parts, which I found late one night…around 3 A.M., knowing me. Laurie also wanted to donate altruistically and was going through testing at Northwestern Hospital in Chicago. Laurie's Dad had received a liver transplant from a deceased donor in 2011, and she wanted to pay it forward to honor the gift he had received. Together they started a nonprofit in Chicago called Transplant Village. They are an inspired group of organ recipients, donors, and their families united in their mission to support the future of organ transplantation at Northwestern Medicine while connecting and supporting the transplant community.

I laughed and also cried while reading Laurie's blog. It was as if I had found my "soul sister." We were going through so many of the same emotions and experiences. I sent Laurie a message, and we became fast friends. Then along came Rebecca and her recipient, Kelly. They were also going through the testing at the same time. We all became friends, and I wanted to meet them in person. I donated my kidney on September 29, 2016, and Laurie donated at Northwestern on November 22nd, to a stranger, kicking off a 6-person kidney chain. Rebecca donated part of her liver, also at Northwestern, to her friend from high school, Kelly, on December 7, 2016.

After we had all recovered, I planned a meetup at the Cloud Gate, called "The Bean," in Millennium Park in Chicago, in April 2017, to celebrate National Donate Life Month. I chose "The Bean" because it looks like a kidney bean, and I thought it was a perfect place to meet to symbolize kidney donors. It was a wonderful first meeting. I finally had friends who got me—they understood and shared my passion.

After that meeting, Laurie and I decided we would plan an even bigger meetup at "The Bean" the following year to set a Guinness World Record. Because of organ donation, we set the record for "The Largest Gathering of Organ Transplant Donors" on April 21, 2018, with 410 living donors. It was one of the proudest moments of my life.

This event also raised $40,000 for Transplant Village to help with the expenses of future living donors.

Later, I helped my donor friend, Brenda Cortez, with promoting her mascot, Howl the Owl, from her children's book series. Howl stands for "Help Others With Love." Brenda is also a contributor to, and the inspiration behind, this book. Together we created a project called "Howl the Owl on the Prowl" and have sent Howl to dozens of hosts all over the world. Howl has touched down on every continent in the world! Because of Organ Donation, he enjoyed traveling with a fellow living donor sister, Leah, to Antarctica, and with Shannon on a 6-week trek through 5 countries in Southeast Asia.

None of this would have been possible had I not donated my kidney. It has been so much fun to see Howl's adventures in places I'll never see in my lifetime. My dream is to take Howl on my number one bucket list trip to the Maldives someday!! He's just dying to go down one of those slides on a bungalow in the middle of the Indian Ocean and to sit on a swing soaking up the sunshine. Someday! I have a map of the world with stick pins in it of where all of my organ donation awareness projects have reached. I'm so proud to look at that map with pins sticking in it signifying where all my decals have reached, where my banners have been, and where Howl the Owl has traveled.

Brenda Cortez and I also recently started a new club for donors called Worldwide Organ Donors. Our goal is to honor each donor as they celebrate their milestone donor anniversaries. The longest donor I know so far donated over 50 years ago! This incredible woman donated in 1971 to her then 16-year-old daughter, which allowed her to lead a normal life. She gave birth 15 years later to her daughter, who also became a living donor 48 years after her grandma donated to her mother. Had this woman not donated to her daughter, she never would have had a child who would later save another life. Living donation is truly an incredible and beautiful thing. Grandma will be 92 years old this October!

These projects have introduced me to so many new friends all over the world. Some I've met, and many more I plan on meeting. Every two years, there's an event called the Transplant Games of America that mainly transplant recipients attend, but they also welcome living donors. The event is like the Olympics in that there's an opening ceremony, a closing ceremony, and competitions in various sports for medals. I attended my first Games in 2018 in Salt Lake City. It was the most amazing experience of my life. I met so many people who knew me from my projects. It was so awesome to have people that I didn't even know, yelling my name from afar and coming up to me for hugs and high fives. I almost felt like a celebrity! I didn't compete in the Games that year as I only signed up to be a team supporter. I had taken up several sports to compete in the Games in New Jersey in July 2020 with Team Indiana, but they canceled the event because of COVID-19. It also saddened me to hear the news recently that the 2021 Transplant Games have also been canceled, but it gives me extra time to work on the sports I plan to compete in. Hopefully, the Transplant Games of America, now scheduled for July 2022 in San Diego, will happen.

Sadly, the World Transplant Games in Houston in 2021 have also been canceled because of fear of COVID-19. It would have been the first time in over 30 years that the World Transplant Games were in the United States., It is now my dream to win a medal at the Transplant Games of America in San Diego in 2022, and the World Transplant Games in Perth, Australia in 2023.

These wonderful things happened to me because of organ donation. None of it would have happened had I not donated my kidney. Even though the journey was a rough one, I would most definitely do it again in a heartbeat. I don't know where I would be without my happiness projects and all the friends I have made through them. I am blessed and grateful beyond measure.

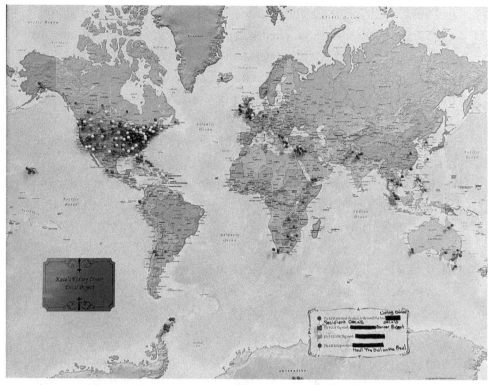

The map of everywhere her decals have gone: all over the world.

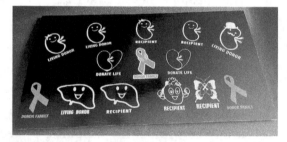

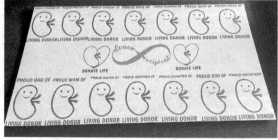

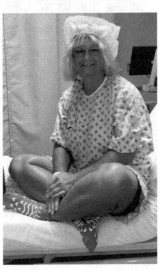

Living Donors Setting the Guinness World Record
April 21, 2018 at The Bean in Chicago.

Laurie and Kate celebrating after setting
the Guinness World Record in Chicago.

About Kate

Kate Griggs is an altruistic living kidney donor and organ donation awareness advocate. She is the owner of a traveling forensics company serving Indiana counties since 2007 and also manages her husband's medical, legal practice since 2003. Kate found her passion shortly after donating her kidney in 2016, to start what she calls her "happiness projects."

A few days after donating her kidney, she started her first of many philanthropy projects called Kate Cares Kidney Donor Care Packages. She has given dozens of care packages for soon-to-be kidney donors around the United States and Canada. From there she started the most rewarding of all her projects, the Living Donor Kidney Decal project, in February 2017.

Kate has put together many donor and recipient meetups around the country the past several years, including the annual meetup at The Cloud Gate, aka "The Bean," in Chicago, and most recently the Cruising for Organ Donation Awareness Cruise to the Bahamas in February 2020. She has given several interviews for news stations and magazines, and her projects have been written about in several articles and a book. Kate is a private kidney coach, mentoring future living donors. She is an Ambassador for Team Indiana and for Howl the Owl. She is also the organizer of the Worldwide Organ Donors club.

Kate lives in Bloomington, Indiana, with her husband, son, two dogs, and a cat named Kitty Square. When not working in her company and on her many donor projects, Kate enjoys traveling, boating, golfing, tennis, bowling, hiking, and spending time with her family and with her living donor and recipient friends.

You can connect with Kate on her Facebook page called Kate's Journey to Donate a Kidney, or by email at:
kidneydonorkate@yahoo.com.

Brittany Elliser

Three Heroes, Three Blessings

How does a person say "thank you" enough? Is it enough? Will it ever be enough? I can use any other synonym—grateful, relieved, blessed, etc.—but it never feels adequate. My son Briggs was blessed with three liver transplants all before the age of six months, and it never feels like I can properly thank his lifesaving heroes. They gave us the world, their world, and allowed us hope to one day see our son grow up, move mountains, and accomplish goals. How do you tell the person who lost their precious loved one, the most important person in the world to them, you are eternally grateful for the gift they gave to your son? As a family, we find sometimes it's easier to show, rather than say. So we are here to show the world the good things that can happen, all because a hero said yes.

I'll start with a little backstory. Our son Briggs was born December 29, 2014, and is the second-born son to my husband and me. His older brother Brady is just 17 months older than he is, and we were so excited to have two under two! However, we quickly learned that something wasn't right when his lab values were not what they were supposed to be, and they sent us to a specialist. We found out he was born with a rare liver disease named "Biliary Atresia." At one month old, he had the Kasai, which is a surgery where they directly connected his intestines to his liver in hopes of draining the bile. Around four months old, we found out the surgery was no longer working, so they placed him on the National Transplant Waiting List. At five months old, on June 24, 2015, we got the call that there was a liver for Briggs, and our lives were about to change forever.

Briggs made it through the first transplant with flying colors. He was extubated almost immediately. We got to hold him and see him open his eyes. It was in those moments that it really hit us, while we were so overjoyed and thankful, there was a mom out there who was living her darkest days. I couldn't help but admire her strength, and that somehow, someone far away from us said *yes* to organ donation, and that decision had a direct impact on our lives.

The next day, we found out Briggs had a clot in his portal vein. They sent him back for surgery to clear it; however, it was during surgery when they found they could not reestablish blood flow. We were told, ten hours later, that they were going to do everything they possibly could do to make him comfortable, but we needed to say our goodbyes.

As a parent, I was devastated. It was hard to wrap my brain around the fact that our brightest day had turned so quickly into one of our darkest days. I found myself thinking a lot about the parent of our hero, and how she had so much strength. We were told at that time that he had about 24 hours to live, and they weren't even sure if he could handle another surgery at this point.

The days following were a blur. I am not sure we ate or drank, and we mostly cried. Our baby boy was sick—VERY SICK! We feared he might not be able to hold on long enough to find another liver. He was in complete liver failure. It was hard to comprehend and to think just three days before he was sitting up and flirting with the nurses.

But we were still so thankful we had those days with him and that a hero saved him.

I just couldn't believe the laughing, cheerful baby I had brought into the hospital might never wake up. Briggs was re-listed the following day, and just two days later, July 1, 2015, we received the second call that would change our lives again. The rollercoaster of emotions was gearing up, and again it was a time when I thought a lot about our heroes and their loved ones. We were overjoyed again that someone's decision to say *YES* was impacting our lives and giving us hope again. I couldn't believe there were two strangers out there that saved my son's life in a matter of days!

We found out, however, that transplant surgery is a hard surgery, and while the liver from our second donor saved his life, something was not going right AGAIN ... his liver labs were in the 6,000's when they should have been 45. We knew when he came back upstairs that he was going to be immediately listed again for another transplant, and we went from super high to another super low.

I sat and listened as doctor after doctor told me to prepare for his funeral, and if he ever woke up, be prepared for him to never walk or talk, and to be even more honest, that he might not make it to the next surgery. And trust me, what *could* go wrong *went* wrong. He was heavily sedated, intubated, had a seizure, a GI bleed, and his arm turned completely black. I am a numbers person, so I sat watching his labs, and when I say there were so many numbers coming back to me, I am not even sure how I kept it all straight. His brain showed signs of swelling and having fluid on it. He started retaining fluid all over. One doctor did a bladder test and discovered he had compartment syndrome. They rushed him to surgery again where he was left with his abdomen open and a vacuum continuously draining fluid (about a liter a day) from his stomach. He had a bowel surgery and many biopsies. But all the while he was holding on and making slight improvements. We witnessed many miracles during this time, and to this day, I am still in shock how much we went through and made it through.

But even through all of that, we kept insisting that we were going to take our baby boy out of that hospital and take him home to play with his brother. Both my husband and I had an overwhelming sense of peace that it was all going to be OK, and it helped that we had the entire world praying for him. I literally mean the whole world was praying for him. We had set up a Facebook page to share news and updates on Briggs, and we found that our posts and prayer requests were getting over 100,000 views from all over the country and the world. People we never met or heard of were sending in messages of support and offering prayers. It was overwhelming, when I think about it, but it helped get us through those difficult times. I've heard that some people shy away from asking for prayers, or don't want to share bad news. However, we took a different approach. We knew this was going to be a time for God to shine, and we needed every prayer warrior out there. We were bold in our prayer request and knew that no mountain was too high.

On July 17, 2015, we got the final call, which I believe truly set us on the path of healing. When he came back up from surgery, I could see the pinks of his toes; something I hadn't seen over the last few weeks since he was extremely jaundice. It was at this point we knew we could finally let out the breath we had been holding for weeks.

So much happened before our hospital exit, but on October 20, 2015, we finally got to go home to our family. After spending that long in the hospital, it was like we finally saw the light at the end of the tunnel. But we knew we had work to do. We needed to heal, and we were going to make an impact on this world.

From that day forward, I have made it my life's goal to educate others about organ donation and tell people about the miracle we witnessed. You read about miracles in the Bible, and you hear stories of Jesus performing miracles, but these days I don't feel you see a large miracle on the scale which we did. When doctors, science, and everything you know says your son should not be walking, or even alive today, and then you carry him home; something changes in you. I know deep in my soul, that only God could have had a hand in Briggs' healing.

This past summer made FIVE years since Briggs received all three of his life-saving liver transplants. We don't say the first two didn't work, because he wouldn't be here without them. Each one of them saved his life. Was it a little bumpy? Sure. But it took all three heroes to have Briggs with us today.

Because of organ donation, we got to see our son roll over, crawl, take his first steps, run, play with his brother, go to the beach, go to a birthday party, start school, go on play dates, dress up for Halloween, learn how to shoot a basketball—I could go on!

We even got to meet his second donor's family. Her name was Trinity Hoblit, and she was an amazing young girl. She was 14 years old and was an advocate for organ donation, so when the time came, her parents knew right away that she would want to help others.

That was a day, as a recipient mom, I will never forget. It was my chance to tell the family of the hero that saved my son's life exactly what their decision did for our family, and for our son. Of course, I was completely speechless, but as the weekend went on, we were able to connect and really show them just how much their gift changed and shaped our lives. There will always be a part of Trinity that is with Briggs. Her liver kept Briggs alive until his last transplant. While it was a short time in between the second and third transplant, her life still made one of the biggest impacts on our lives. I can never say thank you enough to them, and they have certainly gotten to see how much we live life to the fullest!

We have had some pretty big moments with our boy Briggs! We watched him compete in the Transplant Games in 2018 in Utah, where he brought home three gold medals to Team Louisiana, and he got to sit in the pilot's seat on the airplane. Briggs has been featured in commercials, has been on TV with the local news, and so many more exciting things! He was even invited to play on a basketball team this year. We have seen time and time again, doctors and therapists tell us he would not be able to do something, and then a few months later we see him mastering the skill.

But it doesn't end there. All the little moments, you know the ones, where you look in your review mirror and you see your boys holding hands or making faces at each other; or when you are dancing in the kitchen making dinner and he comes running in there to dance with you; or when you peek in the room and see his brother and him playing in the tent, the older one teaching him how to say *bear*, or what color it is, or where to put the puzzle piece in; the moments when you think back to five years ago and realize all the progress he has made, all the odds he has beaten, and you wonder *where did the time go* and *how did we get here*; the moments when he reaches for you, hugs you super tight and says, "Mama." All these little things I get to have because of an organ donor, and I don't take them for granted for one tiny second.

Briggs' life wasn't the only one saved those days. These heroes saved all of us. They saved both my husband and me from losing our child, and they saved my son from growing up without a brother, his grandparents, aunts, uncles, and cousins, literally all of us. I can't wait to experience more "firsts" with him, even at five years old. Every day is a day we don't take for granted, and every day is truly a miracle. Not a day goes by when I don't think of our heroes and how I am so thankful they gave me these moments. I cannot wait to see, and keep showing the world, all the things Briggs will do in his life— all because of organ donation.

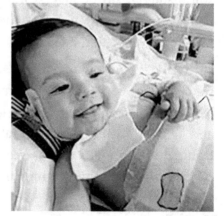

Smiling after his last surgery.

*Briggs as a newborn before his
Biliary Atresia diagnosis.*

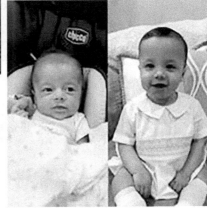

Before and after transplant.

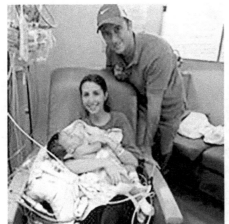

*First time holding our baby
after his three transplants.*

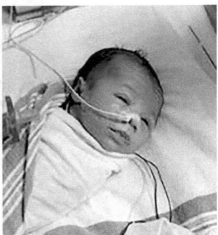

*Briggs after his Kasai surgery—where
doctors connected his intestines directly to
his liver in hopes to help him grow before
needing a transplant.*

Family of Four.

Briggs all grown up and enjoying life thanks to his heroes.

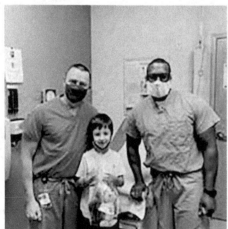

Briggs five years later with the guys that flew to retrieve his gift of life!

About Brittany

Brittany Elliser joined the BA mom's club back in 2014 when her son Briggs was born and diagnosed with Biliary Atresia. He is a three-time liver recipient and ever since they made it back home from the hospital; she has been a huge advocate of telling her son's miraculous story and speaking about the great things that come from organ donation. Brittany frequently speaks to schools, nursing classes, and can be seen on the news and radio shows to talk to anyone who will listen to their story. She loves to tell the amazing story of all that her son has overcome and finds great joy in connecting with other "liver moms."

Brittany is married to the love of her life, Bryan Elliser, and they have two amazing boys, Brady and Briggs. She is a CPA by day. Brittany and her family loves life and lives it to the fullest—they don't take a single moment for granted.

You can connect with Brittany through social media or email:

Briggs' Facebook page:

https://www.facebook.com/blessingsforbriggs

Personal Facebook: https://www.facebook.com/bkelliser

Instagram: https://www.instagram.com/bkelliser

Email: brittany.kinsley@gmail.com

George Franklin

Blessed With 45 More Years and Counting!

The Beginning

It all started at Frederick Douglass Junior High school. I attended school in Washington DC and I remember always being on the weak side, not quite able to keep up with the other kids. I was in the ninth grade and pretty scrawny. I missed a lot of classes from staying home sick and I failed my final exams! Thankfully, my mom heard about Sharpe Health School. They came out to tutor me at home during that summer break. Their tutoring me throughout the entire summer allowed me to retake my finals, which I then passed, and advanced on to high school! I had never had to repeat a grade in school, and I was so glad that I didn't have to do another year in junior high. THANK YOU, Sharpe Health School!

Once in the realm called senior high school, Frank W. Ballou Senior High in Washington, DC, things seemed so different. There seemed to be a seriousness that might have been missing in junior high. Maybe I just missed it? I majored in Business Administration, and enjoyed meeting new kids, and hanging with "old" friends from junior high. I also joined Cadets in my senior high school, but I never seemed to keep up. My marching cadence was always a bit off, and I just didn't seem to fit in. I was in Cadets for two years but decided it was not for me. The stress was giving me headaches all the time.

My senior year was a breeze! I had all my credits to graduate, but I took a few classes just to give me a reason to get up and go to school! Finally . . . GRADUATION! I'd planned, along with several classmates, to go into the military service. Yes, I was the one that could never march correctly! The one that turned left when we were to turn right. First, I continued my summer job. I'd been a pool manager or a lifeguard since eighth grade, and I loved it! Towards the end of the summer of 1972, my only sister announced she was getting married in the fall, so I put off my plans to enter the military until after the wedding. Then September came and my life, as I knew it, changed forever.

The Middle

The wedding went off without a hitch, except I wasn't able to be there because I was in the hospital. It started out as a serious cough. My mom took me to the community hospital, not wanting me to disturb my sister's wedding, hacking all over the place. There they discovered my blood pressure was sky high! It took them several days to get it down low enough to where they felt comfortable to transport me 30 minutes away to the George Washington University (GWU) Hospital in DC. Once at GWU Hospital, they found a whole new set of problems. Besides my blood pressure still being dangerously high, they discovered I was born with just one kidney, and that one was shutting down! They got my blood pressure under control, thankfully. I remember being in a four-bed ward. I guess none of us were very sick, that is, until "the cough."

I had stopped down at the nurse's station to get a sleeping pill and some cough medicine, after playing a card game with another patient I'd met. Once back in my room, I was coughing a lot, so up came the sleeping pill. A doctor wandered into our room and noticed the red phlegm I was coughing up. Next thing I knew, a nurse came in and told me I was being moved to another room. I called my mom to let her know I was being moved to another floor. The last thing I remember is the elevator door closing. While on the brief elevator ride, I lapsed into a coma.

The red phlegm was not red from the cough medicine; it was from the blood I'd been coughing up.

I believe the coma lasted a bit over a week. While I was in the coma, my heart stopped several times. To this day, I remember the pain from those paddles they used to jumpstart my heart. I remember being told that once I came out of the coma, they had to tape my eyes shut because, whenever I looked around the room and saw all the tubes, wires, and machines in there, my heart would do flips, or so it seemed. I also remember that one of my dialysis doctors stayed in my room for several days. My grandmother told me he would not leave my side. So many years have gone by that I can't remember which doctor stayed with me, but to this day, I am grateful!

"George is not going to make it." That is what they told my mother. While in the coma, I had developed a viral pneumonia that had only a 5% survival rate. Coma, heart stopping, and now a viral pneumonia, was all just a way for God to show off in my praying grandmother's opinion. I'm told they sedated my mom after telling her that her 18-year-old son would not make it through the night. My mom got in touch with my father, who lived in Philly. He and my grandfather, and a cousin, came down to see me. I had seen none of them since I was five years old. I remember seeing my dad and my cousin, and I only knew it was my cousin by his piercing gray eyes. My dad had to wear two hospital gowns because of his height and size, and they both had to wear face masks. But I had a praying grandmother! I remember her telling me how she'd wandered down the hall past my room and had seen the doctor bouncing up and down on my chest. I had coded again. She began praying and called her church. There was a church service that night, and they asked everyone to pray. Several days later, I came out of the coma and was going to survive. I told my mom I'd dreamed of a real red and white Christmas. Miraculously, I was home for Christmas! My mom had found a pure white Christmas tree, which was rare in 1972, and she decorated it in red bulbs! The drapes at the balcony window were white with red stripes, which made it even more beautiful. It was a Christmas I was never supposed to see, and yet my dream had come true! Certainly, my mom's and grandmother's had too! Not to mention, my mom and dad were together...for a little while anyway. The Christmas of 1972 will always remain in my heart!

The Dialysis Years

I was on hemodialysis at the George Washington University Hospital for exactly three years. In that three-year period, I had to have surgery, every six months, for something or another. Two shunts, in and out, a fistula, a kidney nephrectomy. My native kidney was causing blood pressure issues, so they removed it prior to transplant.

While on dialysis, I met Jerri, Yolanda, and Maureen. The four of us were on the "machine" together. I was the oldest, at 18. Later, we also met Steve Carey, Robert Bell, William Goodloe, Joseph Hughes, and several others. Many have passed on, but the memories of those three years will always be with me. Without question, I truly had the best nurses on the planet during my hospital stays and while on dialysis. Pat Shine, Ethel Jamison, Sandy Madison, Rodney, and several others were the best. But it was Pat, Ethel, and Rodney who got me through three tough years and eight surgeries, along with Dr. Pierpont, Dr. Parrish, Dr. Kramer, and Dr. Anne Thompson.

I remember driving down to the hospital late in the evening, on non-dialysis days. I could not sleep at home, so I'd drive down, and the nurses on the fourth floor would always find a bed for me to sleep in. They would call my Mom in the morning and let her know I was there and safe. The George Washington University Hospital and staff were just getting started in my life!

The Transplant Years

It was November 4th, 1975, and the day started out normal. I was working for a company where I'd drive up to Baltimore from Washington, DC, about a 45-minute drive, and pick up blood samples. I'd pack them in dry ice and then mail them to a lab. It had snowed the night before, so there was snow everywhere. While I was in Baltimore, my beeper went off. Back in those days, long before personal cell phones, everyone had a beeper. This beeper was not for my job, but for my transplant center. If it beeped, you were to call them right away. It had never beeped before! I called my hospital, and they instructed me to get there soon, because there might be a kidney for me! Well, in my excitement to get there, I slid off the road and into a snow embankment. *Oh, no, what am I going to do,* I thought. While I was sitting in my car alone, and totally unsure of how to get my car unstuck, God sent an Angel who helped me get my car back on the road. I have no idea what his name was, but I've never forgotten that act of kindness. Remembering that moment makes me think of *Howl the Owl®* and his special message of *Help Others With Love.* Someone did just that for me!

I finally got down to Washington, DC, to the transplant and dialysis center, at GWU Hospital, where I was met by the transplant team. It terrified me. I had another transplant just six months before, and sadly, it never worked. They had to take it out the day after Mother's Day. It devastated me. I think it was the worst day in my life, up to that point. I had never missed a day on dialysis, had finally gotten a transplant, and then they had to take it out. So, for six months, I recovered, went back to work, and was back on dialysis three times a week, six hours each time. When I told my surgeon, Dr.

Glenn W. Geelhoed, that I wasn't sure I wanted to do this again, he said to me, "George, do NOT turn down this kidney. This kidney is YOURS." Those words changed my life!

The surgery took place that evening and into the next morning, and I woke up peeing all over the place! So many people take certain body functions for granted, but I will NEVER take for granted the ability to just PEE! It was everywhere, and I even took pictures. I mean, after all, it had been three years, and I was only 21 years old, so it was exciting to pee so much. The transplant was a success and has remained that way for forty-five YEARS!

Because of organ donation I have LIVED! There are so many things I have been able to do, and places I have been able to visit, because an organ donor saved my life!

The birth of my son, Waylon Q. Robinson, would never have happened without organ donation! My grandchildren would not exist without organ donation. I developed a relationship with my father, George E. Franklin, Jr., and his side of the family, because of organ donation. My dad remarried and had another son, Gordon, who loved me and I loved him. Sadly, he passed away at 13, but I never would have known him, had it not been for organ donation.

Since my transplant, I have been invited by the American Kidney Fund to attend the 1st International Transplant Games, along with two ladies I'd been on dialysis with, Jerri and Yolonda, in Southsea, England. I would not have been able to attend, had it not been for organ donation! The Gold, Silver, and Bronze medals I've won at our National Transplant Games were only possible because of organ donation. The Games (previously operated by the National Kidney Foundation for 20 years and have been taken to a new level by Bill Ryan and the Transplant Games of America group) have been a big part of my life. I have attended the Games every two years and also founded the Quarter Century Club, of which I am still the president. The Quarter Century Club recognizes transplant recipients who have had their transplanted organ for 25 years or more. There is a special reception for these members to celebrate their gift of life during the Transplant Games. None of this would be possible had it not been for organ donation!

To be alive to see my mom reach 89 years of life would not have been possible without organ donation. Without God, my mom, my grandmother, brother Brian, and my sister Carolyn, I don't think I would have lived past the age of 25. So many of the people I was on dialysis with passed on in those three years while I was on "the machine." For an 18-year-old, it was very tough. My brother had to come downtown often to pick me up because I would be sunblind when I got off of "the machine," and couldn't see to drive myself back home. However, because of organ donation, my life was saved. I can still see and breathe and drive all over the place!

There are still so many things I want to do, and so many places I want to visit, but for FORTY-FIVE YEARS my kidney, named Retread, along with God's mercy and blessings, have kept me alive! I think often of my unknown donor. I wish my local Organ Procurement Organization would honor her. All I know about my kidney is that it is from a woman who was killed in an auto accident in the great state of Tennessee. A kidney I almost turned down. **I am, among men, most blessed.**

As I write this, I've decided I'm going to drive across America to San Diego, California, for the 2022 Transplant Games! Why fly and miss so much, when I can get an RV with my wonderful friend Barbara Witt and me to go road tripping to California! Barb is a two-time recipient. Her first kidney came from her dad and functioned for 36 years. She then received her current kidney through a kidney paired exchange program. Her sister's son, Brian, was not a direct match for her so they entered the program to allow her to receive a kidney from a living donor. She's had this kidney for over 10 years!

About George

George Edward Franklin 3rd was born and raised in Washington, DC, along with his brother, Brian, and their sister, Carolyn. He currently lives in Cumberland, Maryland.

George graduated from Frank W. Ballou Senior High, in Washington, DC, and a few months later started hemodialysis at the George Washington University Medical Center, in Foggy Bottom in DC. George received a deceased donor kidney in April 1975, but unfortunately the kidney had to be removed the next month. He continued on hemodialysis till November of the same year, when he received another deceased donor kidney, which is still functioning to this day!

George is now the longest deceased donor kidney recipient in the State of Maryland. He has had his kidney for 45 years and his best friend Barbara Witt is cheering for 50 years!

George has slowed down a bit the last few years, but he still volunteers with the Living Legacy Foundation, the OPO in Baltimore, and the WRTC OPO in Falls Church, Virginia, when he can. He also volunteers with the National Kidney Foundation in Maryland and Delaware. George participates in the Transplant Games of America with Team Maryland. He also is the Co-Founder of the Quarter Century Club (along with Barb Witt) which celebrates organ transplant longevity. He currently serves as President. George serves on several patient affairs committees, to help disseminate the information those committees provide. He is also the Chairman of the Athletes Advisory Council of the Transplant Games of America, an organization he loves and fully supports any way he can.

You can connect with George Franklin on Facebook or email: gef3rd@gmail.com

George with Howl the Owl.

Geroge and his brother.

George's son, Waylon, George, his father, and his grandfather.

George and his Transplant Surgeon, Dr. Glenn W. Geelhoed, meet at GWU Medical Center, Summer of 1976, 9 months after George's November 4th, 1975 Kidney Transplant

George and his Transplant Surgeon, Dr. Glenn W. Geelhoed, meet again, to celebrate the 40th Anniversary of George's Kidney Transplant, at the NKF of Maryland Offices, in Lutherville, Maryland, on December 22, 2015

Geroge's brother Brian, and Geroge's 31 year poster...these posters were displayed in the subway system in DC, Mayland, and Virgina. Also as a trailer in movie theaters!

George with his brother, sister, mother...and Snowball!

Brandi Thornton

Double Donor

As a child growing up in a small mountain town in Colorado, I didn't know of anyone who ever needed an organ transplant, but that would change as I got older. While I was in middle school and high school, I was fortunate to live next door to an amazing family that I babysat for. I spent several days a week caring for Michael and Jessi. Jessi was born with Cystic Fibrosis, but that diagnosis never stopped her, or her family, from living an incredible life.

When Jessi was 19 years old, she required a lung transplant in order to survive. She had spent 19 years thriving, but her lungs could take no more. As she waited in Children's Hospital for a donor, she knew what would happen if lungs did not become available. She knew there was a very good chance that she would die and wrote about it in a journal she kept during those last days.

A donor did not become available for Jessi, and she passed away. I remember thinking at the time how unfair it was. This beautiful and amazing creature deserved to live! She deserved a new set of lungs, and at the time I wished that I could have given them to her.

It was at Jessi's memorial service that I registered to be an organ donor after death. I couldn't stand the thought of another family waiting for a lifesaving organ transplant, only to have their loved one die because an organ didn't become available. At the time, I didn't know that living donation was an option for some organs, but I knew I wanted to help someone in the event of my death. It seemed like such a simple thing to do in order to save a life.

Many years later, in 2014, I was invited to like a page on Facebook. The page was created to help a local woman, named Christy, find a kidney donor. I didn't know her, but after scrolling through her page and reading her story, I learned more about her and couldn't get her out of my mind. I thought of her constantly, wondering what would happen if she didn't receive her kidney, and worried that I would be the only one who would get tested. If I didn't get tested, would she die? I spent the entire evening thinking about her and called the transplant center the next day to inquire about testing.

Once I completed the initial testing, I found out I was not a blood match for my potential recipient. As devastating as that was to hear, it encouraged me to learn that we could join the paired kidney exchange, and get Christy a new kidney that way. We were hopeful a match would be found, and that Christy could begin a new and healthy life.

We remained in the paired kidney exchange off and on for about two years. Christy's health declined, and during that time she was no longer considered a good transplant candidate, so they removed us from the exchange. When her health improved, they would enter us back into the database.

I never got to meet Christy in person, but we would communicate on Facebook, where she expressed her desire to find a match, and we would joke about our future hospital stay. She had hopes and dreams for the future with her husband and her son, and I was more than ready to help her fulfill them.

Sadly, Christy passed away in December 2016 before we could ever find our match. I was confident we could save her, and I would have done anything to make that happen. When it didn't, it devastated me. I couldn't understand, at the time, how we could go through two years of waiting, only to have Christy die before we ever made our match. I know that everything happens for a reason, but that wouldn't become apparent until later.

After Christy's death, I immediately entered the paired kidney exchange without a partner. I was already willing to donate to a stranger, and entering on my own would ensure that my kidney would go to someone in need. I couldn't imagine another family going through what Jessi's and Christy's did, and I couldn't get rid of the feeling that this was something I was destined to do.

Once I entered the database, I matched immediately with a man in Ohio. That's all I knew, that a man in Ohio needed my kidney. Unless my recipient and I agreed to allow communication with one another, all I would ever know is that my kidney's new home would be Ohio.

My kidney donation surgery took place on March 15, 2017, at UC Health Anschutz in Aurora, Colorado. Minus a brief layover for my kidney in Chicago on its way to Ohio, everything went according to plan. The kidney started working right away in its new home and my remaining kidney did the same. After a brief stay in the hospital, I was on my way home to recover, and to wonder about my recipient and his recovery.

When donating anonymously, or altruistically, you are given the option to reach out to your recipient. If they choose, they can respond and begin communication with you. I always thought of it like an adoption. My kidney went to its new home, and one day, when it was older, I might get to know who's been caring for it. I wrote my recipient a letter hoping I would find out how he was doing, but never expecting a response.

About four months after my surgery, I received a letter in the mail from my recipient. Rob was the new home for my kidney, and both were doing amazingly well. This was his second kidney transplant, so he'd been down this road before, but with one difference. His first kidney came from a friend, and this kidney came from a stranger.

During the next several months, Rob, his wife Becky, and I built a relationship. I got to know him and his family, and he got to know mine. I heard about Stacey, who donated to a stranger so that Rob could receive my kidney, and about his first kidney donor Matt. We planned a trip to Ohio, during the summer of 2018, so I could meet my amazing recipient, his family, and his donors in person.

During our trip to Ohio, I could see the direct impact of living organ donation. I had never been around anyone who had received an organ transplant, so I had no idea how lives could be impacted. I talked with Rob's family members and friends, and I watched Rob live his life, which is something he would not have been able to do without organ donation. I met Stacey who donated on his behalf, and also Matt who was his first living donor.

I wasn't the only person in my family who witnessed the direct impact of living organ donation during that trip to Ohio. My daughters, Jailyn and Adelyn, got to know Rob and Becky via Facebook and phone calls. The girls knew of Rob's story and knew how I came to give Rob my kidney. They watched our story come full circle and saw firsthand how important organ donation is for the recipient and their families. They also understood how important it is to help others, even though you might need to take something from yourself in order to make that happen.

Because of my trip to Ohio, the desire to do more became stronger. It had always been there, that feeling that I hadn't yet done enough, and it only got stronger after meeting Rob and seeing how his life had changed because of my gift. At my two-year kidney donation checkup, I decided I wanted to help another stranger.

I had heard that UC Health had successfully completed a handful of liver donation surgeries on previous kidney donors. Since I didn't feel that I was done giving, I brought it up to my living kidney donor coordinator at my final kidney donation checkup. The risks were laid out very clearly to me, but I insisted that I wanted to continue with testing. I couldn't help but feel this was something I was destined to do, so I knew I needed to try.

It took several weeks to complete testing and then wait for results. It's much more difficult to get approved as a liver donor, so I had doubts they would accept me. I was told before testing began that my liver lobe would go to a small child or baby, so becoming a living donor once more was something I did not want to give up on.

After a week of waiting, I finally received the phone call I had been waiting for! I had been approved to donate a portion of my liver, and any lobe could be successfully donated. Since all of my liver was suitable, my transplant team found the perfect match out of several potential recipients.

On May 2, 2019, my left liver lobe went to a baby boy. Once again, that's all I knew. A baby boy needed a portion of my liver in order to live. I knew he was very sick, and that this was his last chance. The fear I felt going into surgery soon faded when I thought of this little boy and his family, and how their lives would soon change.

Liver donation surgery is much more difficult than kidney donation. I spent two days in ICU and several more in the hospital. I went through some very dark days, but always had in the back of my mind that little baby boy, his family, and his new chance at life. I got reports about how he was doing, how his health was improving, and that kept me going. I knew that all the discomfort and pain would be worth it, because another life was saved because of organ donation.

Just like I had done after my kidney donation, I wrote a letter to my recipient's family. This was a much more difficult letter to write, as my liver lobe had gone to a baby. What do you say to a family who almost lost their child? As a mother myself, I couldn't imagine the emotional toll this entire experience had taken on them. I was desperate to know how my recipient was doing, but knew that I may hear nothing back.

Four months after I sent my letter out, I received one in return. My left liver lobe had gone to a baby boy named Greyson. Greyson was born with biliary atresia, and without a liver transplant would have died. About a month after that letter arrived, our families met. Greyson is the most beautiful little boy! Because of organ donation, he's able to grow and thrive! He's in school, and has celebrated two birthdays with his new liver, which we have named Leo. He's created a very special bond with my daughters, and they think the world of him. I can't wait to watch them all grow together and thrive. They will forever know how very special life is, and how special they are to each other.

Some would say that I gave so much to my recipients and their families, but I have never seen it that way. To me, this was something I was supposed to do, and in my reality, they've given me so much more. They've enhanced my life in immeasurable ways. Because of organ donation, they have become extended members of my family, and have shown me the meaning of perseverance and survival. Donating my kidney and liver was never a big deal to me. I don't feel like a hero or anyone special. I just feel like someone who did something they were just put on this earth to do.

My living donor story would never have happened without Christy. After she passed away, I questioned her death, and felt that it was so unfair. Today, I can't help but think that several people received lifesaving organs because of her. Without her passing, my recipients wouldn't have been able to receive my organs. Without

Christy's gift, the other recipients in our kidney donation chain wouldn't have received their lifesaving organs either.

My journey never would have started if it hadn't been for an amazing team at UC Health. Without that incredible team, I never would have felt comfortable donating once, let alone twice. My visits with them are never clinical, but more like visiting a friend, and I value that. My surgeons and team of doctors, coordinators, and caseworkers are the genuine heroes of my story. Without them, so many organ donations would never happen.

Brandi's kidney recipient Rob and his wife Becky.

From L to R: Brandi's kidney recipients—first living donor Matthew; Stacey, who donated her kidney to a stranger in order for Rob to receive Brandi's kidney; Brandi, and Rob.

Rob on his and Bradi's first kidneyversary.

Greyson, Brandi's liver recipient.

Greyson and Brandi the first time they met.

Greyson and Brandi on their one year liverversary.

Greyson with his mom Tara and dad Michael.

Daughter Adelyn, Brandi, and daughter Jailyn.

Greyson and Brandi during one of their visits.

Jailyn, Brandi, and Adelyn.

About Brandi

Brandi Thornton is a mother and double donor who grew up in Salida, Colorado. She has always had a passion for helping others and has been a living donor mentor since she donated her kidney in 2017 and a portion of her liver in 2019.

Brandi lives in Erie, Colorado, with her two daughters Jailyn and Adelyn. In her free time, she enjoys spending time her with children, exercising, reading, and crafting.

You can connect with Brandi via social media on Facebook and Instagram under brandidai, and through email at brandidai@msn.com. Be sure to check out Brandi's Etsy shop featuring a variety of organ donation items and more! https://www.etsy.com/shop/BrandiDaiDesigns

Ellen Tuech

Geoff's Legacy

"Because of organ donation, I honor my son and help save lives."

On the morning of February 15th, 2016, my 19-year-old son Geoff took his own life. On this day he also gave the gift of life, as he became a tissue donor. His corneas provided sight to a 45-year-old woman and a 70-year-old man. We also donated his heart valve, which most likely saved the life of a child. Geoff has helped heal as many as 75 people with his bone and tissue donations. Geoff did not die in a hospital, so the first contact I had with the procurement team was when they called me to discuss his medical history and lifestyle. They called because Geoff was designated as an organ donor on his driver's license. As a teenager, I registered to be an organ donor when I received my driver's license, and Geoff made the same decision when he received his. Did you know you can register anytime as a donor without having to wait to receive or renew your driver's license? Register today at www.

registerme.org. When we had concluded our conversation, I thought to myself, it's wonderful how Geoff is helping others, and I figured that would be the end. I didn't realize how his act of kindness was about to impact and influence my life.

About a month after his death, emotions overflowed upon opening a box I received in the mail. It was a care package that included a Hero's Medal, a keepsake box, an invitation to join a group called the Donor Family Circle, and many resources for healing. I would soon discover something I didn't expect…I was gaining a second family.

Through the organization OurLegacy (they are the organ procurement organization 'OPO' that handled Geoff's donation), I have met so many incredible people and am blessed to continue my son's legacy. The staff, donor families, volunteers, and transplant recipients have enriched my life in ways I never expected. Every staff member has always greeted me with a smile, expressed genuine concern for my feelings, and been eager to help me honor Geoff. Donor family members are a constant system of support. When I attended my first event, I felt so comforted by the other donor family members. They saw how upset I was and reached out with tissues and hugs, and shared their stories. I've used what they taught me that day to help other donor family members as we continue to gather and honor our loved ones.

When I heard about a volunteer orientation being offered, I knew I wanted to learn more about how I could help spread the mission of organ, eye, and tissue donation. As a believer and long-standing registered donor, I often talk to family and friends, and post on social media, but I never knew there was a team of donation champions who went out to educate the public and private sectors to increase registrations. Through volunteering and working events with organ recipients, I've gained a lot of knowledge and a greater understanding of how they live their lives before and after receiving a transplant. This has helped me in educating the public; and these experiences, interactions, and relationships have helped me in the healing process. I can only imagine where this journey will lead me when I meet some of Geoff's recipients.

I've always hoped to meet Geoff's recipients, but it took over three years to write my donor mom letter. On March 14th, 2019, (National Write Your Story Day) I was ready to tell his recipients about him. Some words I used to describe Geoff included adorable, kind, athletic, endearing, funny, and stubborn. When I meet his recipients, I will tell them a lot more about him…like how the 4th of July was his favorite holiday. I will share how he loved to set off firecrackers, bottle rockets, and mortars. I cannot wait for them to know his name and picture were selected to be displayed on the hood of a race car. I will describe to them our family's exciting day at the races. OurLegacy contacted me and said they had nominated our family to receive a special opportunity. A race car driver wanted to honor Geoff on the hood of his car at the NASCAR Daytona Firecracker 250 race during the 4th of July weekend. How ironic that this race took place 4th of July weekend which was Geoff's favorite holiday. It stunned me that from the entire state of Florida, we were one of two donor families who would have our sons' pictures displayed on the hood of Joey Gase's car. Joey Gase is an up-and-coming driver, sponsored by Donate Life. He became an advocate at 18 after his mother died suddenly of a brain aneurysm. For most races, Joey honors his mom, along with a transplant recipient, living donor, or deceased donor, on his car. In the Firecracker 250 X-finity race, he prominently displayed the Donate Life Florida logo and two photos on the hood area of his race car. Geoff's name and picture, along with "Tissue Donor," adorned one half of the hood, and another young man's name and photo, along with "Organ Donor," were placed on the other half. The other young man's name is Justyn, and he lived in the Ocala, Florida, area. Each family received two all-access passes for the race, which gave us a behind-the-scenes look into the racing world. Memories were made as we spent the entire day with Joey, his family, and his crew. We toured garages, attended the driver's meeting, and had a prime spot on the infield during driver introductions. I will always treasure this day, our photoshoot on the track before the race, and our best seats in the house from the pit box! I beamed with joy and was so proud watching that car speed around the track, knowing that Geoff was spreading the import message of organ, eye, and tissue donation on an international level. After the race, my husband asked Joey if we could have the hood as a keepsake. We wondered if and how they would cut it in half so each family would forever have a memento. We were all thrilled when Joey said, "Yes!"

I could share endless stories with Geoff's recipients, like his successes, troubles he endured, and memories he left behind of his kind soul; all of which inspired me to establish a Facebook page in his memory. I created "Geoff's Legacy" (https://www.facebook.com/geoffslegacy) as a platform to educate about organ, eye, and tissue donation, and to bring awareness to the importance of mental health/suicide prevention. The page is also a vessel to promote self-love and acts of kindness.

Borrowing the idea I got from another mom who lost her son, I designed kindness cards in Geoff's memory. Every year, on his "Angelversary" and his Birthday, I do at least one act of kindness in his memory. When doing so, I give the recipient a card, tell them about Geoff, and ask them to pay it forward. I have two versions of Geoff's cards. On the back of one, I included the Suicide Prevention Hotline Number, and on the other one I included the national Donate Life website, www.donatelife.net.

Because of organ donation, people's lives have been improved, I honor my son and help save lives, and Geoff's legacy lives on...

Ellen holding a picture of Geoff taken of him a few weeks before he passed.

Geoff loved playing sports.

Forever in my heart

Ellen, husband Tim and driver Joey Gase at a NASCAR X-finity race, July 2018.

137

Ellen and fellow donation champions
at a Daytona Beach Tortugas baseball
game, June 8, 2019.

Donate Life flag raising ceremony
speech, Leedsburg, Florida,
April 23, 2019

Ellen with the American Foundation
for Suicide Preventions (Central
Florida Chapter) memory quilt.

Geoff and his older brother, Greg,
August 15, 2015.

TEAM FEFF (Geoff's nickname).
Friends and family at AFSP Out of
the Darkness Walk, Feburary 2018.

About Ellen

Ellen Tuech is a mother and wife who is an advocate for organ, eye, and tissue donation, mental health awareness, and suicide prevention. She has been a volunteer for OneLegacy, her local OPO, since 2017. They awarded her Rookie Volunteer of the Year for her efforts in 2017, and the Mary Carpenter Award of Excellence in 2018. Ellen is a committee member of the GR8 To DON8 8k/5k Run for Organ Donation. The latest race raised over $130,000 to go towards vital community education. Ellen also volunteers and fundraises for the American Foundation for Suicide Prevention. She has taken part in her Community Out of the Darkness Walk each year since 2017, and aspires to join a national overnight walk in the future.

Ellen lives in Longwood, Florida, with her husband Tim and their dog Slash. Tim and Ellen have been married since 2015. Besides Geoff, Ellen has one older son, and Tim has three grown sons. Ellen works a full-time job as a Sales Assistant. She is a huge fan of *Outlander*, and in her spare time she enjoys watching the show and hosting *Outlander* events. You can find her crafting, playing with her dog, attending rock concerts and sporting events, frequenting arts and crafts festivals, and shopping at vintage/antique stores with Tim in her free time.

You can connect with Ellen through social media on Facebook, via her personal page, or by email at ellen.twish@aol.com. If you feel inspired to help AFSP (American Foundation for Suicide Prevention) reach a bold goal to reduce suicide 20% by 2025, please visit afsp.donordrive.com. Search for Ellen's personal fundraising page or GEOFF'S LEGACY team fundraising page to make a donation. Be sure to *like* and *follow* "Geoff's Legacy" on Facebook and post your story about organ donation or mental health.

"When you stand and share your story in an empowering way, your story will heal you and your story will heal somebody else."

–Iyanla Vanzant

Lisa Barker

Two Moms, Two Letters

February 2014 changed my life forever in the most unexpected way.

My husband, Reid, and I were married for a year and a half, and had our lives planned out. Our plans included living in our cute apartment for a couple years and then buying our first home. We would continue our mission trips to Africa, traveling, and enjoying just the two of us before we started having children. We planned to start our family year five of our marriage with two biological children, and then, one day, adopt from Africa. As you can see, we made many plans. We always think we know what is best for our lives, right? We had our dream jobs; I was a dental hygienist, and Reid was a middle school teacher and coach. We were 25 years old, healthy, and had our entire lives ahead of us.

In January 2014, we had a friend pass away because of a stroke. We were heartbroken. I remember telling Reid as we were preparing for the funeral, and still in complete shock, "It is scary how you never really know what is going on in your own body." Little did Reid and I know the irony of my statement. Our own storm was brewing inside of my body that would hit six short weeks after the funeral of our friend. Our storm would reveal that I was the one now in dire need of a miracle and the gift of life to survive.

It all happened suddenly and unexpected. Until this point, I was healthy, or so I thought. On Super Bowl weekend, I suddenly became so ill that we rushed to the hospital. Upon evaluation, we learned my gallbladder had thickened, and I needed surgery to remove it. During that procedure, they removed a liter and a half of fluid (bile) from around my liver, and we learned I was in acute liver failure. Liver failure? Reid and I looked at each other, shocked. How can this be happening? An MRI revealed I had a liver condition that only one in a million people develop! This rare liver condition had caused my liver to fail at 25 years old.

They told us we needed to be at a hospital that has a liver specialist who is familiar with my disease. They airlifted me to a hospital in Dallas, Texas, and I was put into a medically induced coma so my body could rest. The doctors told Reid that my only chance for survival was going to be a complete liver transplant from a deceased donor. I can only imagine what was going through my husband's mind.

The transplant team informed Reid I was being placed on the top of the transplant waiting list as Status 1A, which meant I had 48 hours or fewer to live if I did not receive a new organ. My body was suffering and needed a complete miracle to function again.

A mere 10 hours after being listed, Reid got the phone call that would change our lives forever. A healthy liver was available for me from a 15-year-old female who had passed away in a car accident. My life-saving surgery would be the next morning.

On February 6, 2014, new life came to me through the blessing of organ donation. A miracle saved me, but another family was experiencing the deepest of suffering, losing a child.

God would show me the power and miracle of the gift of life. Through it all, He would teach me what it looks like to hurt, carry hope, and live expectant!

The next six months after my life-saving surgery was full of suffering; learning I could no longer travel for missions to third world countries, and that I could never carry our own children. I endured the challenges of rehabilitation and learning to walk in my "new normal" of being a liver transplant recipient.

Sometimes I questioned, *Where is the goodness amid this suffering?* I imagine, at some point, you have asked a question like that before too. Those plans Reid and I had made would no longer happen. But during my pain, God revealed to me how He hand-picked me for this miracle and journey.

I remember one night looking at Reid as he sat on my hospital bed, tears streaming down my face, and said, "Someone had to die so I could live." The magnitude of that thought was so heavy on my heart. I had already graduated high school, college, fallen in love, and married the love of my life—things that Courtney would not get to do. I will never forget his reply to me while wiping away my tears. He said, "That is the gospel. Christ died so we can all live." He said that we are all in need of a heart transplant. We need our cold, stone hearts removed and for a new, softened heart put in its place through inviting Christ to live in our hearts. This can only happen by having a personal relationship with Him. A correlation I was so thankful for. Organ donation reflects the gospel.

I looked at this call on my life and asked, "Why not me?" We can carry hope in our sufferings, and it committed me to doing that the best I could. I believe God finds joy in the way we respond to our sufferings.

About six months after my transplant, I heard from the Lord that it was time to write to my donor mom. It was one of those moments where you hear the Lord loud and clear. Not that my donor dad did not need this letter, but it was clear my donor mom did, and she needed it right now. I wrote the letter and mailed it. I needed this family to know how thankful I was for the gift their daughter, Courtney Sterling, had given me. After communication through mail and the phone, we met five months later.

When we met, my donor mom, Dawn, told me she received my letter in the mail on a Tuesday afternoon, and that, on Friday of the same week, she was planning on taking her own life by suicide. Her suffering seemed too much to bear. She had lost not only her daughter, my organ donor, Courtney, but she also lost her oldest daughter, Connely, and her unborn child, Tyson, in the car accident.

She knew from my letter that Courtney was still living on and she needed to continue to live for her girls. Her daughter saved my life, and she would tell you that in return . . . I saved her life. Another miracle revealed amid the suffering.

We have developed the most beautiful relationship with the Sterlings. It is a relationship neither of us ever wanted or desired. They never desired to be a donor family, and I never wanted to be a transplant recipient, but our relationship is a silver lining to our journey. I will never bring back their precious Courtney, but I know it brings them joy knowing she is still living on in me, and the four other organ recipients she saved. Reid and I call them our Godparents, and they call us their Godchildren. We FaceTime, call, text, and try to see each other in person at least every two months as we live five hours away from each other. We are grateful for the Sterling family letting us into their lives and for their being a part of our day-to-day life. It is a special bond like no other.

Another miracle took place in December 2018 when my husband donated his kidney to a former coworker. Through the miracle gifted to me and seeing my life saved, Reid felt called to give that gift back to another. There were concerns I would need a kidney someday, and many people asked, "What if you need his kidney one day?" Reid was a universal blood donor and might be a match for me, if ever needed. This is where faith comes in. We had to put what we believe about God's character into action. We trusted that if the need arose, God would provide. For now, however, this man needed a kidney, and Reid could donate. He donated his kidney so a father of four could have his life back with his children, off of machines and dialysis every night. Reid lived out his faith through donation. The transplant was a success and his recipient, Jon, is back to living an active lifestyle with his children.

A few years after my transplant, we felt God calling us to adopt. After two-and-a-half years of planning, we received another miracle when we brought our boys home from Burundi, Africa, in October 2019. Our boys are Frank, 6 years old, and Blaise 4 years old. These sweet boys radiate joy and have the most infectious spirits.

It was time to write another letter, this time to the birth mother of my sons.

Two moms; two letters. One mom gave me the gift of life through her daughter's organ donation, and another mother, halfway across the world, gave life to my sons and joy to my world.

Courtney's gift has given me seven more birthdays, seven more wedding anniversaries, allowed me to see the birth of my three nieces and to enjoy my duties as an aunt to the fullest. It has allowed me to travel, to spend time with family and friends, and to make so many fresh memories. Most of all, it has given me the blessing of experiencing life—new life. Her selfless gift also allowed new life to my sweet boys. I am a mom because of organ donation. My donor parents are now grandparents to my boys. The boys call them MawMaw and PawPaw and adore them. How full circle is that? I cannot wait for the day when Frank and Blaise are old enough to understand the magnitude and depth of what Courtney did for their Mama. Because of her gift and the grace of God, I am alive to have the honor of being called Mama. I am thankful my boys will know a world with the Sterling family in it.

Our journey is not the one we ever expected, and as you can see, the plans we had made for our lives did not happen. However, our life has still been beautiful in each new season. Organ donation has a ripple effect. It begins with the donor and extends to the recipient and to everyone impacted by this generous act—family, friends, neighbors, acquaintances, and even strangers who hear the impact this ultimate gift has granted. It is an ultimate act of love, showing the gift of true generosity. Organ donation is a miracle, a selfless gift that grants new life. A gift to treasure and share with the world. Because of organ donation, my life has forever changed, and I am grateful.

In honor of the greatest hero I never knew,
my organ donor, Courtney Ray Sterling, who saved my life.

Lisa with her silent strength, organ donor, Courtney

Lisa at her organ donor, Courtney's grave site.

Team Barker: Reid, Frank, Blaise, Lisa

Lisa with her sons, Frank and Blaise

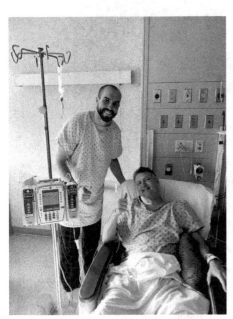

Reid with his kidney recipient, Jon

Lisa and Reid volunteering for
Donate Life Texas

Team Barker with Lisa's organ donor, Courtney's, parents:
Dawn and Michael Sterling

Lisa and Reid with her organ donor Courtney's
parents: Michael & Dawn Sterling at
Courtney's high school graduation ceremony.

About Lisa

Lisa Barker is a wife, mom, liver transplant recipient, author, and a passionate advocate for organ, eye, and tissue donation. Lisa and her husband Reid, along with their two sons, Frank and Blaise, live in Dallas, Texas.

In 2014, at 25, Lisa was hours away from dying because of acute liver failure when she received a life-saving liver transplant from her donor, Courtney Sterling.

Four years later, her husband, Reid, being so touched by the extra life, time, and memories given to Lisa through organ donation, paid it forward and became a living kidney donor to save a friend in need.

In 2019, Reid and Lisa welcomed home their sons, Frank and Blaise from Burundi, Africa, through adoption. If it weren't for the gift of life that Courtney gave to Lisa, they could not have given new life to their boys.

Organ donation has impacted every part of their lives, and the Barker's will continue honoring their journey. You can connect with Lisa through email at teambarkerdelivered@gmail.com

Be sure to follow her on social media through Facebook or Instagram, at Team Barker Delivered, and visit their website at www.teambarkerdelivered.com.

Hailey Steimel

Hailey's Valentine Heart

I was born at 34 weeks, a premature twin with a congenital heart defect called transposition of the great arteries, which is where the two major arteries that carry blood away from the heart (the aorta and the pulmonary artery) are reversed. My identical twin sister, Hope, was born with a hole in her heart, but not the severe defect that I had. Doctors don't know why one of us had a serious congenital heart defect, and the other born only with a hole in her heart. The hole in Hope's heart closed up, and she has had no problems. I had a procedure at three days old to keep me alive, and another open heart surgery at one. From then, I lived a normal life until the fall of 2012.

In the fall of 2012, I was sixteen years old and contracted a respiratory infection that persisted. The illness lasted a couple weeks and nothing made me better. Doctors performed tests to find what was going on, and we were told to go to the children's hospital. They hospitalized me at the University of Iowa (U of I). This was the first time I remember being admitted to a hospital. I had no issues with my heart until this point. Before being discharged from the hospital, I received the shocking news. During an echocardiogram, one cardiologist shared that most children born with my heart defect, and who had the same procedure that I did (Mustard Procedure) at a year old, later needed a heart transplant. My mom and I were both in shock. We were to continue with my local cardiologist and then meet with the transplant team at the University of Iowa.

Transplant was foreign to me. A sophomore in high school shouldn't need a heart transplant. Denial set in, and I carried on trying to be a normal teenager. Soon I felt better as life returned to normal, but by the next summer I felt far from normal. Things happened quicker than I could have imagined. I became tired more frequently; extra fluid, known as edema, built up in my body; and the summer heat made things worse. I didn't want to believe my heart was failing and only a transplant could save my life.

On August 19, 2013, we met the transplant team to discuss adding me to the transplant list. I packed a bag, just in case, because it became obvious my health was declining. They admitted me that day and did a multitude of tests over a two-week period to see if I was a suitable candidate to get listed for a heart transplant. They planned to have testing done and send me home to wait for the call, but right before they set me for discharge, I became ill and coded. The cardiac team determined the best choice for me was to have a ventricular assist device (heart pump) placed to do the work of my failing heart. I learned later I was the first pediatric patient to have this device placed on the right side of my heart. After two months in the hospital, they released me on November 4, 2013. My parents preferred bringing me home instead of waiting in the hospital.

On February 13, 2014, at 6:07 p.m., that call came, and my life changed forever. My family had just sat down to have dinner when the phone rang. My mom answered. I could hear excitement in her voice, and my dad's face lit up. It was the call we were waiting for! Within a half hour, we were heading to the University of Iowa. As I always tell everyone, transplants are bittersweet. I pondered this on the car ride to the University. I learned from talking to my cardiologist that an ideal donor for me was a child or young adult, so while the excitement grew for my second chance at life, it meant someone else's family had lost a loved one—more than likely a child. Waiting for the gift of life is the hardest part about a heart transplant, because you are waiting for someone to pass away.

At the hospital, many preparations took place before the transplant surgery and then waiting. At 1:00 p.m., on February 14, 2014, they took me to the operating room. It was Valentine's Day and also National Donor Day! The surgery lasted a grueling twelve hours, and then I started recovery in the PICU (Pediatric Intensive Care Unit). Everything went as expected for the first 24 hours, but then things changed. My blood pressure was out of control, and I became very sick. My condition became grave, and I nearly died. They determined I had a hospital-acquired infection and placed me on a ventilator until February 26th. I also came down with PICU psychosis, which made it difficult for me to sleep. My donor's heart worked perfectly, with a strong heartbeat! This amazing gift not only saved my life by the transplantation, but it came at the perfect moment. If the infection in my lungs had presented before receiving my gifted heart, I never would have survived. My donor saved my life two times!

Two weeks after transplant, I moved from the PICU to a regular room. They discharged me on March 14th, 2014, exactly one month after my transplant surgery.

I was a junior in high school when first admitted to the hospital. Because of my risks of getting sick, and having a heart pump, I could not attend regular classes. I attended a few online classes through my high school, but in reality I missed my entire junior year. There was a strong possibility I could not graduate with my class; these kids had been my classmates since kindergarten. I didn't even want to think about the possibility of not graduating with my sister Hope. I continued to work hard with my online classes and tutor because I desperately missed school. Towards the end of the school year, I attended half-days with Hope, and I was overjoyed to see everyone! I had missed my junior year homecoming but did not want to miss my prom. In fact, this was my first major goal after transplant, and, because of organ donation, I got to enjoy my prom! I even stayed for most of the after-prom celebration. That summer, I also took part in a physical education class, which counted towards class credit. It felt so good to be active! I enjoyed the rest of summer and caught up with friends and family. I was a normal teenager again.

With a brand new heart, I started my senior year in August 2014 with my class. Because of my donor, and tons of hard work, I graduated on time—and with my sister! After graduation, I attended college at our local community college and then transferred to Upper Iowa University. I received my Bachelor's degree in Communications in May 2020!

Before my transplant, I was granted a wish from Make-A-Wish. My family and I enjoyed a fabulous Make-A-Wish trip to Hawaii. In the Spring following the transplant, they invited my family and me to attend a local Gala for Make-A-Wish, where I received the Circle of Inspiration award. I threw out the first pitch of the season at a Kernel's baseball game (our local minor league team). It was Donate Life Night! I will always treasure these extra special moments!

After my heart transplant, I set a goal to spread awareness for organ donation. Because of my miracle, I could sit in a dunk tank for a fundraiser called Cleaning Up Cancer Carnival, and it honored me to be the Grand Marshall in our local town's parade. Donate life was the theme, and Iowa Donor Network benefited from the street dance that year. I've been able to speak at hospitals and driver education classes about organ donation and take part in the American Heart Association Go Red events. It has always been an honor to speak about the impact of organ donation! It is the perfect way to honor my donor and his family, and to give back.

My volunteer work for Iowa Donor Network has always fulfilled me and is one of my favorite things. Through them, I can share my story and help raise awareness for organ donation in our community. Iowa Donor Network is an amazing organization! They have supported me along my journey, and it's obvious the employees love what they do. They offered me an internship with Iowa Donor Network in the summer of 2015, and I enjoyed learning about the different careers at the donor network.

I experienced another amazing opportunity: riding on the Donate Life Rose Parade Float. Iowa Donor Network nominated me to represent our state on the float. My family and I worked on the Donate Life Float with other recipients, recipient families, living donors, and donor families. I rode on the float with other recipients, while living donors walked alongside the float. The beauty of the flora-graphs on the float, representing donors from Iowa and other states, is etched in my mind forever! It was a once-in-a-lifetime experience I will never forget! Besides the parade, we attended the Rose Bowl game that day. I treasured the day and meeting so many people connected to organ donation. Every organ recipient, living donor, donor family, and supporter had a story to share, how their life changed because of organ donation.

Iowa Donor Network also supports Team Iowa. Our team comprises organ, eye, tissue recipients, and living donors. We take part in the Transplant Games of America every two years. It is an Olympic style event for the transplant world. I attended my first games in Cleveland, Ohio, in 2016, and again in Salt Lake City, Utah, in 2018, participating in track and field events, basketball, and volleyball. Because of the Corona virus, they reschedule the 2020 Transplant Games in New Jersey for 2021, which will be a virtual event. I am looking forward to attending the Transplant Games in 2022, in San Diego, California.

On August 14, 2014, six months after my transplant, I wrote a letter to my donor family. Transplant Centers recommend waiting six months before you write to your donor family. I couldn't wait to connect with them, even though it was the hardest letter I had ever written. How do you thank a family for giving you the gift of life, when they lost their loved one in order for you to receive that gift? I did not hear from them right away, but in summer of 2016, I received a letter from my donor family. A year later we had direct contact with each other through email. After emailing back and forth for a while, our families met in person. I met my donor family for the first time on August 13, 2017. Nervousness and excitement filled me as I learned about the person who saved my life. They shared how their son, my donor, enjoyed playing sports, telling jokes, hunting, fishing, and being with his family and friends. Everyone who met him loved him, and he will forever be an inspiration. I have stayed in contact with my donor family, and we have met a couple more times since that first meeting. We plan to meet again, which makes me happy.

Organ donation has affected my life in so many ways! I have met so many amazing people connected to organ donation, including my wonderful donor family. Without my transplant, none of this would have happened. The best part is getting to share my story and inspire others to donate life. Transplant life has its difficulties, but the positives outweigh the negatives because I am alive today. Every day is a gift! I think God chose me because I am more than a recipient. I am a voice for organ donation.

Since my transplant, I have wanted a career doing something with organ donation or helping people. The Iowa Donor Network employees have played a part in why I want a career that helps bring awareness for organ donation. Their employees are so amazing and kind! While I search for my dream job, I will continue to share my story and inspire others to be an organ donor. Are you hesitant about registering as an organ donor? If so, I ask you this: What if you or a loved one needed a life-saving organ transplant? Would you want someone to donate? If your answer is yes, please consider registering.

Make-A-Wish trip to Hawaii.

First picture taken when Hailey was admitted to the hospital for heart failure; with her twin sister Hope.

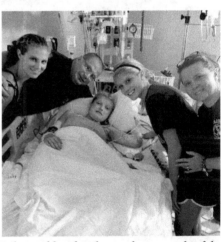

Hailey and her family together a couple of days before her RVAD (heart pump) surgery.

Hailey in the hospital listening to her RVAD. The heart pump sounded like a motor running.

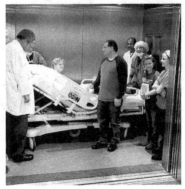

Heading down to surgery.

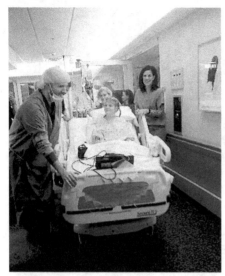

At the 2018 Transplant Games of America in Salt Lake City, Utah. The basketball team from Team Iowa!

Valentine's Day 2014! On her way to receive her new heart!

Go Red For Women Luncheon!

Hanging out with Brenda Cortez, Joey Gase, and HOWL the Owl for their book signing!

The 2018 Rose Bowl Parade! "I got to ride on the Donate Life Float with other transplant recipients and living donors! Met so many amazing people!"

About Hailey

Hailey was born and raised in Cedar Rapids, Iowa, by her parents Mike and Brigitte. She has two sisters, Hannah, her older sister, and Hope, her identical twin; and she has three dogs named Lucy, Molly, and Millie. Hailey graduated Prairie High School in 2015, a year after her heart transplant; and in the spring of 2020, she graduated from Upper Iowa University with a degree in Communications.

Hailey hasn't landed her dream job, but when she does she hopes to use that position to promote organ donor awareness, or to give back to the community that supported her so much during her heart journey.

Hailey enjoys spending time with friends, shopping, traveling, volunteering at the Iowa Donor Network, being with family, and playing with her dogs. She also enjoys binge-watching shows on Netflix and Hulu, and her favorites so far have been *The Office* and *Impractical Jokers*. If you wish to follow Hailey and learn more about her journey, you can follow her on social media:

Facebook- Hope 4 Hailey's Heart

Instagram- haileysteimel2014 and hearttransplant2014

Twitter- hearthailey2014

Maria Teresa "Terri" Pilawa

Lungs For Life

I considered myself a tomboy growing up in California, always wearing cutoff shorts and a T-shirt. I was active in many sports such as co-ed softball, girls' basketball, and I even tried out for cheerleading. Concert and marching band were a favorite, where I played the clarinet; and I also enjoyed playing the flute, piano, violin, and guitar. Life was good and became even better when I was 25 years old. My son Ryan was born, and he became my pride and joy. I worked in retail management. The business I worked for closed, so I moved to Las Vegas and began a new life with my son. My new venture included going to college and getting my accounting degree. After graduation, in 2005, I purchased a condo and a new car. My accomplishments made me feel proud, but disappointment set in since I was very much overweight. My highest weight of 245 pounds was not healthy for my five-foot stature. After changing my lifestyle, I shed 100 pounds! My career was off to an impressive start as I landed a job with a Home Owners Association as their accounting manager. My life goals were coming together, and I was glowing.

At 38, I met Edward who is now my husband. He became my best friend; it blessed me that he adored both me and my son. Life felt like a party as we enjoyed dinners, concerts, movies, sporting events, and everything that living in Las Vegas offered. We were active, healthy, and living a dream. Then one day, I noticed I had been feeling tired, weak, fatigued, and short of breath. After a trip to my primary care physician, I was diagnosed with Adult Asthma. The doctor prescribed steroids and an inhaler. Nothing too concerning; I just had to take the medications to ease my symptoms. The symptoms persisted, but my doctor kept me on the same regimen of medications. Then emergency room visits for breathing treatments became the norm. It didn't stop me from going to the gym, and I continued with my dance classes. Dancing brought out life in me, and I would go to the clubs and dance for hours! Life and work continued on, but deep down I knew things weren't right because I was having symptoms.

My dream wedding came true on August 1, 2009, as I married Eddie in a Catholic church surrounded by family and friends. It was magical except for a scary episode of shortness of breath. I kept it to myself because I didn't want to alarm anyone and assumed it resulted from my heavy beaded wedding dress and exhaustion from all the excitement. Our honeymoon to Manhattan, New York, was amazing! We filled our days with all the amazing sites, subway rides, and a Yankee's baseball game. We walked all over the city but then shortness of breath caught up with me and keeping the same walking pace as my husband and the surrounding people proved too difficult. Not wanting to ruin our honeymoon, I ignored my symptoms. After the baseball game, we headed back to the subway, and the feeling of suffocating consumed me. Eddie was panicked, and I could barely walk, but we made it to our hotel room. He called 911, and the ambulance took me to Roosevelt Hospital. They did an x-ray, gave me two breathing treatments, and advised I see a specialist when I got home. The x-ray showed something in my lungs, but they didn't know what it was. When I returned home, I went to my primary care physician, but, again, she did not refer me to a specialist. Fear set in; my health was declining. After that appointment, I made my way to my belly dancing class but had to excuse myself because I couldn't finish my routine. At that point, I quit my dancing class and also stopped going to the gym. Soon after, walking up the stairs at my house became a chore. I realized this was not asthma.

After a while in denial, I made my way to see a specialist and had a CT scan and an open lung biopsy. My heart sank when they placed me on 2 liters of oxygen. Relying on oxygen at such a young age terrified me. I had to learn oxygen therapy, how a pulse oximeter worked, and how to keep my oxygen levels up. It was a lot, but I knew it was the best thing to allow me to walk, exercise, and continue to work. A couple days later, I received a phone call from my doctor saying he wanted to see me right away. Tears filled my eyes, and I panicked, knowing in my heart and soul something was wrong with my lungs. The next day at the doctor's office I learned I had ILD (Interstitial Lung Disease). Filled with fear again, I had questions. "What is ILD?" "Can it be cured?" "Can you fix me?" They shared literature about the disease, and I would have to go to UCLA for a lung transplant evaluation. This shattering news continued as I heard the words, "This disease will get worse, and you may only have five years to live." No cure—only medications to slow down the disease. Time stood still! I couldn't cry, and I was in shock from the news that just filled my ears. How will I tell my husband and son? What will they think when I say, "I may not be able to walk or to drive anymore, and someday, I might need a caregiver?" I was just married, had a son in high school, and about to embark on the biggest battle of my life. In preparation, the doctor gave me an application for a handicap sign for my vehicle. I remember going to the DMV. My face turned white as a ghost as they punched out the expiration date of September 2020. Terrified once again . . . *am I even going to live that long?* This memory remains with me.

Later that week, I received a letter from the Mayo Clinic in Arizona stating what my diagnosis was. The letter stated that my accurate diagnosis is NSIP (Non-Specific Interstitial Pneumonia) Pulmonary Fibrosis. I will never forget how I felt reading that letter. My life as I knew it forever changed. A couple of months later brought the first of many painful changes. They let me go from my job because my work performance was slowing down, because of my exhaustion, fatigue, and constant coughing. It devastated me. I carried the insurance, so how was I going to provide for my family? My husband's business closed because of the housing crash. We would have to start over. After that troublesome time, we opened up a small business called Centennial Glass and Glazing. I was paying a fortune for extended health insurance through Cobra, and I was trying to get any kind of help in Las Vegas, Nevada. We had household expenses, and my medical and prescription costs, but I could not find any financial help.

In 2013, I applied for Social Security Disability. I went into the office with oxygen tanks lined up in the back of my wheelchair. I was on 4 liters of oxygen. Another blow came my way, as I was told that I would have to wait two years to receive Social Security Disability. I told them I was going to die. I needed oxygen therapy and prescription medications to slow down this disease. There was nothing they could do for me. We were running out of money because we had to use our savings for my medications and oxygen. I resorted to begging for discounts from my oxygen supplier. I felt so alone with no one to help me or to talk to.

I got my paperwork together for my death, added my husband's name on all of my accounts, and deeded the house over to him. I created a spreadsheet with all the information my husband would need in the event of my death. Reality was setting in and I wasn't getting better. This disease was progressing fast, and I continued to deteriorate. The doctors in Las Vegas were at a loss for how to help me. There was talk of removing the lower lobe of my lung, but they didn't think I would survive. They hospitalized me for a long time, and when I was released, we hired my niece to be my caregiver.

The time had come for a visit to UCLA, where I met Dr. Joseph Lynch III. Test after test was performed, which proved my health continued deteriorating. Thankfully, I felt I was in a safe place. It was time to consider transplant, but because I was on Prednisone, I had gained some weight. In order to be listed for transplant, I needed to shed some pounds. They placed me on pulmonary rehab, and I changed my eating habits, which helped. My husband and son remained in Las Vegas, and I moved back to California to stay with my mom. I received the help to pay for my prescriptions, which cost $2,000 a month. A hospital bed was ordered, and all the medical equipment I would need for help. I couldn't be alone and longed for my independence. My sisters were great caretakers. They cooked, made shakes, washed my hair, bathed, and dressed me. My spirits remained high, despite not feeling well. Coughing spasms and feelings of suffocation often caused me to panic. I had faith in my Lord and that faith grew stronger praising God.

The pulmonary team at UCLA was amazing! Because my diagnosis was Non-Specific, they ordered more tests to rule out other possibilities. Those tests revealed I had acid reflux and that the acid was going into my lungs, scarring them. The transplant evaluation began, but because of my insurance, I had to transfer to USC Keck Medical for evaluation and future transplant. Having to start all over again with testing and getting to know my new transplant team scared me. The transfer was denied because I was 30 pounds overweight. Again, I blamed it on the Prednisone . . . the steroid that causes people to gain weight. It upset me, but also motivated me to lose the weight. I deserved a second chance at life! Life was strenuous, but I had to remain strong. I cried in bed at night when my family was sleeping and begged God to please save me. The loneliness and despair I felt was overwhelming.

Mission accomplished! I had reached my goal weight of 160 pounds and a BMI of 30 and couldn't have been more proud. I wore a lacey, cream-colored dress that day to celebrate that I was being sent to USC Keck Medical. Testing for transplant evaluation started in June 2014. Weight loss continued, and I was excited to begin this new journey. My new goal was 130 pounds, and I had 15 more to go. I went from a size 14 to a size 8! It thrilled the transplant team. Pomona Valley Hospital even used me as a model for their promotional brochure!

For our fifth wedding anniversary, my husband took me to my favorite place in Oceanside Beach, California, and we rented a beach-side house for a week. It wasn't easy traveling with my wheelchair, all my oxygen, and medication needs. Eddie would carry me to the beach because walking in the sand was too difficult. I marveled as I stood in the sand and watched the waves come up over my feet, while my husband held on to my oxygen tank. It brought tears to my eyes. We made memories, not knowing what the future held.

After the trip, I had to meet with a psychologist for an evaluation. The meeting went well; She could see I was keeping myself strong and healthy, and I WAS READY!!! Now there was only one more test, called the Sniff Test, since I had MAC (Mycobacterium Avium Complex) which destroyed my right lung. They needed to be sure my diaphragm was working.

We completed all my testing on October 13, 2014, and I received my acceptance letter placing me on the UNOS (United Network for Organ Sharing) transplant list. My LAS (Lung Allocation Score) was 38, and the higher the score, the closer you are to receiving a transplant. My lung capacity was only at 24%, and with my coughing spasms getting worse and lasting longer, I needed 20 liters of oxygen to recover. I would shake violently from the coughing, sometimes causing a rib to break, and my eyes would tear up. Tons of mucus came out of me; I was flustered, unable to talk or move. My chest would get tight and my back hurt. I was dizzy, my head ached, my heart would race. I was tired, so tired of it all. I continued to pray and to worship God . . . and to wait.

After feeling alone, not knowing anyone going through the same struggles I was, I found a support group called One Breath Foundation. I wasn't alone on this journey anymore. Other people in the group were going through a similar journey and some had already received their gift of life, which provided hope to us still waiting.

As I waited for my gift of new lungs, my family helped by fundraising to help pay for post-transplant housing, since staying in Los Angeles, California, is expensive. I would dream that I received my call, and in these dreams, I would receive visitors from heaven like my Grandpa John. He would hug me tight and then he would leave. I knew it wasn't my time to go. I made a promise to my son Ryan that I would never leave him.

In May 2015, I began needing more oxygen support and was admitted to USC Keck Medical and diagnosed with Pulmonary Hypertension. To keep me comfortable while I waited for my transplant, they placed me in hospice. I hated being there and begged my doctor to send me home. After three weeks, I called the oxygen company and asked for another concentrator and a high regulator for my oxygen tank, which allowed me to get back home. My mom and I had a deep conversation, and I told her I was sorry if I were to die in her home. She assured me I would not die! I asked my mom if she spoke with God and was He was going to take me. She replied God would not take me.

I celebrated my 46th birthday on June 17, 2015, and a couple of days later my lungs failed me and an ambulance rushed me to Riverside County Hospital. They placed me on a high-flow machine which saved my life, and the next morning they transferred me to USC Keck Medical. My family and a priest were there to witness my last rites blessing and communion. It worried my family, but I felt at peace.

I was admitted at USC, awaiting for my much needed lung transplant. My husband was in hospital room with me when my surgeon Dr. Amy Hackmann called me with amazing news. She told me they had lungs for me! They were high-risk lungs from a young lady who was on dialysis, and her family would end ventilator support at midnight. She advised me to call my family and to get ready to be in surgery in a few of hours. My miracle had finally come! I told my husband; he called our family members, and I was in surgery at 2:00 am the next day, after waiting a terrifying eight months and eleven days.

Recovery was rough because I was still very weak and sick. Physical therapy helped me gain my strength back, and I learned how to breathe and live life again. Occupational therapy helped me with life skills post-transplant. I was in and out of the hospital for about three years. There were some complications—pneumonia, lung collapses, CMV—and I had a few GI surgeries. Since the transplant, I've had 16 surgeries.

Almost four years after receiving my miracle gift of life in April 2019, I had the privilege to meet my donor family. We had written a couple times, but now my family and I were excited to meet them. I needed to know who my donor was. Maria Berfelia Quinteros was her name; she was 22 years old and had a young son. She was from El Salvador but had been living in Los Angeles. She overdosed on pills and didn't wake up. Ventilator support kept her alive for a few days, and then her family donated her organs. Maria shared her wishes with her mom (also named Maria) and told her, if anything should happen to her, she wanted to help others. She saved two lives: my life, with her beautiful pink lungs, and the life of another with her heart. Maria leaves a legacy and lives on within me, and I honor her and her family every day.

Besides my lung transplant, I am also the recipient of donor tissue. Following my transplant, I had chronic bone infections and inflammation because of long-term use of Prednisone. My cartilage disappeared through the years and my nose collapsed, which caused difficulty breathing. I had reconstructive nose surgery using donor rib cartilage tissue. It was a blessing, and I am humbled and grateful to another donor. This donation has allowed me to breathe again and has given me back my self-esteem. I never imagined organ and tissue donation would touch me twice!

Because of organ donation, I have been able to live life to its fullest. I am an ambassador with OneLegacy Foundation; a Nevada Donor Network advocate; and now, the CEO of One Breath Foundation. I am a Howl the Owl Ambassador, UNOS Ambassador, and Class of 2020 Donate Life Float Rose Parade Rider. Maybe you've seen me in my red-hot Camaro, walking around New York City, or on a cruise to Mexico. I have been zip-lining at Catalina Island; and I have attended rock concerts, and football and baseball games. My son attended college and the transplant allowed me to be there for him. I am now five years post-transplant, have made it to my 51st birthday, and have celebrated 10 years of marriage. Growing old is a reality, and I look forward to the day when I will be a grandma.

In the summer of 2020, I went to visit my donor Maria's grave for the first time and gave her flowers. As I sat beside her headstone and talked to her, I shed tears of joy and sadness. Everything I do is because of her. I will continue to educate the community about organ, eye, and tissue donation, and share my journey to inspire others to say "yes" to donation and to saving lives. I continue to live a life of service and helping those in need who are living with a lung or other organ disease. Every day, I'm living my best transplant life and thanking my God for all that He has blessed me with. It gave me a second chance to be with my friends and family.

> "I am forever grateful beyond all the stars
> in the sky because of you, Maria."

Baby Terri at 1 year old, 1970.

Ryan, Terri, and Eddie. Terri's first walk on the beach 2016 no oxygen needed!

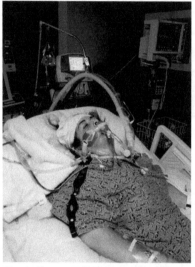

Terri radio news interview holding her Donor Maria.

Terri after a 13 hour surgery 6/24/15.

Class of 2020 Tournament of Roses Donate Life float parade rider.

OneLegacy Executive first look of the Donate Life float, Donor Maria, and Howl.

Terri was honored and sponsored by OneLegacy Foundation to be a Recipient Rider for Class of 2020.

Terri's dream came true to honor her donor, Maria, and her donor family spreading the message of organ, eye, and tissue donation.

Terri holding a banner created by Kate Griggs honoring her donor giving her a second chance of life.

About Terri

Terri was born in Upland, California, and grew up in Ontario, California. When she was 12 years old, her family moved to Fontana, California. She has three younger sisters, Angelina and, identical twins, Esther and Estella. Terri now lives in Las Vegas, Nevada, with her husband Eddie and her son Ryan.

Terri is the CEO of One Breath Foundation, and she also runs an online jewelry business. To learn about the foundation, please visit onebreathfoundation.org, or email Terri at terri@ onebreathfoundation.org. If you wish to make a donation to help support the foundation, please write a check payable to One Breath Foundation and send it to One Breath Foundation, P.O. Box 1101, Covina, CA 91722.

You can check out Terri's jewelry business at myparklane.com/ terripilawa or call/text at 702-813-1452.

Jill Dillon and Sara Solinsky

Hope Meets Gratitude

Jill's Journey
"Tell him you'll give him one of yours."

It was an October morning in 2009 and I was busy seeing patients in my optometric office in Wisconsin Rapids, Wisconsin. My next patient was a 64-year-old gentleman by the name of Lonnie who I had known both personally and as a patient for quite a few years. In the course of our usual health discussion, Lonnie told me his kidneys were failing and his doctor mentioned he would need a kidney transplant sooner than later. What happened next is still incredulous to me. A voice clearly said the words, "Tell him you'll give him one of yours." Lonnie and I were the only two in my exam room that morning, but I heard the words loud and clear. I didn't hesitate when I told Lonnie I would do just that, and I am sure he thought I was crazy, based on the look on his face. He just laughed. Although I assured him I was serious, we completed the exam and Lonnie left my office. That night, I went home and told my husband, Mike, that I was donating a kidney to Lonnie. He is used to my crazy antics, so as I recall he simply said, "okay." As I looked back on that encounter years later, I realized that was the moment that would change my life forever. I just didn't know it then.

Six months went by, and although I believe God spoke to me that fall day, I went about my routine life with minor change. I heard nothing from Lonnie or his wife, Ginger. Then March came around, and Lonnie returned to see me for a follow-up appointment. He relayed to me during the exam that his doctors told him it was time to get listed for a kidney transplant. They had checked his daughters for the potential to be his living donor, but that didn't work out. I recall saying to him that day, "I told you I would give you one of mine." With tears in his eyes, Lonnie told me he could never ask me to do such a thing. I replied, "You didn't ask. I offered." Lonnie and Ginger provided me with the information for the hospital where he was listed, and I contacted them right away to set up an evaluation.

Signs

By this time, Mike knew I was quite serious about donating my kidney, and he was supportive. We told our children, Josh and Isaiah, eleven and seven at the time, about my intentions. I also told my sisters and my parents. It thrilled me that each of them told me they would be behind me all the way. I don't believe I ever once doubted answering the "call" to be a living donor, but if I had, the "signs" I kept seeing everywhere confirmed that I was fulfilling my purpose. From news articles that would pop up in my inbox, to evaluation dates at the hospital coordinating with a time I could easily leave my practice for a day, it seemed like everything was lining up for a smooth donation. I had to laugh the day my family and I stopped at a local fast-food restaurant for lunch. Literally, there were signs everywhere in the place that said, "Be a Hero for Life, Donate a

Kidney." It turned out one of their employees needed a kidney, but it sure seemed like those signs pointed right at me that day!

Evaluating and Waiting

On a beautiful May morning, Mike and I traveled to the transplant center, where Lonnie was a patient, to have my donor evaluation. To say that a donor evaluation is a comprehensive physical would be an understatement. We met with doctors, nurses, a social worker, a psychiatrist, a donor advocate, and more. My physical, emotional, psychological, and mental health was scrutinized, and they determined that I was healthy enough to be a living donor. The feeling of excitement was incredible! After my visit, the transplant team met and approved me to be a donor. This opened the door for us to proceed, and we set the date for July 13, 2010. It overjoyed my heart. And then came the first of so many obstacles.

Lonnie needed to go through a routine CT scan prior to transplant. During that scan, they discovered a mass on his kidney. The doctors felt sure that it was a cancerous mass. I will never forget the day he called to tell me. Neither one of us knew what this meant but knew we had to remain hopeful even as we were both crushed. They did a biopsy, and we were all amazed to find out that the doctors were wrong . . . it was NOT cancer! The transplant was back on . . . or so we thought. Just two weeks prior to surgery, and less than 24 hours prior to our pre-operative appointments, Lonnie and I both received phone calls from the transplant center. They were canceling our surgeries. They had decided that Lonnie just wasn't healthy enough for a transplant and may never be. As much as this broke my heart, I couldn't even imagine how Lonnie felt. Here was a guy who was just two weeks from receiving a life-saving transplant and destined to survive only with the help of dialysis. I knew that just wasn't acceptable. I needed to help him find another answer.

Late that night, I was desperately searching the internet for an option. I stumbled upon the website of the University of Wisconsin

Health system. Their transplant page contained these words, **"UW Health Transplant consistently leads the nation in patient outcomes, despite taking patients whose conditions are so complex that other centers may not consider them for transplant."** I must have read that sentence five times before I was sure that it said what I thought it did. WE had a case that another center wouldn't take. Was it possible that changing centers would solve our problem? I found a "Contact Us" area of the site and sent off an email. I felt a small glimmer of hope once again! The very next day I received an email back from a coordinator at UW by the name of Chris. She asked me to have all of our records transferred to UW for review. I didn't know it then, but Chris would be an absolute rock and support for me from that point on.

Soon after, Lonnie was told he could come to UW for an evaluation. His family and I went along and were so encouraged by everyone we met that day, including a young fantastic surgeon by the name of Dr. Joshua Mezrich. What one center thought would be a deal breaker, Dr. Mezrich shrugged his shoulders and said, "It might be a little more difficult, but I can do it." Again, our hopes soared! All the information was gathered and compiled, and the transplant teams once again held our fate in their hands.

Crushed, but Never Broken

At the end of August, Chris called me and told me she had some tough news for me. It turns out that there was a mismatch between Lonnie and me in the DQ gene. I told Chris she must be wrong because I loved Dairy Queen and I was pretty sure Lonnie did too! She laughed but said this DQ was not one that determined how much we loved ice cream. And it could have devastating effects on our transplant. It turns out there was a very high chance that Lonnie's body would reject my kidney. There was no way I could be a direct donor to him. I hung up the phone and sobbed. But then I realized what almost happened. If the other center hadn't backed out on us, we would have had a disaster on our hands. Maybe everything that had happened had been a blessing in disguise. God must have a plan, and I needed to keep the faith!

During that call from Chris, she mentioned that the new "swap" program was soon to go online, and UW would join it. This might allow me to donate to another recipient, and that recipient's donor would give a kidney to Lonnie. This was a momentous occasion in the world of transplant, and it was just around the corner. I was so sure God had asked me to give a kidney to Lonnie, but maybe this was the intention instead. I knew I had to at least try it. So, in late November, when UW was gearing up to join, Lonnie and I gave permission to enter us into the system. Chris told us that after the start of the new year they would add us.

As January rolled around, my excitement was building once again. I couldn't wait to see what the swap program would bring. Then on January 11th, 2011, at 11:00 p.m., Lonnie received a call from UW. They had a deceased donor kidney available for him and wanted to know if he wanted it. Although he had me waiting in the wings, they recommended he take the kidney as his health had become precarious at that point. The next day we all traveled to Madison to be with Lonnie as he received this precious gift of life. The surgery was an amazing success. When Dr. Luis Fernandez came to the waiting room to speak to us afterwards, Lonnie's wife Ginger told him I was the original donor. Dr. Fernandez turned to me and said, "So, what do you plan to do now?" Wow. What did I plan to do? What a brilliant question! That night as I walked out of the hospital, light snow started falling. As I looked to the sky, tears ran down my face, and I realized the miracle that had just taken place. I said a prayer for the donor's family as they had just suffered a tremendous loss. The decision that donor made prior to their death had just saved Lonnie's life. I was so grateful. On the way home I called my best friend since Kindergarten, Jolene. Together we laughed, cried, and marveled at the amazing gift of life.

The next four months I went on living my life, checking in on Lonnie, and thinking and praying about what to do next. I was SO sure that God asked me to donate a kidney to Lonnie. But yet, here I was, still carrying around two kidneys while Lonnie received a kidney from another donor. One option was to donate and kick off a chain, which was like the swap program. Mike worried that without a connection to my recipient, I wouldn't have the same experience I had so far on this incredible journey. But, by mid-May, I just felt that God was telling me to make a move. So, on May 19th, 2011, I called Chris and told her my plan was to kick off a chain. She agreed to get the ball rolling. The next day, I was finishing up in my office for the day when one of my staff members, Laura, and I found ourselves alone for a few minutes. I had this sudden urge to tell Laura what my plans were. I will never forget her look as a smile came over her face. She told me that her friend Sara, a classmate of hers from high school, had just posted on Facebook that she needed a kidney. Laura asked if I wanted her to ask Sara to get in touch with me. My answer, of course, was, "Yes, please do!" Once again, my life was about to change in a way I could never imagine.

Sara's Story
The Long Road to Transplant

In the year 2000, at 20, they diagnosed me with renal agenesis. I was born with only one kidney. In addition, they gave me a secondary diagnosis of Henoch Schoenlein Purpura (HSP), which shares features with IgA nephropathy. IgA is an antibody (infection fighting protein) that was making deposits in my kidney. With the initial diagnosis, I didn't show many signs or symptoms. However, my doctor placed me on an immunosuppressant to help maintain my kidney function. For ten years this helped, but then my health deteriorated.

In the spring of 2010, I found myself in and out of the hospital several times, receiving blood transfusions at each visit. At first, the doctors just couldn't figure out what was happening. They diagnosed me with cytomegalovirus (CMV), which resulted in symptoms of fatigue, fever, and gastroenterology issues. I began losing weight, strength, and energy. Over the course of the next couple of months I dropped a substantial amount of weight, and my overall kidney function declined significantly.

In the fall of that year, one of my biggest fears materialized. I was told I was going to need a kidney transplant . . . and soon. My creatinine level, which was used to measure my overall kidney function, was rising fast. This was causing me to have fatigue and nausea daily. The higher my creatinine rose, the worse I felt. Minor tasks became big chores. Running into the grocery store for a few items took every ounce of strength I had. I was missing out on the small joys of being a mother. Taking a walk or a bike ride with my daughter Ashlyn was too much for me. I wasn't the mother I wanted to be nor the one Ashlyn needed. This went on for months and months and was exhausting.

After my diagnosis, Craig, my sister Carrie, and I had traveled to the University of Wisconsin Clinic and Hospital for a transplant evaluation. I cannot tell you how nervous I was. They reviewed my entire life history. While we were there, they tested my sister Carrie to be my living donor. Unfortunately, she was not a match. My brother Joe, and many families and friends also tested without success. I am forever grateful to those who stepped up to say, "Yes, I will."

Transplant Becomes Imminent

In early May 2011, my kidney function deteriorated to the point of permanent renal failure. My doctor advised me I would need to begin dialysis very soon. I tried my very best to hold off as long as I could. I dreaded the idea and never thought I would start having to rely on a machine to keep me alive. My cousin Wanda told me, in the days before she passed away from a long battle with cancer, "You never know how strong you are until being strong is the only choice you have." I soon realized how right she was.

They scheduled a consultation with the dialysis unit and explained my dialysis options. I had to choose from peritoneal or hemodialysis. Peritoneal dialysis uses a membrane inside your body as a filter to clear wastes and extra fluid from your body and to return electrolyte levels to normal. Hemodialysis relies on a central line placed in your chest that pulls blood through a machine to filter out toxins and return the blood to your body. Neither option sounded good to me. But peritoneal seemed like the best choice, since I could do it at home while I slept.

I left the consultation that day with marks drawn all over my abdomen showing where they would place the catheter. Feeling overwhelmed and scared, I sobbed the entire way home. The next day, my husband Craig and I attended another consultation with the surgeon to talk about how and when the catheter would be placed. I had doubts that peritoneal was the route I wanted to take. My biggest concern was Ashlyn. It would scare her to see me hooked up to a machine. She was only five years old. I know it sounds silly, but I didn't know if it was the thought of being hooked up to tubes or concealing them so that no one would notice them. The surgeon reassured me that this was my decision, and I could choose whichever treatment I wanted. We left his office that day with the ultimate decision that I would switch treatment options and revisit the idea of hemodialysis. This would require me to attend dialysis sessions 3 times per week for several hours at a time. At that point, I knew this was not something I could sustain as a young mom and wife. I knew I needed to think about long-term treatment options. I could not imagine forever depending on a machine to keep me alive.

On Thursday, May 19, 2011, I decided it was time to recruit for a kidney donor. I started with a simple Facebook post mentioning I was going to be starting dialysis soon and was being added to the United Network for Organ Sharing (UNOS) waiting list for a potential deceased donor. That one post changed my life forever.

A Living Donor Comes Along

Two days after my Facebook post, I received a private message from my high school friend, Laura. It read something like this, "I have someone that you may want to contact about being a donor. Her name is Jill!" I immediately sent Jill a Facebook Friend Request and waited. Soon Jill accepted my request and sent me a message. In that moment, my journey became our journey. Jill and I became instant friends. For hours we chatted online, getting to know each other. We talked about our husbands, families, kids, and just about everything else! Jill explained to me she was already an approved donor. As you know from the first part of this chapter, Jill's original intention was to donate to her patient and family friend, Lonnie. When that fell through, Jill knew she still wanted to make a difference and donate her kidney to someone in need.

Just a few days later, Jill contacted UW and asked that our labs and antibodies be tested against each other. UW had blood samples in storage for both of us, so it required no visit. I was so excited and nervous at the same time. I needed to stay positive that this would work out, yet I didn't want to get my hopes up and set myself up for a huge letdown. Jill was told that because of the upcoming Memorial Day holiday, we may not get results from UW for 2 full weeks. I could not think about anything other than those results as I went about the next couple of days. To my surprise, I arrived home from work just three days later and found Craig standing by the door with the phone. He wouldn't say who was on the other end of the phone. To my surprise, it was Jill!

We had never spoken in person at that point. We only shared conversations through Facebook. Jill started out by saying that UW had already called her, and they had our results. I had a terrible feeling that meant she had bad news to report. When they perform matching testing, the DSA (donor specific antigens) is a crucial number. This is used to determine how strong a person's antibody level is against a specific donor and helps to know if the recipient will reject or react to the new organ. To be a viable recipient, that number must be less than 3,000. Tears filled my eyes as Jill gave me the news. Our DSA was just 57! WE WERE A MATCH!

Meeting Jill

Jill and I took a trip to Madison together in early June for additional testing. This was the first time we met, and I was so nervous. As I traveled to her house, armed with flowers for her, I kept thinking, *What if she changes her mind?* We hit it off very well. Our last tests were confirmed, and we set a transplant date of July 21, 2011.

I called my doctor to give him the news of my newly found donor and was hoping he would say I could hold off on starting dialysis. I was determined to change his mind! However, as he explained, dialysis treatments would help give the new kidney a fresh start after transplant. A couple of days later I had the dialysis port placed in my chest so I could start making the three times a week trip to the dialysis center. Some treatments were better than others, but they all left me feeling exhausted. During this time, Jill checked on me through calls, texts, or Facebook messages, just to make sure I was doing okay.

When life settled down a bit and I started gaining a little strength, Jill and I introduced our families over dinner. Everyone had a great time getting to know each other. I loved seeing Ashlyn interact with Jill's two boys. They were the brothers she always wanted!

Transplant Time

The next several weeks seemed to take forever. Finally, it was the day before our surgeries, and Craig and I made our way to Madison. I was trying to stay positive, but the closer we got, the more nervous I was. I had so many thoughts running through my head. *What if I don't make it? What will happen to Craig and Ashlyn?* The list went on and on. That night, we had dinner with Jill and Mike, and Jill's parents, Janet and Bob. Then we all spent some time in the lobby of our hotel talking. Craig and I called Ashlyn, and Jill and Mike called their boys, Josh and Ike. We all went to bed early, knowing sleep might be elusive!

In the morning, we all gathered at the hospital; joined by my mom, Carol, and two of my best friends, Teri and Angie. We said goodbye, and they wheeled Jill into surgery. Shortly after, I was brought to a surgical suite nearby. A transplant surgery should take about four hours, but for anyone who knows me, it isn't often that things go the way they should! Complications arose during surgery. One vessel in Jill's kidney tore. The surgeons worked hard to come up with a solution to the problem. They removed the kidney, got a donor vessel from the tissue bank (from an unknown deceased donor), and used that to reconnect the kidney. Eight hours later, the transplant was complete.

I spent the next three days in the ICU. The transplanted kidney didn't start working right away, but after a few days, it woke up. The surgery itself had been hard on me. I was just 92 pounds when I went in that day. When they finally discharged me into a regular room from ICU, I found myself 50 pounds heavier from all the fluids they had pushed through my system, trying to keep all of my other organs going during the extensive surgery. I ended up spending over a week in the hospital, each day gaining a bit more strength. By the time they discharged me, I was feeling so much better. I knew I was on the road to getting my life back.

Raising Awareness Together

In the time leading up to our surgeries, we both had been through so much preparation that we didn't have time to think, it seemed. Once we had both recovered, we truly realized the significance of what had taken place on that July day in Madison. Our worlds had merged, and we were both so grateful for it all. About a year after our surgeries, they invited Jill to share her story at a local organ donation awareness group's annual scavenger hunt. We attended the event together, and we just knew we needed to get more involved. The next couple of years we entered a team into this event and had an absolute blast. Soon we learned that group was planning to discontinue their hunt. We knew this was our time to make a move to create our own awareness.

Over lunch with Sara's cousin Kathy, an idea formed. What if we started our own organ and tissue donation awareness group? Would we even know where to begin? For help, we turned to the people who had performed our life-giving and life-saving surgeries at the University of Wisconsin Health, specifically UW Organ and Tissue Donation (UW OTD). It thrilled them to hear we wanted to help them spread awareness. They connected us with Trey Schwab, their Community Outreach Coordinator. Trey was himself a double lung recipient, so he knew firsthand about the miracle of transplant. Out of this partnership, Central Wisconsin Gift of Life was born.

Our group comprises recipients, living donors, donor families, their family members, and people who just care about making a difference. Through several years of scavenger hunts and other events, we have raised tens of thousands of dollars and tirelessly spread awareness of the vast need for donors. We have chosen two important benefactors, UW OTD, and the Restoring Hope Transplant House in Middleton, Wisconsin, to receive funds from all of our events. Our group also built a Legacy Garden, the only of its kind in Wisconsin, dedicated to honoring and remembering recipients, donors, donor families and those involved in the gift of life. We have experienced the devastating loss of two friends, Trey and Chris, who both suffered complications from their lung transplants. Both men left a lasting mark on our lives, and we know they were eternally grateful for the extra years their donors gave them when they received their lungs.

Both of us travel to many events, do media interviews, and share our stories with as many people as we can. We hope that anyone who spends time with us knows how much we value the gift of life. If even one organ is donated, and we save one life through our work, it will all be worth it.

Last Words From Jill

I often hear from people they feel like I am a hero, or how amazing it is that I saved a life. But I can honestly say that what I gave I have received back at least tenfold. I like to call it "addition by subtraction." They subtracted an organ from my body, but the addition of all that has happened in my life since that day far outweighs any physical change to my body. I know that God showed me one of my greatest purposes in life that October morning, in 2009, as I sat in my office with Lonnie.

I am in awe of the donor moms I know (Patti, Dawn, Megs, Mary, Teri and so many more), who have lost their children and made it their life mission to be sure their children's memories live on just as their organs and tissues did. I have grieved with those who have lost their significant others (Wanda, Diane, Wendy), but who are grateful for the gifts of life they received and shared. I have celebrated as families received the call for their own life-saving transplants (Lonnie and Ginger, Mike and Beth), even while knowing that another family is grieving the loss of one of their own during that same time. And I am so very thankful for those at UW OTD, and UW Health, who work countless hours to make it happen (Chris, Carol, Kathy, Mary, and many, many others).

I will always be grateful for the incredible support of my husband Mike, sons Josh and Isaiah (Ike), parents Bob and Janet, sisters Wendy and Jennifer and their families, and my great support of amazing friends who were, and continue to be, with me through it all. I love every one of you!

To Trey, who helped launch our group, never stopped believing in me, but also never failed to be honest with me. I miss you and love you, my friend.

To Sara, let's keep living our best lives and changing the world, one donor at a time! Gaining you as a sister and friend is one of the greatest blessings in my life. I love you!

Sara's Closing

Being a donor is a brave and generous act, whether it's as routine as a blood donation or as extraordinary as an organ, eye, or tissue donation; whether it comes from a living donor, such as Jill (or friends Connie, June, and Cindy); or whether it's a final gift of the deceased like my dear friend and hero, Janelle. You never know when you could be the answer to someone else's prayers.

Together we can all make a difference by supporting organ donation, whether it is by monetary donating, taking part in fundraisers, or helping our organization bring awareness to the importance of being a donor. These are all ways of increasing quality of life for all of us. We can all do little things to make a big difference for such an important cause.

I am grateful for the amazing care I received from UW Health. I am even more thankful for the support I received from my husband Craig, daughter Ashlyn, parents Joe and Carol, brother Joe, sisters Shelly and Carrie and their families, and my great support of friends who were, and continue to be, with me every step of the way. Love to you all!

To Jill—There are no words, or gifts, that I could ever give to thank you for everything that you have done for me and my family. Because of you, I am the wife, mother, daughter, sister, and friend that I knew I could be. Because of organ donation, I am alive! I am alive because you gave the gift of life!

About Jill

Jill Dillon was born and raised in Nekoosa, Wisconsin. She has a bachelor's degree in Biology from the University of Wisconsin-Oshkosh and a Doctor of Optometry degree from the Illinois College of Optometry in Chicago, Illinois. Jill and her husband Mike returned to Wisconsin shortly after her graduation, where she has practiced with Marshfield Clinic in Wisconsin Rapids for over 20 years. Jill and Mike have two adult sons, Joshua and Isaiah, and live in the Town of Rome. In 2010, Jill's life forever changed when one of her patients informed her of his need for a kidney transplant. In 2011, she donated her left kidney to her new friend Sara. This launched a passion for spreading the word about the need for organ and tissue donors. Together, Jill and Sara, along with Sara's cousin Kathy, formed Central Wisconsin Gift of Life. Jill also volunteers for the University of Wisconsin Organ and Tissue Donation and the National Kidney Foundation of Wisconsin. She is an active speaker, telling her story and sharing the importance of donation to groups all over Wisconsin. She also educates young people in driver's education about the need for donors. In Jill's spare time, she enjoys golfing, riding UTV's with friends, playing with her dog, and watching and attending sporting events.

About Sara

Sara was born and raised in Milladore, Wisconsin. She is an Account Executive for Security Health Plan where she has worked for 20-plus years providing health insurance for Medicare and individual and family plans throughout Wisconsin. Sara and her husband, Craig, have one daughter, Ashlyn. They live in Auburndale. She enjoys gardening, photography, cooking, and spending time with her family.

Jessica Wickersheimer

Fourth Time is a Charm

My life has been spared not once, but four times because of organ donation. I have lived with type 1 diabetes since the young age of nine. Being diagnosed with type 1 diabetes was not an easy road. No child wants to be labeled different with a disease at that young of an age. Childhood can be hard enough, but add four to five finger sticks per day to test blood sugar levels and four shots a day to regulate insulin. It was very challenging. A lot of kids in my elementary school were afraid of my disease. They thought they could catch it by holding my hand or sitting too close to me at the lunch table. I am thankful for the ones who saw past the disease and became friends with me. I also had my cousin, Nicole, in a lot of my classes; she knew the signs of low blood sugar and other side effects of the disease. She always stood up for me, which made school much easier to deal with. To this day, I am still close with a handful of friends from elementary school, and that is a blessing.

When I entered my teenage years, the disease got real. High school was an entirely different monster when you are living with diabetes. I had a lot of friends who understood I had diabetes and all that was involved. Even though I knew that, I still felt different. I wanted to be a "normal" teenager like my friends . . . normal as in my getting to sleep in until whatever time I wanted without worrying about a finger stick, getting to eat meals without having to calculate carbohydrates and give myself insulin; getting to exercise without worrying if I were going to have to deal with low blood sugar, and not having to have candy on me at all times because of it. I wanted to be normal, but that wasn't the case for me.

It was hard for me to deal with the reality; and I admit, I skipped finger pokes, and I ate snacks and candy without an insulin shot. It eventually showed in my lab results. The doctors became concerned when they noticed my hemoglobin A1C (average of blood sugar readings over a three-month period) elevating. My diabetes was always very hard to control on its own, but I am sure I didn't help matters by being irresponsible. My medical team made it very clear to me the complications a diabetic can face in the long run with poor control. They explained that not managing my disease could destroy organs such as my kidneys and pancreas, and lead to disease and failure. It could also affect my eyesight and lead to swelling of the optic nerve and retinopathy (damage to the blood vessels in the eye). It could also cause nerve damage within my legs and feet known as neuropathy. I took what the doctors said seriously, but by the time I became a responsible diabetic, and followed the rules, it was too late. Diabetes is a serious disease that comes with many lifestyle changes and responsibilities. It can be the enemy if you let it.

I experienced all the text book complications my doctors told me would happen with type 1 diabetes in my twenties. I had neuropathy in my legs and feet, major eye issues with optic nerve edema and retinopathy. I had a handful of laser surgeries on my eyes to stop hemorrhages in my blood vessels, and Vitrectomy surgeries on both eyes when I lost eyesight because of bleeding in the back of my eyes. That was just the beginning of a long road ahead. Because of the long-term side effects of diabetes, I also have received multiple organ transplantations. No one can prepare you for the responsibilities you face after a transplant. I had an intimidating box of medications I had to take. I had blood draws twice a week to make sure my body was not rejecting the transplanted organ or organs. It was a definite lifestyle change, but for the better, of course. I believe I would not be here today to talk about my story had it not been for organ donation. The support of my family and friends was the most important element to my staying strong and being able to get through these surgeries, emotions, and recovery to help save my life.

My first transplant took place on July 14, 2003, at UW Health Hospital, in Madison, Wisconsin, which is more than an hour from where I lived. I was 24 years old. I received a pancreas from a deceased donor and hoped that this transplant would work and I would no longer be a diabetic. I spent a month in the hospital, and they put my parents up in a hotel to be close to me through the recovery. Once I was discharged from the hospital, my blood sugars were normal, and I did not have to give myself insulin injections. It worked! I truly felt like a miracle to not be a diabetic after having the disease for fourteen years. I did, however, experience many complications after that transplant, including Cytomegalovirus (also known as CMV), bowel obstruction surgery, and organ rejection. Unfortunately, the onset of rejection elevated my blood sugars, and I was back to being a diabetic. Although my transplanted pancreas was still producing some insulin, it was not enough to keep my blood sugars regulated, so I reverted to injections and finger sticks daily. My miracle disappeared, and it devastated me. It was very hard to deal with having that amazing feeling taken from you. I would have never made it through this time without the support of family and friends. Two years later, in March 2005, I got sick with pancreatitis and my transplanted pancreas had to be removed in an emergency surgery at Froedtert Hospital.

Three years went by and life with diabetes was getting back to being the normal for me. I had labs drawn frequently in Madison, and unfortunately, they showed I was in stage 4 renal (kidney) failure and had chronic kidney disease anemia. My treatment for the kidney failure and anemia consisted of red blood cell injections and numerous medications. This went on for about a year. My kidney function kept diminishing, and I was once again placed back onto the transplant list. This time they listed me to receive a kidney and a pancreas. I ended up getting the phone call that they had organs for me from a deceased donor on July 6th, 2009, and off we went again to UW Health Hospital in Madison. Recovery was much easier this time around, and I was only in the hospital for about a week. However, we noticed my blood sugars elevating again, and I just knew what this meant. All my hopes and excitement diminished. Unfortunately, I was going through organ rejection of the pancreas once again, and I knew it would be back to daily insulin injections and finger sticks. As much as it was a disappointment that this pancreas did not work either, I remained positive because at least my kidney was working strong. It cured me from kidney failure, and that was enough to keep me going!

Over the next four years, a lot of life events happened for me. I purchased a house all on my own, which made me feel strong and independent. A month later came another disappointment when I lost my job at Children's Hospital of Wisconsin after 12 years of service. Shortly after that, my lab draws showed some cellular rejection in my transplanted kidney. My creatinine (kidney function) levels were elevating over this time period, and my doctors started talking about the need for dialysis. This word has always been so scary to me because I knew it was a possibility for my future. I was also, once again, placed on the transplant list for another Pancreas/ Kidney Transplant.

I met with my doctor, and he explained I had two options: hemodialysis or peritoneal dialysis. Both options filter the blood and get rid of any toxins, extra salt, and water in the body that the kidneys can no longer process. They normally do hemodialysis in a medical facility, three days a week for four hours each day. It uses a machine to filter your blood through a port in your chest, or through a fistula placed in your arm, to remove waste and toxins. Peritoneal dialysis is done at home for 11 hours, usually overnight, and uses a machine that pumps fluid through a catheter that is placed in the abdominal area to remove the waste and toxins. After a lot of consideration of the pros and cons of each method, I chose peritoneal dialysis (PD). Once I chose this option, there was a lot to abide by. Classes were required for me to learn how to administer it in my own home, and I had to have someone with me at all times in the home, plus I had a house visit by a representative of the medical facility to make sure my home was a sterile and safe place to do the dialysis and to check that all the equipment was delivered. Next was the procedure to place a catheter, about twelve inches long, in my abdomen to connect to my dialysis machine. My best friend Jill attended all the classes with me and moved into my home. Once everything was in place, I started my dialysis in June 2013. I had to do this every single night for 11 hours. There were huge bags of fluid, called dialysate, strewn out on the floor every night, hooked up to my machine, that was hooked up to my abdomen catheter, to cleanse the excess salt, water, and toxins. Jill was such an amazing "caregiver," and a best friend who was there for me through all of this, along with my parents, family, and friends. Like I said before, a support system is the key to surviving anything like this.

Three months went by on PD, and finally on September 3rd, 2013, I got the phone call once again that the hospital had found a kidney and pancreas for transplant for me. This was my third transplant, but first one being performed at Froedtert Hospital, which was close to my home. The transplant was touch and go at first, and I was in the hospital for almost a month, but it was a success! Finally, no more diabetes, kidney failure, and no more insulin injections or finger sticks. I was back to my medication regimen for transplant recipients. I would take frequent labs and tons of pills over having diabetes and kidney failure any day. It was so nice to be close to home this time, instead of two hours away in Madison. It made a tremendous difference because friends and family could visit me without driving miles and miles, and I knew most of the doctors, nurses, and staff already, which made it feel like home.

Over the next year, although my pancreas and kidney were working great, I dealt with a lot of complications. I ended up having a kidney biopsy because they thought there was mild cellular rejection going on. I battled an infection along my incision from my last transplant because of a stitch that did not heal correctly, and because of no immune system, I could not fight off the infection myself. They wheeled me away for another surgery to remove the stitch, and place a vacuum to heal the wound. The vacuum therapy lasted two months. Once it was healed, I could finally celebrate my one-year anniversary of my kidney-pancreas transplant. My labs were perfect, I felt healthy, and thought I did not have to worry about anything else going wrong. That soon changed.

It was Labor Day weekend; I had gone up north for the holiday weekend. Come Monday, I noticed severe swelling in my ankles. I knew right away that this was not normal since my kidney was working perfectly. Once again, I had a terrible feeling. I contacted my transplant team, and they admitted me to Froedtert Hospital. My kidney was failing, and it was a mystery why. The team ran numerous tests to figure out why this would all of a sudden happen. They suspected it was my immuno-suppressive medication Tacrolimus (Prograf). They took me off of the medication immediately and had to replace it with another form of immuno-suppressive medication called Nulojix (Belatacept). This was not in pill form but rather an infusion every 28 days for the rest of my life. They performed a kidney biopsy to see how much damage there was. Unfortunately, my kidney was not working at all. I was absolutely heartbroken. Thank goodness through all of this, my pancreas was still going strong. I feel you always have to find a bit of positive in a tough situation.

My Doctors have always said there is a question mark hanging over my head because of all the complications I have encountered. There was really no rhyme or reason for the things I have gone through. I do my best, without even trying, to always keep them guessing. I felt if there is a rare complication or side effect, I will experience it. It's just how the ball rolls for me. With that said, we found out the reason my kidney stopped working so abruptly was because of an extremely rare disease called Atypical Hemolytic Uremic Syndrome (aHUS). This means the disease causes abnormal blood clots in small blood vessels that go to the kidney, and can restrict or block blood flow causing kidney failure. The treatment for this disease is an immuno-suppressive drug called Ecluzimab (or the trade chemotherapy drug called Soliris). They administer it through IV every two weeks to prevent my red blood cells from breaking and clotting up the small vessels to my kidney. One major side effect from this medication is the risk of getting Meningitis, therefore I also need to be on a prophylactic antibiotic to keep me protected from the risk of getting it. They also informed me I needed a catheter placed in my chest to start hemodialysis immediately to save the kidney. I believe this was scarier than my first bout with peritoneal dialysis. The thought of removing my own blood into a machine to cleanse it and then putting it back into my body seemed so unreal. I was set up with a dialysis center near my house and this is where I spent half my days, three days a week, for four hours at a time. I had to restrict the amount of water I drank, and food that contained too much salt, magnesium and phosphorus. My legs would swell up to the point of wearing shoes was a challenge. I kept telling myself there was a light at the end of the tunnel, my kidney function would come back, and I would be okay. Strength was a huge part of me getting through this. I knew giving up was not an option.

Throughout this process, I had a CT scan done to see if the damage to the kidney was improving and what our options were. Would I need to pursue another transplant? My nephrology (kidney) doctors explained to me that because of my history with transplants, surgeries, and complications from having diabetes for so long, if I needed another kidney transplant it would be very difficult, if not impossible. My veins and arteries had so much calcification and scar tissue on them it would make for a tough surgery to find a place to connect another kidney. They presented my options, which were getting re-listed for a kidney on the transplant list or finding a live donor. The waiting list for a deceased kidney was close to five years. The doctors explained to me waiting five years would be a race against the clock because of the sclerosis of my arteries and was not an option. All that kept running through my mind was I am going to be on dialysis the rest of my life. It scared me to death. I knew prolonged dialysis treatment was very hard on your heart and body. After all, I have been though I would find a way for this to work if it came down to needing another kidney. I had to.

I survived life with dialysis for about six months. I also continued to receive my Soliris infusions every two weeks to help with the aHUS. By the grace of God, it was all working. The lab tests showed my kidney was responding to the treatments and function was improving. Complete function could not be restored, but it was enough to stop my dialysis. I was so relieved and excited when they told me it was time to see if my kidney could make it without the dialysis anymore. I had the procedure done to remove my chest catheter and hoped for the best in the future ahead.

Over the next three years, I felt my life was back to normal. Although with a half-functioning kidney, a lot of side effects can happen. I overcame a lot of difficulties throughout this time, and was in and out of the hospital many times with high fevers, pneumonia twice, and a gastrointestinal infection that led to a bleed or ulcer. Once I recovered from all of this, I ended up with anemia and had multiple blood transfusions and iron infusions to help my body regenerate the production of red blood cells. At this point in my life, I didn't know how strong I could really be, until being strong was the only option I had.

In March 2017, they placed me back on the kidney transplant list for fear it would take up to five years to find a match. I knew my kidney function was trending downward, so I wanted to start my wait time as soon as possible and remain hopeful one would become available. Living day to day, knowing your kidney is getting worse by the hour is hard to swallow. But if you take one day at a time, and a deep breath every morning, it is worth it! I dealt with lots of swollen ankles, fatigue, high blood pressure, and more medications to regulate what my kidney could not do anymore. It was a challenging waiting game. A game I did not want to play anymore.

After being active on the list for almost a year, I started my search for a living kidney donor. It felt like the best option, so in the spring of 2018 I brainstormed ideas on how to spread the word of my quest for a kidney donor. I imagined yard signs, bracelets, and magnetic signs for cars. I decided to start a GoFundMe page to help raise money for my ideas, and I raised enough money to go through with all of it. I also saw a man on the news who used t-shirts at a Brewer's game to get his word out. Brilliant! So I then designed my own t-shirt, and had a group outing at a Brewer's game with family and friends in April to promote National Donate Life Month, and advertise my need for a kidney with our t-shirts. Thinking I needed to go a step further, I thought, *what better way to have my desperate need for a live kidney donor seen than a billboard around Milwaukee?* I called Lamar Advertising Company, and they were amazing and absolutely on board (no pun intended) to help me with the billboard I designed. Amazingly, I was able to rent billboards with the leftover donation money I raised.

Lamar approved to put the billboards up in different locations around Milwaukee. Once the signs went up, they caught the eye of local news channels, and the spread of the word, of my search for a live kidney donor, skyrocketed. A potential donor, Jennifer, informed me she was moving to the next phase of testing and had a phone interview. Things were looking more positive. I was receiving phone calls to set up interviews with all the local news channels to get the word out about my search for a live kidney donor. I got to share these news interviews with my husband Jason and his two sons, my stepsons, Chase and Eyan, as well. We also got a call from *The Morning Blend* TV show on WTMJ in Milwaukee, Wisconsin, to appear and share my story and the experience of looking for a kidney donor. Jason and I were on together; and they even allowed my Mom, Dad, and Chase and Eyan on set while they interviewed us. It was definitely an experience I will never forget, and to have family there to support me was even better. This is also where I met Brenda Cortez, who has now become a good friend. She had been on the show in the past, and they wanted to bring her back to follow my segment. What a brilliant idea to follow a segment about searching for a living kidney donor with a person who donated their kidney 13 years prior and is doing great!

At the end of April, my transplant team contacted me to discuss the option of a Paired Exchange Program. This is where I enter the program with a potential donor who doesn't exactly match my blood type, but they can donate their kidney to someone in exchange for a kidney which matches my blood type. It would open many more doors in finding a live kidney donor since I am very hard to match because of antibody levels from previous transplants. I also have sclerosis of my arteries, which puts me on a very short timeline to still be eligible for a transplant. We found out Jennifer had my same blood type, but our DNA did not match. Unfortunately, she could not donate to me directly, so we joined the paired program once she was officially approved to be a kidney donor on my behalf.

Jennifer and I continued to keep in contact while waiting to hear if a potential donor came from the Paired Exchange program.

Although it was over text messages, our friendship was already growing. It was a heartfelt feeling to know a complete stranger would give up their kidney for me; I knew it was already a friendship for life. The waiting game is the hardest part of hoping you will find a match. During this time, my kidneys got worse, and function was declining. I ended up having to get a catheter placed in my chest and start hemodialysis once again. This was not my first rodeo on dialysis, but in fact my third time. I was back to three days a week, for four hours each day, at my dialysis center. It was a lot to deal with, but when you have the support and "never give up" attitude like I did, you can make it through anything.

Jennifer and I both received phone calls on June 27th, letting us know a potential donor had come forward. We were so excited and scared at the same time. A few weeks later, however, they notified us that the donor had to be rushed into emergency surgery, so the chain for transplant was broken, and so were our hearts. It was back to hoping and waiting again. We both knew it was always a possibility, since they never promised the paired exchange would work. With that being said, I knew Labor Day weekend was approaching us, and the 115th anniversary of Harley Davidson was also upon us. This would be the perfect opportunity to get my billboards up again, with so many people coming to the Milwaukee area for the occasion. They were approved again, and the billboards went up advertising organ donation . . . and the need for a live kidney donor for me, once again.

My transplant team informed me that there were so many phones calls coming in from people who were interested, not only in donating to me, but wanting to donate to anyone who needed a kidney. It was amazing to me to know not only would I hopefully find a donor, but so many other people who were in need just might find a match because of my billboards. The day after Labor Day, Jennifer and I got another phone call stating there was another chain happening through the Paired Exchange program, and they were getting donors in line. My heart dropped, and I felt this time would be the one. The potential date was October 10th. We had more tests to complete as well.

On October 3rd, I had to have pre-op testing done, and Jennifer had contacted me to share that her pre-op testing was on the same day. I felt it was a coincidence, maybe, and when I was done with my tests and ready to leave, they told me to wait by a door in the hallway. When it opened, there stood Jennifer! We both saw each other for the first time and immediately knew who the other person was. Tears were shed, we hugged each other, and we both knew this was the beginning of a truly amazing milestone in our lives. I knew she was my angel, saving my life in such a special way.

A week later, on October 10th, 2018, Jennifer and I went to Froedtert Hospital, and I received my fourth, and most recent, Kidney Transplant. This was also my first time receiving a kidney from a live donor through the paired exchange program. We had minimal details on how the chain worked, but they informed us Jennifer's kidney went to a recipient in Pennsylvania. Then in Pennsylvania, the donor's kidney went to a recipient at a Children's Hospital in Ohio, and in return, I received my kidney from a donor in Virginia. Not only did I receive my kidney, but others did too—all in one transplant chain. To me, it was truly amazing!

During recovery, Jennifer and I got together to make sure we were both doing well. We met each other's families, and it was the start of a relationship that will last forever. While in the hospital recovering, they set a press conference up to share our story of the importance of organ donation and the paired exchange program. It was the first time Jennifer and I were together, telling our story for nurses and doctors, along with my most amazing doctor, Dr. Ehab Saad. If it were not for Dr. Saad, I would have never made it this far to talk about it. He has been with me through all of my health issues, helping me every way he can. I am so blessed to have a doctor with so much dedication and compassion.

Once discharged, with a perfectly working new kidney, I felt life couldn't be any better. No more dialysis, no more feeling swollen, sick, or like I had no energy. I felt like a new person, all because Jennifer made the ultimate selfless decision to donate her kidney for me. Even though her kidney did not go directly to me, I still feel she is my kidney donor. She saved my life because of organ donation. Three months later, I was invited to be on *The Morning Blend* TV show once again, but this time with Jennifer, to share our story and the importance of organ donation. The story had come full circle.

The friendship between Jennifer and me is a forever bond. We are like family now. We recently celebrated our two year "kidneyversary" together with our families. None of this would have been possible without her and organ donation. It is so important that we spread awareness for organ donation and how great the need is. It saves lives. I am living proof of that.

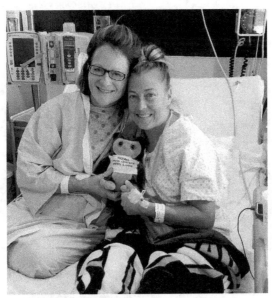

The first time Jennifer and Jessica were able to see each other after surgery. It was a forever bond they immediately had because of Organ Donation. Jennifer saved Jessica's life. Howl the Owl even joined them for the occasion.

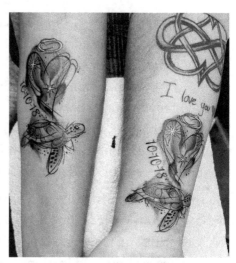

Jennifer and Jessica with her most amazing Transplant Medicine Physician, Dr. Ehab Saad after the donation-transplant surgeries.

Jennifer and Jessica created a tattoo to symbolize their bond. The halo is for Jennifer, Jessica's Angel for saving her life. The green heart represents organ transplantation/donation, and the turtle symbolizes longevity, endurance, persistence, and the continuation of life (sometimes against incredible odds).

Jennifer and Jessica holding the Donate Life t-shirt at Froedtert Hospital with Diane and her kidney recipient, who were another pair blessed with the Gift of Life.

During Jessica's search for a live kidney donor, her billboards around Milwaukee sparked the opportunity for the family to go on the tv show The Morning Blend to raise awareness and tell her story.

My amazing family-husband Jason,
and Stepsons Chase and Eyan.

Jessica with her best Friend Jill. She was
Jessica's rock during her first bout with
Peritoneal Home Dialysis by moving in with
her and learning it all.

Jessica's parents, Cathy and Lee, have been her rocks
and life support through everything she has endured.

Two amazing families bonded forever by the Gift of Life.

About Jessica

Jessica is 41 years old and lives in West Allis, Wisconsin. She is a kidney recipient through the paired exchange program, with her donor Jennifer. They celebrated their two-year "kidneyversary" in October 2020. This is also Jessica's fourth transplant.

Jessica is married to Jason Kanapka, and she has two amazing stepsons, Chase and Eyan. She is an enthusiastic crafter, always making projects to keep her busy. Jessica is a volunteer mentor, at Froedtert Hospital of Wisconsin, for transplant recipients, both pre-transplant and post-transplant.

If you would like to connect with Jessica, you may email her at shareyourspareoneg@gmail.com or reach out to her on her Facebook page. Jessica also raises funds to help others in need of a living kidney donor with advertisements on billboards. If you would like to know more about this, or donate, please contact Jessica.

About Jennifer

Jennifer Shallow is a Nail Technician who owns her own salon. She is also a CNA and phlebotomist at St Luke's Medical Center of Milwaukee, Wisconsin. She has been married to her wonderful husband Greg for eight years, and she has a beautiful daughter named Brehanna.

Jennifer enjoys long motorcycle rides, Caribbean vacations, spending time with friends and family, and sitting on her patio enjoying a warm fire. You can connect with Jennifer through her Facebook page, or email her at breandjen@yahoo.com

Deb Kavanaugh

One Kidney, Two Lives Saved

My journey to become a living organ donor, I believe, started because of my nature of always wanting to help others. I was very shy growing up but I still had a deep desire to do things, see the world, and help others. I was just too scared to venture out and do any of the things I dreamed of doing. I think some of my anxiety stemmed from being teased a lot as I was growing up and not wanting to leave the comfort of my home. As I got older, left for college, and started working, the more courageous I became. I slowly came out of my shell. My confidence grew more; I took part in doing class projects with other students, standing up in front of class, and being around co-workers. I ventured out and started doing a few of the smaller things I always wanted to do, like exploring beautiful trails, old towns, and now, even the world.

I've always had the desire to help others, but just wasn't sure how or what to help with. I remember my father donating blood and being part of the gallon donor club, and I thought that was an amazing thing to be a part of. It was my father's blood donations, and my mother always welcoming the neighborhood kids in for treats and a place to hang out, where I inherited my desire to help others.

As I became more daring, I did small volunteer projects which helped build my self-esteem. One of the first things I remember being a part of was the Christmas toy donation drive at my job, which lead to other volunteering activities outside of work. Years later, through the counseling program I was in after the death of my younger daughter, I learned about foster parenting. I thought, *What a great way to help children who needed caring for*. I took the training and for many years I was a foster parent. It was very rewarding and made my heart feel good.

I don't remember how I found out about living organ donation, but I remember thinking how amazing it would feel to save someone's life. For a long time after learning about it, I kept thinking about my desire to donate a kidney, so I did some research on it. I decided it was time to talk to my parents about my wish to donate. My parents, brothers, sister, my daughter, and myself were sitting around the dining room table at my parents' home talking when I brought up donating a kidney. Everyone became quiet. My father and mother looked at each other and then at all of us. My father then told us they had diagnosed my mom with end stage renal failure about six months prior, and she would need a kidney transplant at some point. They had told none of us yet because my mom did not need to start dialysis yet but was getting close. My mom shared with us how she learned she had kidney failure and what she was going through. One thing I remember her saying is she had to sit down about eight times just to make the bed. She was going through so much, and we did not even know it; yet she continued to work up to about two weeks before the transplant surgery.

Of course, after hearing my mom needed a kidney, I immediately wanted to donate to her if I could. We all talked for hours that night and decided I would be the first one tested of all my siblings and other family members. A few days later, my mom contacted her transplant coordinator and testing started within a week. The closest transplant center then was University of Iowa Hospital, in Iowa City, Iowa. For us, the distance was five hours from my parent's house and eight hours from mine. Testing was done by faxing the needed test to the hospital in the town I lived in, and paperwork to my place of employment. I asked why they didn't just do all the testing at once, because it was taking weeks doing it this way. They did it that way in case a set of tests didn't pass, or if I changed my mind.

At the time of testing, I was taking college classes, and working full time, and raising my daughter as a single parent. I let my professors know I might have to miss some classes, and my employer that I may have to miss some work. They understood and told me to do what I needed to do to get the testing done. They would work around everything during the testing and donation if I was a match. I appreciated how supportive my professors, classmates, coworkers, family, and friends were. My boss and coworkers surprised me by donating their PTO (Paid Time Off) to me if I should need it. The stress of not knowing if I would be a match, and the excitement of being able to save my mom's life if I was a match, caused a constant wave of emotions; so the support I was receiving from everyone I knew was very helpful.

Testing took six weeks and was a breeze for me. The hardest part was waiting to hear if I was moving on to the next test. There were a lot of blood draws, crossmatching, and tissue type tests. With each test, it was exciting knowing I was one step closer to being able to donate. I recall how nice the staff at the hospital were, and they were excited each time they saw the next test come on the fax machine, knowing I could take another step forward to donating.

I was at work when the transplant coordinator called to tell me I had passed all the tests and was a great match for my mom! She explained our next steps and that my mom and I needed to discuss if we wanted to move forward right away with the transplant. If so, we needed to decide on a date. I left work early that day to call my mom to discuss everything. She was at 11% kidney function and still had not started dialysis. Instead of waiting, we moved forward and scheduled the surgery so she could avoid dialysis. Mom and I discussed what would be a suitable date, and decided the end of the school year would be the best, which was only a month away. We called the transplant coordinator to let her know our decision to move forward with the surgery so my mom wouldn't have to do dialysis. The date for surgery was set for June 10, 2004.

We prepared all the last things to get ready to travel to Iowa for the surgery. School was done for the summer, I had my hours covered at work, my daughter would be with relatives, and friends would watch my house. I bought matching robes for my mom and me to wear at the hospital. We were packed, excited, and ready to go!

A few days before the surgery, my parents and I drove down to Iowa City to explore along the way; definitely something we all like to do, taking the back roads to see things one doesn't get to see on the interstate and highway systems. My parents surprised me by taking me to the Amana colonies in Amana, Iowa. The colonies are seven small German villages of shops with handmade candles, blown eggs, soaps, fudge, wines and beers, and many other items made by the locals. The food we had was amazing, and the demonstrations on glass blowing, candle making, and other things were fascinating. What a great treat before the transplant surgery! Something I will always remember and cherish.

We arrived in Iowa City the day before the surgery and checked into the hotel, then made our way to the hospital to meet with the transplant team. They told us what would happen the day of the surgery and asked if we had questions. There was one thing they mentioned I had not previously known. Instead of taking out Mom's left kidney, they would leave it in place, disconnect it, and hook up mine instead. Her old kidney would eventually shrivel up, and it was easier on her body to leave it in. Per hospital instructions, we were told to stay hydrated that night, and they suggested eating popsicles. So, mom and I sat in the hotel room and ate an entire box of cherry popsicles! Cherry is still my favorite flavor.

The rest of my family members, my daughter, and other relatives came to Iowa City the day before surgery. They let me and my mom have time alone that night. We talked about the surgery and how we were surprised neither one of us was nervous about the surgery. I guess we were both more excited to be moving forward with it so she didn't have to do dialysis, and mostly concerned for each other's wellbeing. There was that desire to always help others more than we do ourselves.

The big day had arrived! Surgery day, June 10, 2004! We arrived at the hospital, and they prepared both of us for surgery. They put us in a room together with our family so we could all visit until it was time to start. There were lots of smiles and laughs, then hugs when it was time to begin surgery. My younger brother told me later that once they gave me the medicine to make me sleepy, I was saying funny things, making them all laugh. I don't remember that at all.

They did my donation as laparoscopic nephrectomy, and they said the surgeries would last about 2-3 hours. While both surgeries went well, my surgery took a little longer than expected because they couldn't get my remaining right kidney to pee. It surprised my mom and I because of all the popsicles we ate the night before. My left kidney started working right away in its new home.

The first thing I remember upon waking up was that I was sharing a room with a stranger and not my mom. I don't think we ever asked if we would be in the same hospital room after surgery. I'm one of those few people who enjoys being in the hospital. I saw it as a mini vacation where they would cater to me, and I could call for room service food whenever I wanted. My mom was down the hall from me, and I didn't get to see her until the next day. My dad and my daughter came to see me after seeing my mom and told me she was doing great. I was happy to hear this and was able to go to sleep without worrying. We were both exhausted and slept a lot that first day.

Our family let us rest, and it had been a long day for them too since they were awake and worrying the entire time while we had slept. That night my family members went out to dinner and tried the "Around the World Beer Bucket." I still tease them about that— "Thanks for enjoying yourselves while mom and I lay in the hospital." Truthfully, I was glad they could celebrate our successful surgery and let some stress go.

The morning after surgery, the doctors came in to check on me and were worried because they couldn't figure out why I wasn't responding when they tried to talk to me. When one of them finally touched my arm, I woke up. When I saw they were talking to me, I reached up and took out my earplugs. I could see the relief on their faces when they figured out why I wasn't waking up. I explained that I always wear earplugs when sleeping away from home; I'm a very light sleeper, even the slightest noise wakes me up. The nurse later told me it was a good thing I brought ear plugs because the person I was sharing the room with snored like a freight train. They could hear her down the hall and she was keeping other patients awake. I guess I should have brought ear plugs for everyone!

The doctors said they would release me in a few hours, and I was a little alarmed by that. I expressed my concern that I just woke up and no one had even taken my vitals yet, plus I hadn't gotten up to walk. What would happen if I got back to the hotel and something went wrong? They weren't aware I lived eight hours away, and that I had donated to my mom, who was still in the hospital. They let me stay another day and released me the following day. While getting ready to leave the hospital, I realized I couldn't get my socks and shoes on, so my dad had to do it for me. He laughed since he hadn't done that since I was three years old. Before leaving the hospital, we walked down the hall to see my mom. I was nervous to see her, not knowing what to expect after such an extensive surgery. It made me smile to see her looking the same as before surgery, but she now had more color in her face. We visited for a bit, and then my dad took me to the hotel.

My 13-year-old niece, Kelsey, stayed to help take care of me at the hotel, so my dad could be with my mom at the hospital. She had to stay in the hospital for about a couple of weeks because of some complications. For my niece, it was like a vacation. She said it was like she had her own little apartment. I enjoyed having her there to help me with things like making meals. Everything I ate for the first two weeks tasted salty, but all the things I was craving to eat were salty things, such as chicken noodle soup and potato chips. While I had an appetite, I got full really fast.

My dad came at lunch every day to take my niece and me to the hospital so we could see my mom. It was nice being able to see her progress, and knowing she was getting better every day relieved our worry. My recovery was seamless. I noticed before surgery I would get up six times a night to use the bathroom, but after surgery I only got up a couple times a night. I joked with my mom that I must have given her the kidney that made me get up a lot at night to go to the bathroom. Another thing I noticed after donating was that I stopped having menstrual cycles. My doctor said it was from the stress of surgery and that it would eventually come back, but it never did. I was fine with that! I was 41 years old and glad I was no longer having a period. My doctor felt, because of this, maybe I wouldn't have the symptoms that come along with menopause for so many women, and she was correct. Many of my girlfriends going through menopause got hot flashes, etc. I told them to donate a kidney and save a life, and maybe their menopause ailments would go away.

After they released my mom, we went to their house, and I stayed there for a few days. Both of our recovery periods were going great, and I drove myself home a few days later. Luckily, I didn't need the PTO generously donated by my coworkers. I was back to work in four weeks, working part-time at first and easing back into full time.

I would still tire easily.

Mom started flourishing, and I could see her desire to do all the things she loved to do, like cooking, baking, crafting, spending time with family, and travel, coming back. It quite surprised me when my dad told me they wanted to come with me on the ten-day spring break trip to Italy and Greece that I had booked through the university I was attending. You didn't have to be a student to go, which was perfect. Life is too short, and after what my mom has been through, not going on this trip would be something they would regret. So, I booked the trip, and my daughter also came along. Just nine months after the transplant surgery, we all were off to live life on our first international travel experience. Mom did amazingly well at keeping up with the tour group, and the tour guide slowed the walking down to help her out, which was nice of him. It surprised everyone on the trip that she just had a kidney transplant a few months prior and was doing so well. They were interested in hearing more about kidney disease and the surgery. It was an amazing trip, and we were all grateful we got to experience it together. My mom always said it felt like she was in a dream, and what a beautiful dream it was.

Since the surgery, I have become very involved in advocating for organ donation. For the past five years, I have been on the Board of Advisors for The National Kidney Foundation, serving the Dakotas, Iowa, and Nebraska. I help with all the programs and fundraising events, the kidney walks, and golf tournaments, offered by The National Kidney Foundation that help so many patients, and their families and donors as well.

On April 21, 2018, I helped set a record, for the Guinness Book of World Records, for the most living donors in one place, at the Cloud Gate (Bean Sculpture) in Chicago, Illinois. I am so proud of this, even though I hesitated because I would travel by myself, and it made me anxious to go to a big city. One of the most memorable things from that weekend, besides setting the record and meeting so many amazing people, was the realization of how many people didn't know that you don't have to wait to die to donate. Many people saw our "Living Donor" shirts and asked questions about living donation.

That weekend trip to Chicago really kicked off my living donor advocacy. I now talk to anyone who will listen on how easy being a kidney donor is for most donors. I also advocate to others who are considering becoming a living donor by talking with them, answering questions, and helping ease their minds of any concerns. There are three living donors who donated because of my support to them!

I have met many other living kidney donors, these last five years in particular. It's great having a support group of others in the "One Bean Club." Many from the Guinness World Record event and many new donor friends from a donor awareness cruise I went on in February 2020. It was a blast, and I am looking forward to doing it again! Through our talks and Facebook groups, it surprised me to learn how many named their donated kidney and got pictures taken of the kidney during surgery. Pictures weren't an option when I donated, but maybe I will think up a name for my donated kidney.

I am looking forward to attending the Transplant Games of America and volunteering again at Life Source–Donate Life events. The events help to increase organ donation registration.

Through talking with so many other living kidney donors, I learned that some have not only donated their kidney but also part of their liver. This is something I had never considered since I didn't know you could donate while living. Organ and tissue donation is always evolving, and recently there have been uterus donations for transplant. I reached out to Penn Medicine, one of the few hospitals in United States that performs this type of transplant, to inquiry about donating mine. While they were very appreciative and honored I would want to, especially after having donated my kidney, they denied my request. They explained that after donating your uterus there is a greater risk of kidney and bladder infections. Since I only have one kidney, the risk would be too high for me.

I have now researched donating part of my liver or lung. I find it fascinating that the liver regenerates itself. It is truly amazing what the human body is capable of. Wouldn't it be great if all organs would regenerate, and we could donate again and again?

My mom lived life to the fullest after the transplant, only having slight but manageable issues with anemia. She traveled the world, taught her kids, grandkids, and great-grandkids to enjoy and appreciate every minute life offers you. She took good care of herself and her new kidney, and as health issues popped up, she addressed them. In 2016, after having some leg pain and a hard time walking, she had surgery to unblock a vein. The surgery went well, and she was excited she could keep up with the great-grandkids once again. But within a few days after being released, complications set in, and she was in the hospital for six months. She recovered and flew through rehab and went home. Unfortunately, she was back in the hospital a short time afterwards. While not having issues with the kidney, she had a lot of fluid buildup, so the doctor did dialysis. He explained they would teach my dad how to do home dialysis if she would need it. Doctors explained eventually the kidney would figure out there was nothing for it to do and we could decide to donate it to someone else or I could have it back. That surprised my dad and me.

My mom started dialysis the next day. They did two more rounds the following two days, but on the third treatment, her heart could not take it, and she started having problems. The kidney was still strong. My dad decided it was too hard on her and transitioned her to hospice care. They called the family to the hospital, and we sat with her. The doctor explained that when she passed, we would have to decide if we wanted to give my kidney to someone else or for me to take it back. I called my nephrologist, and she advised against me getting it back because I was doing fine. If I did get it back, I would have to be on anti-rejection medicine for the rest of my life. Mom passed away peacefully just a few hours later. We donated the kidney to help another person in need. I still do not know who that person is, but I feel honored to have saved my mom and another person with my one kidney.

My mom is looking down, and I know she is proud I have led my life with a mission to help others and advocate for things that are important to me. Deep down, I am proud too. Once a shy, scared little girl growing up, to now being an outgoing spokesperson for living organ donation! Dreams do come true if you work hard enough at them.

In Honor of my Mother—Diane Kavanaugh

Deb and her mom on their 10th kidneyversary.

Deb's niece Kelsey and Caitlin.

Kristen, Seamus, Harper and Peyton at the Kidney Walk - National Kidney Foundation Serving SD, ND, IA, NE.

Because of Organ Donation

Living Donors Guiness World Record Holders Group Picture .

My Parents
Tom & Diane
on their
Wedding Day

Mom, Me and
my Siblings,
Duane, Angie
and Doug

Deb's Father Tom releasing a Chinese Lantern to her mom on World Kidney Day.

Deb's Mom Diane, Daughter Kristen, and Deb...at Deb's Daughter's Wedding.

Star Wars *Warriors, friend Brenda and Deb. Warriors in the Fight to End Kidney Disease and Advocates of Organ Donation - one Star Wars Warrior donated his kidney to another one.*

Celebrating after helping set the Guinness Book World Record for the Most Living Donors in One Place on April 21, 2018.

About Deb

Deb is a Living Kidney Donor who donated to her mother in 2004. She has always had a strong desire to help others and, after her kidney donation, she wanted to do more to help others waiting for a kidney transplant. Deb serves on the Board of Advisors for The National Kidney Foundation serving the Dakotas, Iowa, and Nebraska. She also helps with many programs and events for The National Kidney Foundation to help raise awareness with both kidney health and living organ donation. She educates patients on how to ask for a kidney, the many programs available to them, and other questions they have. Deb supports, listens, and answers questions for those considering living donation, and is active in the One Kidney Club in her area. She is an advocate for all organ, tissue, eye, etc., donations. If you have the desire to be a living kidney donor, learn more about kidney health, or finding a kidney donor, you can learn about the program The Big Ask the Big Give at kidney. org. You can also register at RegisterMe.org to donate organs, tissue, etc., upon your death.

Deb lives in Sioux Falls, South Dakota, and enjoys traveling, exploring unknown places, spending time with her family and friends, and spoiling her two granddaughters, Harper and Peyton. If you have interest in living kidney donation, Deb would be happy to talk with you! You can connect with her through social media on Facebook or by email at debnkf@yahoo.com.

DONATE LIFE!

HEART YOUR KIDNEYS!
♥

ShirLey Scott Brill

New Lungs, New Life!

SUFFOCATION. I felt like I was walking around suffocating! I felt like a fish flopping on the floor, out of its aquarium, waiting for someone to rescue it and place it back in the water! Too many steps would cause me to lean on the wall, gasping for any available air passing near where I stood. If breathlessness had a familiar aroma, I'm sure it would be like that of a skunk or an untidy gas station restroom used by hundreds of travelers without being cleaned. There is nothing pleasant about the fear of not being able to catch your breath . . . not being able to breathe!

DENIAL. The red flags that waved danger in my mind were signaling to get help, but I marinated in the comfort of I'm okay. Even though I realized this was not how I moved about daily, I permitted myself to believe it was nothing to worry about. It would fix itself, and my breathing would return to normal; it's probably just the few extra pounds that I've added on—probably.

Where is this debilitating feeling coming from? What have I done to bring such misery to my no-worries lifestyle? HAKUNA MATATA . . . no worries. There was worry, because the shortness-of-breath feeling had settled into my body, and it seemed like it was there to stay; like a guest that has worn out their welcome and refused to leave.

As a certified public-school educator, it became difficult to walk with a group of active fifth graders at their pace, and to go up and down a flight of stairs at least five to six times a day. Something I had done just a month ago. It became even harder to camouflage my inability to keep up, and I'd frequently stop and motion for them to continue moving forward without me. I would pretend to stop and say hello to a fellow teacher or lean over to tie my shoe when I was out of breath and my heart was beating so fast as it depleted my energy.

I was the Minister of Music at my church. The walk from the parking lot to the sanctuary became a challenge during the two weekly choir rehearsals and the Sunday morning worship service. It wasn't until I had finally had enough, and faced the fact that something was seriously wrong, that I told myself if I still felt this way when service was over, it was time to pay a visit to the emergency room."

JOURNEY. Little did I realize on that day my journey toward healing would begin. The stench of fear saturated both nostrils and caused my eyes to fill with water. All I could think about was the thought of my life coming to an abrupt end much sooner than I expected. At age 49, I thought of saying goodbye to the people I loved so dearly. I was so close to 50 and looking forward to family, friends, co-workers and everyone who had my well-being at heart, coming together to celebrate fifty years of my life. I had been seeing the shiny party ball, hearing the party music, and laughter and noise of good times being had by all; but now I visualized a glim hospital room and the smell of death creeping upon me like a snail crawling up a hot brick wall.

As the benediction was said, and church ended, I headed to the ER. With no conclusive information other than being told to schedule a follow-up appointment with my primary care physician, I was frustrated. This appointment could not come quick enough. The agonizing thoughts of what was going on with my body taunted me like a mosquito buzzing in my ear on a hot summer night.

My primary care physician and fellow church member, Dr. Sykes, will always have a special place in my heart because he prescribed oxygen for me during my very first visit. My oxygen saturation dropped each time I took a step or attempted to do anything. After four visits, two or three inhalers, and various prescriptions, Dr. Sykes thought it best that he refer me to a pulmonologist who could help me understand what was causing this drastic drop in my oxygen saturation.

Dr. McDonough, a gentleman of a guy, reminded me so much of Chuck Norris. He spoke with a quiet, friendly, yet firm voice. I looked forward to each appointment because I was eager to hear the doctor say that within just a few more visits this problem would be over and I could resume my regular life and lifestyle. I wouldn't have to carry an oxygen tank on my shoulder and people wouldn't give me that look and think, *poor ShirLey, she needs to lose some weight.* Or, *she used to smoke, didn't she?* After six months of appointments, there was no improvement in my condition. It was worsening, and my oxygen usage had increased from 2 liters to 3 liters. I had many X-rays taken of my lungs, and they showed the white spaces were getting larger. The words of Dr. McDonough clearly resonated with me. I needed a lung transplant. My thought was, *you are mistaken, for that is something far too complicated for my simple yet happy life.* WHAT? You read or hear about these things, but never would I think that this would happen to me. I signed up to be an organ donor as a teenager, when I got my first driver's license, but that was just to help someone else when I died. *This can't be happening to me . . . he's mistaken,* I thought as I chuckled in my spirit.

A few more months passed, and it became more difficult to move about at a slow pace, and my energy level was declining rapidly each day. It was not getting better. I had tanks in my car trunk to last throughout the day for school, for choir rehearsal, for the grocery store, for home—oxygen tanks everywhere.

I was facing head-on the fact that my situation was not improving. I requested a third opinion about this lung transplant, and they referred me to Dr. Cury and Dr. D'Agostino. Those two advised me of what was going on in my body and why it was not getting better. After two visits, they referred me to the Mayo Clinic for evaluation for a lung transplant.

Knowing that I was not getting better, I began my transplant quest but was declined because my condition was not severe enough. As time passed, it became more difficult to breathe, and I could no longer hide the struggle to pull oxygen into my lungs. The green E-tanks that I pulled behind me everywhere were my lifeline. Even at home, from the kitchen to the living room, there were concentrators everywhere—24/7, 365 days a year. Even to sleep, I had a concentrator in my bedroom. To teach, they allowed me to park in front of my classroom (thank you Principal Blackshear) to save oxygen from my mobile E tank. When I pulled up, a student would turn my classroom concentrator on and meet me at the car with my classroom oxygen line to connect to it and enter my classroom. My students were understanding and always looked out for me. They appreciated that it took me nearly three hours to get up, shower, fix a little breakfast, drive two miles to the school, and make it into the classroom to help them prepare for the then FCAT to pass on to the next grade. Little did they know, my love for them kept me getting up each morning, trying to hang in there, and to continue to be a role model and an outstanding teacher for them. Making learning fun, and anything but routine, was what I did, and I didn't want to let them down, even if it cost me my life. They diagnosed me in 2007 with Interstitial Lung Disease (ILD) which is a group of disorders that cause progressive scarring of lung tissue. Long-term exposure to hazardous materials or an autoimmune disease can cause it. Once lung scarring occurs, it's irreversible. My fingertips were clubbing; I experienced fatigue, shortness of breath, and the inability to get enough oxygen into my bloodstream. I began evaluation for a lung transplant near the end of the year. The fibrosis severely damaged my left lung. It was a thorough investigation of every aspect of my health, both physical and mental. Everything was evaluated to make sure I was a stable candidate for the transplant and could maintain physical and emotional endurance, purchase my medications for the rest of my life, and take care of the gift IF I were to receive it—I mean everything. No stone was unturned. But the kicker was I had to lose more weight to be a suitable candidate.

The struggle was real when, in January 2008, I was declared to be in ESLD (End-Stage Lung Disease) from Idiopathic Pulmonary Fibrosis (IPF) by my transplant team at Mayo. They then placed me on the lung transplant list and moved me closer to the top. By the way, the lung transplant is only a treatment. I don't think people realized how sick I really was because I continued to get up each Sunday morning to play the organ at church; I continued to teach at school and prepare the class for the FCAT; and, at the end of testing, I would need a leave of absence because my body was too weak to continue working.

Life, as I had known and celebrated it, seemed to now be cradled by death—the excessive hospital visits, the calls for the EMTs, the collapsing of my left lung twice, the excruciating pain when they pierced my body and inserted the chest tube into my flesh, the look of despair on my friends Rose and Cheryl's faces as they tried to hold back the tears in the ER—it was all too much—the calls for Diva Transportation to take me to the hospital again; the Sundays when I scanned the pulpit and pews at church, caressing fond memories of people who have been such an influential part of my life, and thinking, *this will probably be my last Sunday to play the organ, share communion, and sing "There is a Fountain Filled with Blood" with my church family.* If only they knew how difficult it was to fight back tears while saying my mental goodbyes to people I love, some people I had known all my life.

NO BARK—NO BITE. Netti and Rose drove me to the beach. We had a wonderful time until I played a round of I've Got a Secret. I rode in the front seat and enjoyed the time away from the confinement of my home. Considering how weak I had become, it was nice when friends think of you and just stop by to take you for a ride. Friendly conversation, pleasant company, and the idea to not tell them I picked up the wrong oxygen tank. My tank was already low when I left and now was empty. I sat as still as I could so I would breathe the cool air from the car. I pretended to be a little hot and asked if they could turn the air up. I sat directly in front of the vent. It was on the ride back, around 15-20 minutes away from my home, and I was feeling the pressure in my chest from no oxygen circulating in my body. Netti turned into the driveway, and I thanked them for the fun-filled time together, and announced that I could not get out of the car. The puzzled look on their faces amused me, and I had to laugh. Someone would have to go in, walk past Shirdolfphe, my Rottweiler, cut on an oxygen tank, and then bring the flowing line with oxygen out to the car so I could move and get in the house. Rose was the designated volunteer to walk in and become an active player of Fear Factor, because she had a fear of my loving dog. She entered the front door and begged the dog to not make her a snack. She needed to get my oxygen line so I could get in the house. I yelled for Rose to please hurry! She grabbed the oxygen line and ran out the door. Great! I placed my line in my nose, wrapped it around my ears and took a deep breath to allow the oxygen to flow throughout my body . . . or so I thought. In rushing to bring the line to me, Rose forgot to turn the oxygen on. OMG!

FAITH. From the little portable oxygen tanks, to D tanks, to E tanks, to the concentrators and the two huge liquid oxygen reservoirs that sat in my front room supplying the oxygen to my lungs . . . from 2 liters increasing to 4, 6, 8, 10, 12, and then 15 liters of oxygen to maneuver throughout the day of mostly sitting still, my familiar friend, Fear, was creeping up on me again. It's funny how you can adjust to whatever situation you may go through in your life and accept it. I can see the poster of the kitty saying, HANG ON IN THERE! Okay, I'll probably be on oxygen for the rest of my life, however long that might be. It now becomes a lonely life sitting at home with the clicking sounds of my oxygen tanks, my oxymizer pendant, and the company of my 13-year-old devoted Rottweiler, Shirdolfphe. So many days I cried out to God for His help to endure the discomfort of not being able to breathe. One day, I pretended to be the woman with the issue of blood, and I reached and reached for my ceiling, trying to get to the hem of His garment. It was during these times at home, waiting on my miracle, that I drew closer to a Savior that I diligently asked to help me. It brings to my memory the day I asked God for patience. I often wondered if this lesson, this three-year class, was His response to my request. Be careful what you ask God for. When would I become the recipient of a gift given by a heavenly God from an earthly angel?

THE CALL. It was a Monday morning, and I remember it well because on Sunday, Shirdolfphe walked out the patio door to never return to our home again, giving me the freedom to not have to worry about how I would care for her. After a tearful goodbye, I was set for God's plan to catapult into motion. "Weeping may endure for a night, but joy cometh in the morning."

My morning had arrived. My daughter Shaunda, four grandchildren, and a friend, were visiting from Memphis when the call arrived from one of my transplant doctors. I thought it was a little unusual for him to call, but I hadn't put the pieces together. He has that type of personality that makes you forget, for a moment, there is something wrong and can get a little laughter out of a rock. I was told I had to stay within two hours of the hospital at all times, just in case a lung became available. All of this played back in my mind when he said, "We have a lung available for you—head to the hospital."

It's funny how you wait for a call, and when the call finally arrives you almost disregard it. I think fear sets in and you have an inner conversation with yourself that you need to do this, and you realize you don't have a choice. I DIDN'T have a choice because, if I didn't have the transplant, I would die. A transplant was my only hope to continue living, to spend time with my family, to continue attending church services, and to go back to teaching. After my momentary hesitation, I knew I had to accept the offer to continue to live. My daughter encouraged me to get ready to go as I sat staring at The Price is Right on TV, working up that courage to take the step towards healing. Hopefully, this wasn't just a trial run like I had heard others talk about, where you get a call, but then it doesn't pan out. I threw on comfortable clothes and called my friends to let them know I got the call and was heading to the hospital for my new lungs. Can you believe they beat me to the hospital and then asked me what took so long! After completing necessary paperwork, I headed to my floor and was advised by the transplant team that it was a go—it was going to happen! I thanked God and, although my prayer had been answered, I was still frightened. But my determination to live and my faith in God were much stronger than my fear of not surviving the surgery.

At 9:00 pm, Pastor Mitchell offered up a prayer for me, my family, and my friends. We bowed our heads to our God, who would bring me safely through this life-saving ordeal. As they took me out of the room, I could feel the tension of everyone behind me until I reached the OR doors. I remember the staff telling my pastor that he would have to stop there, and I chuckled as he headed back to the group. The anesthesia and countdown began . . . 10, 9, 8 . . .

RECOVERY AND RESTORATION. The staff informed my friends that the first lung was in, and they were starting on the other one. A MIRACLE—I ended up receiving a double lung transplant! There was a nurse at my bedside for the first 24 hours to monitor data and the equipment. I had programmed my mind to respond, no matter what shape I would be in, with thumbs up to let them know I was okay. Sure enough, although they intubated me, I could hear the conversations, and I did it . . . I raised my right thumb!

After eight days of hospitalization, my son, Edward, signed papers for my release. On my way home, I stopped at my church. Wrapped in my blanket, I wanted to be the one to tell God thank you for bringing me through the dangers, both seen and unseen. I sat before the altar and gave God His glory! When all is said and done, how do you adequately thank your primary care physician who made correct choices concerning those critical care moments, placed you on oxygen, and referred you to the perfect pulmonologist? How do you thank the pulmonologist that referred you to a second opinion that suggested a third referral to the location of your transplant center? How do you give thanks for a gift from a heavenly God, received from an earthly angel . . . the ultimate gift of organ donation to restore my life that was slowly dwindling away?

A multitude of thank you's, or barrels of cash, would not place a value on a transplant team prepared for my surgery, which took place on May 6, 2008. How do you express gratitude to your family, friends, pastor, church congregation, principal, co-workers, students, and even strangers that kept you lifted in prayer? Because of organ donation, I am able to thank these people, and I have been able to accomplish some amazing things.

Educating Minorities About Transplants, Inc. (EMAT)

When my face is framed with strands of gray hair and my motions have slowed with age, I'll still remember May 6, 2008, when the gift of life was given to me. Restoration of my health caused me to look at life through affirmative vision. Blessed to continue to spend time with family, attend church, and return to work, it thrilled me to be able to enjoy life to the fullest. I wanted to share with others the blessings God has given to me, and the gifts my donor left for me. I am active with Donate Life Florida and Life Quest, and I participated with The Multicultural Task Force led by Amy. During one of our meetings, we discussed data which indicated the lack of organ donation among minorities, especially African Americans. On June 15, 2015, I started a Facebook page, with the help of Walter Hill, and we decided on the name—Educating Minorities About Transplants (EMAT). We felt we needed this group to share information about the truth concerning organ donation, because both of us had experienced aspects of the transplant life. Mr. Hill was caregiver to his wife, Beverly, who encouraged me during my journey, and I am now the recipient of a bilateral lung transplant. Each day I post pertinent information and stories about people who have had a transplant or are waiting for a transplant. I have invited my friends, church members, co-workers, family, and anyone else who wants to, to join the group. Our membership has grown, and as I write this, we have over 700 members. We would love for you to join our group too!

EMAT was formed to (1) give minority transplanted individuals a place to communicate with other people of color; (2) discuss issues, offer inspiration to caregivers, donor families, and those who are on a waiting list for transplant; (3) discuss ways to increase organ and tissue donations among minorities; (4) appreciate living donors and donor families; (5) share experiences with those waiting for a transplant; and (6) eliminate myths and misconceptions about organ and tissue donation among minority communities. I incorporated it in the State of Florida in 2018, and it is a 501c3 non-profit organization. Since our inception in 2015, we have a Board of Directors, Officers, regular local meetings, and prior to the pandemic, we took part in local health fairs and church/community events. EMAT continues to post daily on our Facebook page to educate the public about transplant news, to give current information, and to share positive success stories.

It is an absolute joy to wake each day knowing someone embraced the opportunity to provide another human being the second chance to continue to live. What do you do with each day that was gifted to you? How do you express your gratitude to a person who no longer lives on this side of mortal? You begin each day with a prayer to God, thanking Him for one more day to share with your fellow man by helping make just one person's day a little brighter.

The Gift has allowed me to spend more time with my family and enjoy a granddaughter Lyrik, born on my first Lungaversary — 5/6/2009.

DAVIDA'S GRANDS & SHIRLEY'S GREAT-GRANDS

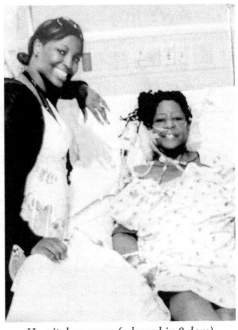

Hospital recovery (released in 8 days).

Celebrating Blue & Green Day

St. Stephen AMEC Musicians
ShirLey on organ and her son on drums.

About ShirLey

ShirLey earned a Bachelor of Arts degree in Elementary Education from Edward Waters College in 1986, and a degree of Master of Education in Elementary Education from the University of North Florida in 2004. She is a retired educator from the Duval County Public Schools.

ShirLey began her service with St. Stephen AME Church in Jacksonville, Florida, at the tender age of 7 as a Sunday school musician. She continues to serve the congregation faithfully as the Music & Christian Arts Ministry (MCAM) Director, a Steward, local PME Director of The Catherine Dawson Missionary Society, and Bible Discovery Hour Instructor.

In 2005, she showed symptoms of Interstitial Lung Disease (ILD) resulting in a diagnosis of Idiopathic Pulmonary Fibrosis (IDF). The disease progressed rapidly, and in January 2008 the diagnosis advanced to End-Stage Lung Disease (ESLD), qualifying her to be placed on the lung transplant list.

On May 6, 2008, she received a bilateral lung transplant and has not been admitted again to the hospital since her life-saving gift from an anonymous donor, along with the Lung Transplant Team of Mayo Clinic/Jacksonville, and an almighty prayer-answering God.

ShirLey is the founder/president of Educating Minorities About Transplants, Inc. (EMAT), and is a UNOS and LifeQuest Ambassador. She is a member of Jacksonville Transplant Alliance, Mayo Lung Transplant Support Group, and volunteers with Donate Life Florida.

Besides being the mother of Roshaunda, Monique, and King Edward, she is a grandmother and great-grandmother who enjoys implementing creative projects with her local MCAM, and a lifelong learner.

To learn more about EMAT, please visit the website at https://emat-inc.org and Facebook and Instagram pages #transplantssavelivesemat and #emat.inc

You can connect with ShirLey via email at: emat.inc185@gmail.com

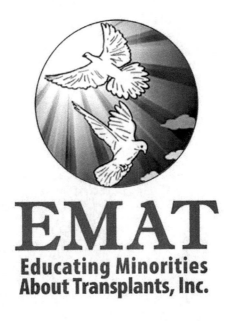

Paul Osterholm
With Foreword by Sarah Razner

God's Whispers

Foreword

In Fall 2018, I walked into Marian University's Common Grounds for an interview. It was not the first I had done there in my time as a reporter, but it became the most impactful. That night, I had the pleasure of meeting Nicole Braatz, Paul Osterholm, and their families, who were coming together to talk about kidney donation.

Nineteen years before, work had brought Paul and Nicole together to meet at the cafe, and the connection—and social media—had reunited them, this time for a different purpose: for Paul to donate his kidney to Nicole.

As they told me the story of their donation journey, I remember the chills running through my body, even though we were sitting in front of a fire. It wasn't only all the ways their match seemed fated, but also the family dynamic that had formed between them and their loved ones, and Nicole and Paul's powerful determination to help others.

That resolve paid off. The donation was not only life changing for Nicole and Paul, but also for the many lives their story touched—including me. Since that meeting, I have had the honor of watching their impact spread around Wisconsin and the world. Paul and Nicole took me along with them on their journey, and, although all I had done was to tell their story on paper, they treated me as if I had gone through the rigors of donation with them, offering more kindness and generosity than was necessary. From academic symposiums, to flag raisings, to Rotary lunches, to social media groups, they shared their important message of encouraging others to "share your spare," and people listened.

I answered calls from those who were seeking transplants; who, because of Paul, Nicole, and the rest of the Fond du Lac kidney donation community, also had a word of their need shared. I received emails from others who, inspired by Paul and Nicole's transplant, went on to save the lives of complete strangers, and I had the chance to write some of their stories. With each interaction, I was moved by the domino effect of goodwill Paul and Nicole had helped to fuel and felt even more privileged to bear witness to it, and allow others to do so as well.

In a time when negativity can overwhelm the good, it's easy to forget the lengths human beings will go to help each other. But Paul and Nicole's story never let me forget this. Instead, it has taught me how one act can truly change the world, and I know they are far from done inspiring.

Paul's Story

When I met Nicole Braatz in 2001, I had no idea over 15 years later I would save her life through a kidney donation. They hired me to run Marian University's Common Grounds when it opened in 1999, and the president of the university, Dr. Richard Ridenour, commissioned Nicole to design the logo and sign through her small business, Nicole's Sign Works.

Years later, we gathered with our families beneath that sign in the weeks leading up to our transplant, wearing shirts reading "Share Your Spare Kidney," and we couldn't help but see the hand fate was playing throughout the process. God had a plan, and He still has a plan. This journey has helped me to listen to His whispers more.

Nicole's Journey Begins Here

It was an unexpected diagnosis for Nicole, then 48, who had no major health issues throughout her life. When she began experiencing symptoms of kidney failure, both Nicole and her doctors didn't recognize them. At the doctor's office on December 20, 2017, she said she had a sinus infection which wasn't going away. Amid flu season, the doctor told her she, too, had the virus. But her symptoms persisted. She couldn't keep down whatever she consumed. Food tasted odd. She couldn't catch her breath. Her legs swelled from her knees to her ankles, to an extent where her jeans no longer fit. Going to the doctor multiple times, the doctor continued to tell her she had the flu. One day, a month into being sick, she took a sip of coffee and threw it up. She knew she had to get to the bottom of her illness.

On her fourth visit to the doctor, she went to urgent care instead and told that doctor something was wrong. He ran blood tests and put her on an IV as she waited for the results. An hour later, her life completely changed as the doctor told her she was days, or even hours, away from going into cardiac arrest, and her kidneys were functioning at three percent. People start dialysis at 15% on average.

The cause for her kidney failure was — and is still — unknown.

The shock set in first. "When he told me that, I was like, no, no," she said.

The kidney failure made Nicole one of about 1,200 people waiting for a kidney in Wisconsin, according to the United Network for Organ Sharing, or UNOS. Nicole looked first to her seven sisters. With a blood type O, while Nicole can donate to anyone, only those with O blood type can donate to her. In her family, matching sisters either had high blood pressure or juvenile diabetes, disqualifying them from giving. The rest of her sisters had blood type A or B.

"We weren't even thinking. We thought for sure someone was going to be an O," said Candy Braatz-Markert, Nicole's sister.

In the United States, the average wait time for a kidney is three to five years "at most centers," according to the National Kidney Foundation. At UW Health, where Nicole was being treated, the median time for patients to receive a transplant from 2010 to 2015 was about 20 months. But this differs with blood type. Wait times for those in need of a kidney with type A or B blood came in around two to three years, but with O, it was five years or more.

From Facebook Friend to Kidney Donation

Not wanting to wait years for a deceased donor, Nicole's family took to social media to get the word out, writing a letter about her story and posting it on Facebook. They received hundreds of replies, according to her mother, Mary, with almost 30 stating they had her blood type. The response left them all in tears. My wife Janet was one of those who saw the post. She went to school with Nicole's sisters growing up. Since Common Grounds, Nicole and I had only seen each other once or twice, but when we learned about her health problems, we donated to her GoFundMe page. Then, on Memorial Day weekend 2018, as Janet scrolled through Facebook, the post crafted by Nicole and her family appeared.

"Honey, what do you think?" she asked me.

I thought we were going to buy more raffle tickets. But when I read the post, knowing I was a blood match, I messaged Nicole, and then reached out to UW Health's Living Donor Program. Having taught our children Paul Jr. and Maggie Rose to give back, our kids were supportive of my decision to pursue donation. Maggie, around that same time, was trying to donate her own kidney to a man in Chilton, Wisconsin. However, in the phone interview, she was told she could not donate because of being allergic to Tylenol, since following kidney donation her body could not metabolize ibuprofen.

A month later, I received a call from UW Health Transplant Coordinator, Leza Warnke, and we spoke on the phone for nearly an hour before she asked if I could come down for further tests. Going through a day of tests, I passed one after another. The only time I came close to failing was because of my blood pressure. They told me I could drink coffee while waiting for my next test, and I had sipped two shots of espresso and two cups of coffee.

In case I wasn't a match for Nicole, I had agreed that I would donate to somebody else to move her up the list as part of the match donation program. In this way, if I matched someone in Iowa, we would "flip," and they would send my kidney to Iowa and Nicole's donor's kidney would come to Wisconsin.

Following the battery of tests, the team of doctors smiled as my wife Janet and I were leaving. About seven percent of people who go through the process actually match. She could tell they saw something positive in my test results.

"I think you're coming back," she whispered.

Soon, UW Health called. Nicole and I had matched four out of six antigens; family members typically match from zero to two antigens. Rarely do people match six out of six, and I matched four out of six. They said that's just a bonus because it means less chance of rejection. When I received the news that I was a match, I called my wife. She told me not to call Nicole until she was home from work. Not able to contain myself, I called her anyway, reaching her on the road. I told her to pull over, but she didn't have time before I shared the news. She was shocked! Nicole had gotten her hopes up. After all, the other 28 individuals that tested before me did not match her.

"I thought you were just calling to talk," Nicole said to me.

The hand of God was at work. Outside our house that day, looking over the lake as the sun set, I felt compelled to take a picture of an early sunset sky. In it, an angel-shaped cloud appeared, kneeling and praying. The spiritual journey has been remarkable. I feel blessed to have been able to do this. We feel honored that we were able to give Nicole new life.

My wife and I met in La Crosse, Wisconsin, in 1985. I was born and raised in Waukon, Iowa, and Janet was born and raised in Fond du Lac, Wisconsin. When we met, Janet was a student at Viterbo College, and I worked third shift at the nearby Kwik Trip.

Janet shared with me, "Who thought I would meet an Iowa boy, be where we are today, and be here to help Nicole?"

The date of the transplant also carries significance. Given the option to choose October 10 or 11 for the transplant, I picked October 10 so I could be home to watch the Iowa Hawkeyes play football, and would be one day closer to recovery for when our son Paul Jr. and daughter-in-law Katie were due with their first child. Our granddaughter Oakleigh was born Monday, October 15th. However, for Nicole and the Braatz family, the date meant much more than football. When Nicole was 21, her father, Harold, passed away, and her mom gave Nicole his briefcase as she started Nicole's Sign Works. The pass code was his birthday . . . 10-10. Ever since, that number has been a constant in her life.

"I almost fell over," Nicole said.

The number only grew in meaning as UW Health told her that while my surgery would take place at 8:00 a.m., Nicole's would be at

10:10 a.m. Nicole remembers that the nurse told her 10:10 represents new beginnings. On the way home, Nicole searched what the nurse had shared, finding that it was "a strong angel number." When you look it up, the very first line is, "If you are consistently seeing 10-10, it's not a coincidence. Your guardian angels are bringing you to new beginnings."

Time for a New Beginning

With our surgery approaching, I started counting down the days, and Nicole was counting down the pokes left for dialysis, which she underwent for four hours a day, three days a week. Throughout this process, our families grew closer.

"My heart is overwhelmed with love for this family. They have been so loving and kind," said Nicole.

Paul said, "She's going to be my sister."

"Mom finally got her boy," Nicole joked.

We saw a symbol of that love in the gift the Braatz family gave me when we first met as a group. In 2003, I donated bone marrow at Froedtert Hospital in Milwaukee, Wisconsin. Years ago, I had checked the "Be the Match" box while donating blood. They sent my bone marrow to a young lady in Barcelona, Spain. To date, I do not know who she is or how she is feeling. In the hospital, after the donation, I used a bell to summon help. Adding to this tradition, the Braatz family gave me a personalized cow bell to convey their gratitude, although they say they don't feel they can ever convey it enough.

"I don't even know what to say to you half the time. What do you say to somebody who gave you the gift of life?" said Nicole.

On Wednesday, October 10, 2018, my family came from as far as California, Iowa, and Minnesota to gather in Madison, and as my kidney was removed and placed in Nicole, a new beginning started for both of us. We were both out of the hospital by the weekend.

Today

"Jesus looked at them and said, 'With man this is impossible, but with God all things are possible.'" Matthew 19:26.

As I reflect on the past two years, we have much to be thankful for because of organ donation. Nicole is doing great! I'm doing great! We have met so many wonderful people and friends since our story came out. I would like to give special thanks to Sarah Razner, a gifted writer and a dear friend. Nicole and I invited Sarah to join us and our families on our journey. Without her telling our story, I believe that there would not be as many donors and recipients, today, who are celebrating their new lives.

To my beautiful wife Janet, my anchor, our family anchor; THANK YOU for all you have done and continue to do for me and our family. To Paul Jr., Katie, Oakleigh, Maggie, and Adam; I love you all very much. You are all so special to me!

To my recipient Nicole, her mom Mary & Ken, Candy & Phil and her wonderful family; I thank you for your love, new friendships, support, and prayers.

To my siblings Amy and Trish, nieces Nicole, Alicia, and Lori, and Ron, and Joyce who traveled to Madison to be with me that day, thank you from the bottom of my heart. Mom was smiling down upon us that day.

To the Dave and Lillian King family (my in-laws), thank you for your love and support. Thank you to Aunt Sam for bringing Sitto and Maggie to visit, and thank you Uncle Markie, Katie B., and Miss A for visiting me in the hospital.

THANK YOU to Dr. Fernandez and the UW-Madison Transplant Team. Leza Warnke, my coordinator; you will always hold a special place in my heart for all you did. Thank you for your love, faith, and support.

To Dr. Colmenares, SSM/Agnesian HealthCare; THANK YOU for taking good care of me for all these years. Who would have thought?!

THANK YOU to everyone in Waukon, Iowa, Fond du Lac, Wisconsin, Marian University, and on Facebook who lifted us up in prayers and thoughts. Your prayers were answered.

To my dear friends: Tracy, Ger, Maranda, Colleen, Rebecca, Eric, Barbara, Brenda, HOWL, Tia, Josie, Carol, Share the Spare of Fond du Lac, and the 1 Kidney Club of Wisconsin . . . love you all very much!

There are so many family and friends that were there for us that day/week/months. If I missed you, please know that I THANK YOU and you mean the world to me. Your love and friendship are dear to me.

Recently, I have become an Organ Tissue Donor advocate and volunteer with UW-Madison Transplant Hospital. Nicole and I enjoy sharing our story and encouraging others to DONATE LIFE.

Be still and listen to God's Whispers.

Praying Angel, God's Whisper. Photo was taken by Paul, August 6, 2018, the day he was told that he was a match for Nicole.

Family.
Day of donation. October 10, 2018;
UW-Health Madison.

Paul and Nicole at Common
Grounds CoffeeHouse, Marian
University—where they met each
other for the first time 15 years ago.

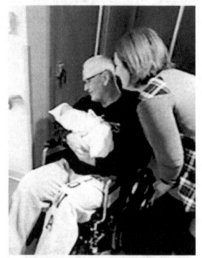

Granddaughter, Oakleigh.
Arrived five days after donation.
October 15, 2018.

The next day.

Common Grounds, where Paul and Nicole first meet.
Back row (L-R) Maggie, Paul's daughter; Candy, Nicole's sister.
Front row (L-R) Janet, Paul's wife; Paul, Nicole, recipient; Mary, Nicole's mom.

Leaving hospital two days after donating.

Living Donor Ceremony.

Howl joins Nicole & Paul on a speaking tour.

Marian University Friends (L-R) Ger, recipient; Tracy, Ger's donor; Nicole, Paul's recipient; Paul.

About Paul

Paul Osterholm, Sr., is a living kidney donor and bone marrow donor (2003). He donated his kidney to Nicole Braatz on October 10, 2018, at UW-Madison Health Transplant Center.

Paul grew up in Waukon, Iowa. He and his wife Janet have been married for 34 years, and live in Pipe, Wisconsin, north of Fond du Lac. They have been blessed with an amazing family: Paul Jr., daughter-in-law Katie, and granddaughter Oakleigh, who was born five days after her grandpa's kidney donation; daughter Marguerite (Maggie), and future son-in-law Adam Geiser. Adam's parents are Donnie and Ruthie Geiser, Chilton, WI

Paul is the founder of the Facebook page, Share the Spare, Fond du Lac, and you can connect with Paul there, or on his personal page, or by email at pwosterholm@gmail.com.

James Myers

Advocate For Life

I had the day off on April 26th, 2016. It was an ordinary Tuesday. I was home puttering around on my computer, updating my social media accounts, and advocating for awareness about kidney disease. I received a call from IU Health in Indianapolis. I had received calls from them many times before. IU was one of three places that I was listed for a kidney transplant. The other hospitals were Rush Medical in Chicago, and UW in Madison, Wisconsin. Typically, when I received calls from IU Health, it was about testing to remain listed. I had already done my testing for the year. IU and UW accepted each other's tests, while Rush did everything independently. This meant I was doing two complete sets of transplant testing every year. I had recently had a colonoscopy at Rush and the driver I had lined up bailed out on me at the last minute. I was supposed to take anesthesia before the surgery and the driver would take me home. I went up to Rush and took the test anyway, but without the anesthesia. I thought this may be the reason

IU was calling me. Maybe they wanted me to take the test over. This had happened to me in the past, so it prepared me when I saw the caller ID.

I had also received calls for a kidney two times prior. Both times, I was fifth or sixth on the list, and was told to fast and wait. On a moment's notice, I would have to head to Chicago or Indianapolis. Both times, I moved up the list to third, but it was just not my time. It conditioned me to be very patient, not to get too high or too low, when I received such a call. I had also met with my pre-transplant doctor in early April, and he had told me it would be another two to three years before I would receive my kidney transplant at IU.

My pre-transplant coordinator, Kristy Williams, was on the phone. At first, it was just some general chit-chat, but then she paused. I thought to myself, here it comes. "What test am I retaking?"

"We have a kidney for you!" She finally blurted out.

It was my turn to pause in disbelief. It is usually at times like this I say something stupid, or try to be funny, while I process the other person's statement.

I finally replied, "You would not kid your Uncle Jim, would you?" Uncle Jim is my advocacy nickname, which many people know me by.

"No, Jim. Can you get here by this afternoon? We would like to do the surgery later tonight or tomorrow," she stated.

"Yes, I can," I shouted with excitement. "My bags are already packed!" I added as I hung up the phone in a daze and looked at my roommate at the time.

"I'll drive!" she said.

All I did was talk fast and grin from ear to ear on the two-and-a-half-hour ride to Indianapolis. I was not particularly nervous until I saw the sign on the wall that read *Organ Transplant*. It became very real to me then; this was really happening. I checked into the hospital and was taken to my room, a wide, odd-shaped room for people with wheelchairs. (I'm an ambulatory guy.) And then the wait started. It was about 4 o'clock in the afternoon. I was not allowed to eat and I could only drink very little. As I lay in the bed, in my gown, talking, watching TV, and staring at the clock, my son, Jim, arrived from Cincinnati. It was good to see him, and we talked and laughed. He helped me to relax a bit.

The Anesthesiologist came in, talked for a while, and we signed papers. Dr. Goggins, the Surgeon, and his Resident then came in. We talked, and I signed some more papers. Around two o'clock in the morning, they finally came for me. No mistake now, no false alarm, no bad kidney. They were taking me down to surgery to have my kidney transplant. The past swirled through my mind. I thought back to the blow I felt when I was diagnosed with polycystic kidney disease just a few months after my father died from it; fighting to stay off of dialysis for nearly 30 years; finally hitting end-stage and going on dialysis; struggling to get on the transplant list; dealing with anemia many times; issues with my fistula; undergoing angioplasties for the narrowing in my fistula, to the point where a few doctors would not do the procedure and they sent me to a surgeon they referred to as an artist; doing dialysis out of town; dealing with vertigo when they took too much fluid off; multiple hospitalizations every year from kidney/dialysis-related issues; the general fatigue that comes from dialysis; having my teeth pulled; stress tests; heart tests; and traveling to multiple different transplant centers. I thought of the many things I had to do to get on the transplant list and remain on that list. Anxiousness had settled in and I was breathing hard.

For the first time, I felt fear, anxiety, and a general, "It's out of my hands now" feeling. A quick prayer was said. They wheeled me through a couple of doors and into a very well-lit, bright place. Not my first time here, I knew this was the operating room. They were all trying to calm me, hooking me up to things and putting a mask over my face, monitoring me. They instructed me to count backward from 100.

"100, 99, 98…" I started as I drifted off.

Next thing I remember is being in the Recovery Room. A pleasant nurse was speaking to me calmly. I remember feeling groggy with some pain in my right hip and groin. They then took me back to my room. Recovery went very smoothly and quickly, and I started passing urine almost immediately. I was walking by the next day and went home the day after that. I named my new kidney Woody. Woodrow is a family name, so I did this to honor my father and my grandfather. My kidney transplant has been successful for the last four years.

Last year, I found out that prior to my transplant, Dr. Goggins had conducted an antigen/antibody test, and I flunked. Because my levels bounced between normal and above normal, he went through with the transplant, anyway. I am glad he did. Because of organ donation, I can do the things I love to do: advocate for my fellow kidney patients!

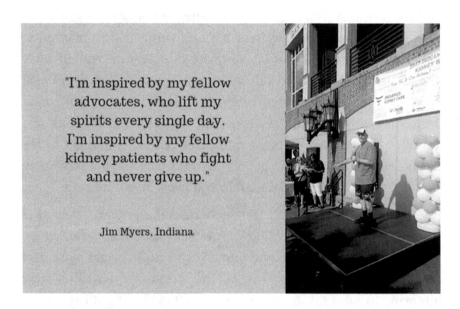

"I'm inspired by my fellow advocates, who lift my spirits every single day. I'm inspired by my fellow kidney patients who fight and never give up."

Jim Myers, Indiana

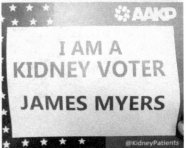

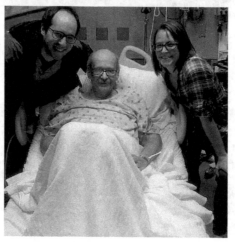

About James

My name is James Myers, and I live in Hammond, Indiana. I graduated from Valparaiso University Law School and I have 2 MBA's in Business and Healthcare Administration. Polycystic Kidney Disease (PKD) runs in my family. I've lost five members of my family to PKD, including my father. I also have PKD, but I am fortunate. Because of my family's history, I was diagnosed at 25 and was able to put off dialysis until the age of 58. I was on dialysis four years and transplanted on April 27th, 2016.

I am a full-time kidney advocate. I am a member of the American Association of Kidney Patients (AAKP). I hold leadership positions with the AAKP as a Member of the Board of Directors, and I am an Ambassador for the State of Indiana. I have won several professional awards and honors, including the Inaugural National Social Media Education and Advocacy Award from the AAKP, and the Robert Felter Memorial Award, which recognizes individual patients who are actively working on behalf of their fellow patients. I have been fortunate to give multiple seminars for the AAKP on social media and kidney disease, and have been a breakout session leader concerning the use of social media to advocate and raise awareness for kidney disease. I have also presented on the use of Facebook to advocate for my fellow kidney patients. I helped to initiate the Pediatric Kidney Patients Initiative (Kidney Pals), and am part of the initiative for Kidneys and Veterans. I am the Chairman of the Strategic Communications Committee, and a member of the 2019 National Patient Meeting Committee.

I am an Advocate for the National Kidney Foundation (NKF), and in 2019, I was named the Advocate of the Year. For the NKF, I am a Statewide Advocate for the State of Indiana, Member of the Kidney Advocacy Committee, Past Leader of the KAC Social Media Group, and Past Regional Leader of Region #5 (MI, OH, IN, KY, TN). I have been influential in bringing about the NKF's Pediatric Kidney Patient Initiative. I am an Ambassador for the AAKP, the Polycystic

Kidney Disease Foundation, the Dialysis Patient Citizens, the Renal Support Network, the National Kidney Foundation of Indiana, More Than Just Your Kidneys, and Waitlist Zero.

My advocate nickname is Uncle Jim. If you have a kidney question or issue you need help with, please do not hesitate to contact me at kidneystories@hotmail.com.

Tonya Gomez

Breathing For Eric

I was born with Cystic Fibrosis (CF) and diagnosed at nine months old. When I was born, my mother knew something just wasn't right about her daughter. I wasn't gaining weight; I was coughing all the time; and every time they fed me, the food would go right through me. She realized I had some type of malabsorption or digestive issue. They had diagnosed me with multiple bouts of bronchitis. I was underweight and failed to thrive. My mother told me if she had not gotten me to the hospital when she did, I would not have survived the weekend. She had made an appointment with some specialists but felt she could not wait for that appointment and took me in without one. Once the doctors determined my diagnosis, they could treat me, and I began responding to treatment very well. This treatment was comprised of postural drainage and percussion, breathing treatments, and a multitude of medication therapy.

My brother was born two years later, and the doctors immediately diagnosed him with CF. We moved around a lot, my parents divorced, and my mother remarried. Unfortunately, my brother's severity of the disease was much greater than mine, and he passed away at the young age of six. He spent more time in the hospital than out. I was always with my grandparents as my mother and step-father were always at the hospital with my brother. This was devastating for my mother, but she did everything in her power to keep me alive. I remember little about that time, but I remember my mother performing postural drainage and breathing treatments on two children, besides making sure we received our medications. We were sleeping in mist tents and always woke up wet. The tents helped break up the overproduction of mucus in our bodies, especially in our lungs. This was a tough time in our family's life. I think I blocked so much out then.

The severity of the disease for me was mild compared to my brother's, and I did very well until I turned 14. I tried my best to be normal. There was a small group of friends I trusted, and they knew about my disease. I didn't want to be different and risk being made fun of. People can be so cruel. I never tried out for sports because I didn't have the confidence in myself that I could succeed at them, and I was terrified that I would get coughing spells and that kids would find out what was wrong with me. I tried my hand at track, however, but it did not last long. I just didn't have the endurance to keep up. I twirled baton as a majorette in high school and was comfortable with a group of friends I could trust. It was then that I landed myself in the hospital four times in one school year. From then on, I spent time in the hospital twice a year for what we called "clean outs." My fellow "CFers" and I would pack our belongings for our two-week-long stay at what we called "the club." We walked the halls with our IV poles, played games, and tried to act like normal kids. The nurses became our family, and the same ones would always take care of us.

When I was younger, the doctors had given me tetracycline to treat my CF symptoms. It discolored my permanent teeth, and because of that, I never smiled big enough to show my teeth. This was one of the biggest reasons I was so reserved growing up. I didn't want to explain why my teeth weren't white. It was hard growing up with Cystic Fibrosis. My sophomore year, the doctors tried to whiten my teeth as much as possible. They tried bleaching them and several other options. Nothing worked until they put composites on my teeth. The composites made my teeth white, and I finally had the confidence to smile again.

Over the years, a bacterium, called B Cepacia, was discovered and was known to cause major lung damage in Cystic Fibrosis patients. Scientists also discovered it was very contagious, so CF patients needed to remain six feet apart to avoid the spread of the bacteria. My friendship circle diminished. Many passed away, or we weren't able to see each other because of the new bacteria. I felt alone again. As the years went on and medical technology advanced, I spent less time in the hospital, but more time doing IV antibiotics at home. After graduating high school, I pursued my dream of attending college. Not knowing if I would end up coming home before even completing a year of college was scary for both my mother and me. She had always been my advocate and had done everything in her power to keep me well and protect me. Mom grieved all these years because she couldn't keep my brother alive, so it was her mission to save me.

Off to college I went, nervous and anxious. I wanted a degree that would allow me to help people, just like the nurses had done for me. I also desired new friends, yet wanted to keep my illness private. I wanted to re-invent myself in a place where no one knew me and wouldn't judge me based on my illness. Things became difficult when I would get flare-ups and cough so hard that I could barely speak, but I worked through it. I continued working as a server, just like I had done throughout high school to earn extra spending money. During this time, I became ill and lost 20 pounds, which left me exhausted and with dark circles under my sunken eyes. I was taking the required nutrition courses for my degree as a dietitian, so I had an idea of what might happen to my body. I was in denial. After all, I already had CF to deal with, so what more could go wrong? The answer is insulin shots and poking my fingers daily. I developed Cystic Fibrosis Related Diabetes, which landed me in the hospital for almost a month. It became clear I couldn't juggle schoolwork, taking care of myself, and working a job. I needed to focus on my health and school foremost, so quitting my job made the most sense.

Living with diabetes was new for me and even scarier than Cystic Fibrosis (at the time). But I learned, thrived, and dealt with the situation. It was difficult, but, as a CF patient, I was strong and determined. I recall doing a Pulmonary Function Test pre-transplant, and the respiratory therapist made the comment that there is just something special about CF patients, that they are resilient and they are fighters. Absolutely, we are! During that time, they asked me to be part of a trial of a new drug, Pulmozyme. It was a major advancement in the treatment of CF that allowed stability in my lung function.

Fast forward after college graduation from THE Ohio State University ... internship, marriage, and the birth of our son. My husband was the baby of 14 children. Imagine having to tell the love of your life, from such a large family, that you might remain childless because of infertility issues. Childless wasn't in the cards for us, and along came our first miracle. We found out we were pregnant, but my doctors were not happy about this. They made it clear they were here to save me, not a child. We put it in God's hands, and He provided a miracle. Our son Eric was born on All Saints' Day. We named him Eric after my brother who passed away. Motherhood was an opportunity I never thought I would get. CF women can have issues with fertility. I was in Heaven!

When Eric was two, my lung function declined again, and it was time for a lung transplant evaluation. They tested me in 1995 and again in 1998. Both times the results showed I was "too healthy" for the National Transplant Waiting List. My mother persisted, so the doctors agreed to follow me annually in order to meet the right timing for listing (not too sick, not too healthy). I worked full time as a dietitian while caring for a young toddler with my husband. Life was challenging. I slept with oxygen at night to provide more energy during the day, which I had been doing since 1998. Just like in college, I felt like a zombie and could barely make it through work. Something wasn't right. During my regular CF check-up, my doctor decided it was time to think about transplant again. My doctor recommended I be open and honest about my situation with the transplant clinic. I had to stop working, and the workup for the transplant list began in September 2003. On December 18, 2003, they listed me for transplant at Cleveland Clinic. I was on oxygen 24/7 by this time. Because of my petite size, I would need a child's lungs and the wait would likely be two years.

It was strenuous caring for an active two-year-old while also trying to take care of myself. It took everything I had to get out of bed and feed my son. During the day, we watched a lot of TV and read a lot of books. If we went to the park, I needed help and had to wait for my husband to get off work so we could take our son to the park, and he could be a two-year-old. Eric was a very smart child. He knew something wasn't right and appeared content most of the time without having to run around too much. It was also winter, so we weren't spending much time outside, anyway. The internet was becoming popular, and sites with support groups were popping up everywhere. I spent time online following fellow CF patients, some of whom had great outcomes and other not so great. It made me sad reading about the poor outcomes, and I would wonder if I was going to survive this disease. I should have died at 14, which was the life expectancy when I was born. Waiting for lifesaving lungs is a tiresome journey. You wonder if you're going to make it or not. I thought raising a boy would be easier for my husband if I were not here anymore. Although I tried not to think about it, the thought crossed my mind many times over.

Breathing is something we take for granted; we just do it. But when you feel you are suffocating every day, it's a terrifying feeling. Coughing until it feels like your head is going to explode, sucks. Fighting for each breath with every ounce of energy you have is tiring. I couldn't give up, not now. I didn't fight this long just to give up. My family needed me, my child needed me! Things continued to spiral downward and got to a point where I was falling asleep in church and could barely take a shower without needing a nap. My sister-in-law called or came over daily to see if I needed help. My husband finally said it would be best if I got off the internet and focused on myself and our son. Continuing to focus on others' stories made me depressed and was not making my situation any better.

I was told to have a bag packed and ready to go because there wouldn't be much time when I received my call. I thought I had more time since they told me I would wait two years. My lung function declined to 19%, and, after five months and one week, on Tuesday, May 25, 2004, at 10:00 am, I received the call from my transplant coordinator that there might be lungs available and did I want them? Knowing if I didn't receive a transplant, I would most likely die, I didn't have to think twice. With tears in my eyes, I said yes, not quite comprehending the full picture of what was happening at that point. They told me to be at Cleveland Clinic by 1:00 pm. It was a two-and-a-half-hour drive, and we had to hustle. I had not showered for several days since it was such a hard task. So, I showered, made some phone calls, and was on the road in 30 minutes with my husband, son, and sister-in-law in tow. I was not leaving my child behind. We made it in time! My parents beat us there, and my sister and brother showed up after I went in to surgery. I did not find out if the lungs were good and surgery was a go until 5:30 pm. After holding my son for what I feared might be the last time, they took me back for surgery at 7:30 pm. I prayed it was the beginning of a whole new life, raising our son together with my husband, and living life better than I had for the past 30 years. I also said a prayer for the donor family who was grieving the loss of their loved one.

During my hospital stay, I requested my post-surgical report, and it was then I found out my donor was a ten-year-old boy. We grieved for my donor family, who had just lost their child. I had my son and could not even imagine losing him. It was an emotional rollercoaster of guilt. I was alive, and this child lost his life. As difficult as it was, we had to move on. They gave me a new life to live for my family and our young son.

My transplant was a success, and I recovered quickly. I had more energy in the months after the transplant than I had in the two years prior. Taking a breath for the first time with my new lungs was indescribable. For years, my lung function had declined so slowly that I just learned to adapt to my abilities and had forgotten what it was like to breathe with ease. I spent a week and a half in the hospital, and then another couple weeks nearby for observation and the removal of the final drainage tube. After a month, I was approved to go home! It was summer, and I felt so good ... so good that I didn't know what to do with myself! We bought our son an inflatable dinosaur pool and instead of blowing it up with a pump; I blew it up with my wonderful new lungs!!!! My recovery went well enough that I could return to my pre-transplant job within a year. I had a powerful urge to give back in any way possible. I reached out to Life Connection of Ohio, my local Organ Procurement Organization (OPO), and started a beautiful long-term relationship as a volunteer advocating for organ, eye, and tissue donation.

After being released from the hospital, while recovering in a nearby hospitality unit, I found a flyer advertising the Transplant Games of America (U.S. Transplant Games at the time). I told my husband, Mario, "I don't know what I can do, but I want to take part!" My first Transplant Games were in 2006, and I have been attending the games ever since. I attended first as a participant, then as a team manager and competitor. I realized abilities in myself that I never knew I had. As a family, we were making amazing memories that I once feared would never be. I was watching my son grow into an amazing man and witnessed all the milestones that came with being a mother.

Prior to transplant, Mario and I had committed that, once I received my transplant and was healthy again, we would take Eric to Disney World. He loved everything about Disney and was eager to go! In April 2005, we made the trek to Disney and had the best family vacation! More memories have been made and milestones reached because of organ donation. Being a mother has been the most amazing gift, and my donor, Adam, gave me that gift.

After transplant, the social workers recommended waiting at least six months before writing a letter to my donor family. With recovering from transplant and taking care of our two-year-old, writing a letter was on my mind, but not at the forefront during recovery. To my surprise, I did not have to wait six months to have contact with my donor family. I had received a letter from them first! Adam was my hero and his mother, Lorie, shared his life with me. Adam was a giver. He told the younger kids in church that, if they behaved, he would give them a quarter. He wanted to be a Green Bay Packer quarterback when he grew up. We wrote letters back and forth. Adam has two sisters who miss him dearly. After six months of back-and-forth letters, my donor family requested to contact me via telephone. Of course, I accepted! This first phone call was with Steve, Adam's dad. It was something very different from writing letters back and forth. During this call, Steve and Lorie asked about meeting me and my family.

Our meeting, in July 2005, was a ball of emotions, but it was a wonderful meeting. Adam's family saw firsthand a three-year-old child who now had both his mother and father to raise him. We met Steve and Lorie at a nearby hotel that had a swimming pool. Eric was young and loved swimming, so when he saw the hotel pool, he cried to go in. We didn't bring swimsuits with us, but Steve said he would take Eric swimming, so we went to a nearby store and bought him swim trunks. This was a very emotional point in the meeting.

Watching Steve swim with Eric, after losing his own son, was both emotional and healing in some respects. They could see what Adam had given our family. Something beautiful came out of something tragic.

During our visit, we learned Adam loved spaghetti and chili. This was interesting because prior to transplant, I would not eat those foods. I just didn't like them, but now, I LOVE THEM!!!! We have found out that, sometimes, a recipient can take on certain characteristics of their donor. So amazing!

We have developed the best relationship with my donor family over the years. We have attended graduations and weddings of my donor's sisters, and my donor family has attended the games with me since 2010 when the games were in Wisconsin, which is where my donor family is from. As time has passed, they have talked more to me about Adam and things that happened in his life. I love them, and they are a part of our family now, and they have accepted us as part of their family. Adam was a ten-year-old boy whose life ended way too soon. In that tragedy, his mother and father chose donation so he could live on in others and continue to give as he did in life. I am a living testament to that.

Today, I am heading into 17 years post-transplant, our son is attending his first year of college. I have been able to enjoy my family, my siblings, and my nieces for much longer than I ever could have expected. We have made memories that wouldn't have been made without Adam. I have been able to do things I never dreamed I could or would ever do. Because of my gift, I am more outgoing and have more confidence in my life. I am an open book which was not the case many years ago. In this life, I have received two beautiful miracles: the birth of my son, and the gift of life which has allowed me to raise our son and spend more time with family. I take nothing for granted and know I am blessed beyond measure. I spend every day living like Adam is watching, because I believe he is and that he would be proud of the life I am living. Adam is my hero.

Please consider registering to be an organ, eye, and tissue donor, if you haven't already. Visit registerme.org or donatelife.net for more information.

Be a hero like Adam. As a grateful and blessed recipient,
I thank you, Adam. Thank You, God.

Tonya and her donor, Adam.

Tonya and her brother, Eric.

Tonya doing CF therapy pre-transplant

Tonya with oxygen pre-transplant.

First Disney trip Post-transplant.

Tonya in Aruba.

Tonya's donor family: Steve, Amber, Tonya, Lorie, and April.

Tonya, Mario and Eric promoting donation.

Tonya with her mom and Lorie.

About Tonya

Tonya Gomez is a Registered Dietitian and Bi-lateral lung transplant recipient. She lives in Archbold, Ohio, with her husband, Mario, son, Eric, and their dogs. They have two huskies; Packer (named in honor of her donor, Adam) and Woodson; a German

Eric off to college, 2020.

Shepherd mix named Rex; and a Beagle named Curtis.

When not working, Tonya spends time with family and friends at the lake and advocates for organ, eye, and tissue donation as a volunteer for Life Connection of Ohio, her local Organ Procurement Organization. Tonya is an Ohio team manager for the Transplant Games of America and volunteers with Hairy Houdini Siberian Husky Rescue.

Her mission, post-transplant, is to breathe deeply and live life to the fullest. She lives like her donor is watching.

You can connect with Tonya via Facebook, Instagram, or Twitter; or email her at: tonyagomez72@gmail.com.

Michelle Schuerman
with Richard Hanusa and Sarah Weaver

Dick, Sarah and Michelle celebrating their kidneyversary at the EAA in Oshkosh, WI.

A Best Friend is a Gift

Introduction

A grandpa, a crazy friendship, a kidney transplant, and a group of kids. You would think these topics would be completely unrelated, but the world is a small place, and the need of one can bring together the many. This is where their story begins, but before you get into the first-hand experiences, here is a general point of view from the younger ones.

As a group, we were all related to the situation in different ways. Some of us the daughters of the best friend who donated the kidney, others the granddaughters of the grandpa who received the kidney. Though our personal experiences may differ, we all felt the same heart-dropping feeling knowing that someone we knew was going to experience something life-changing. Most people know that important "adult" topics don't really phase children at first. They would be more worried about what they were going to do the next day at recess than the important phone calls about hospitals they overheard in the next room. But most people would agree that all kids have a developed "6th sense" that just knows when something important is happening.

Eventually, when the granddaughters were informed of their grandpa's kidney transplant, they felt helpless. As children, they could not donate their kidneys at that young of an age, which was hard for them to understand. And as granddaughters, they could never imagine losing someone so important to them in such a short time. From the perspective of the daughters of the donor, thinking of their mother going into a major surgery made them nervous and frightened. But they also understood that their mother was doing a brave act to save someone's life. After the successful surgery, all the kids felt a new appreciation for helping others and always being by their family's side through thick and thin. Everyone participated in the healing process as amazing caregivers and began to understand how important it is to live life to the fullest, because life can be unpredictable.

Who would have thought that a friendship of over 30 years would lead to a kidney transplant that forever bonded both the donor and recipient's families forever? All the kids are forever grateful for their grandpa and mother, and that they both get to spend more time with each other. Now that you have heard from the kids' perspective, here are the actual stories.

-Alexis, Natalie, Rebecca, Morgan, Emily, and Kayla

Nine Percent

by Sarah Weaver, Recipient's Daughter

Nine percent is a number that will always ring in my ears. I am a numbers person; number three is my favorite number. So, if you take three times three, you get nine. This should be a lucky thing to have nine percent. Not this time. Nine percent was the amount of my father's kidney function. In fact, if this number would get any lower, he would need to start the process of dialysis. I just kept thinking, how is he still able to do all the things he does with only nine percent kidney function?

My dad (aka Pops) is an amazing man. He and my mother have done so much for me, and I don't have words to express how thankful I am to have them as my parents. I decided it was now my turn to do everything possible to find a kidney donor for my Pops.

I started with myself but learned I could not donate. So, my mission began. I started talking to people, anyone who would listen. I decided I would just tell my dad's story. Everyone in the world needed to know how amazing he was, and that it was now his turn to let someone help him. I never asked anyone face to face if they would consider donating to my Pops since I didn't want to make anyone feel uncomfortable by putting them on the spot. Instead, I chose a basic approach on my quest to find a kidney for him. Emails were sent and messages via social media to any family member that I had any sort of contact with. I figured even if they were not interested, the more people who knew, the better. Any chance to speak to anyone was an opportunity to share my dad's story and his need for a life-saving kidney. I took part in various networking events for work and brought up organ donation. I wanted to be sure people were educated and aware of the incredible need for kidney donations. Not just for my dad, but for an additional 100,000+ people in the United States. I needed to spread the word about how a kidney transplant can save a life. Since I work in the medical field, I am comfortable discussing medical topics, and it is something I enjoy. As I was speaking to various individuals at these events, I was so surprised to learn there were several other individuals who also needed a kidney donor.

I heard from a few people through my email and social media efforts, but they all just said they would spread the word. I understood and was okay with that. Living donation is not for everyone, so I never got upset if they were not interested in helping. We all have our reasons for what we will and will not do. My mindset was to just continue sharing my dad's story. Talking and connecting with people can open doors, and we only needed one door to open. I looked into various other medical contacts I had that might be helpful. With Pop's military background, I wanted to see if there were any other fellow veterans who could spread the word.

There were many times I felt discouraged when I wasn't having much luck. I remember one time watching my dad sleep on the couch, covered with a blanket, in the middle of the day. He would tire easily and was cold more often. It tore me up to see him this way, and I just knew I couldn't give up. My daughters all expressed how they wanted to donate to their Gramps. It broke my heart when I told them they were too young. They were not happy to hear that news.

I am very thankful that, by telling his story, I found the door that opened for my Pops. There are no words to let Michelle know how grateful my entire family and I are for her life-saving gift. Because of Michelle, my mission was complete.

My advice, to anyone who is on a mission to save a life like I was, is keep talking . . . just keep talking and spreading the word. All you need is one door to open. You never know who will help.

After the transplant surgery, I was with both my Pops and Michelle in the hospital. The first time I saw him awake and smiling, I saw the twinkle and energy return in my father's eyes. I am thrilled and lucky to say that nine percent is a distant memory now. I have let go of that number and now just see my amazing Pops looking back at me.

About Sarah

Sarah Weaver is a speech pathologist, practicing for over 20 years. She enjoys working with individuals of all ages. Sarah has four amazing children, and together with her wonderful husband Luke, they love to travel as a family. Sarah is an advocate for organ donation and knows the power of a good story.

Positive Mojo

by Michelle Schuerman, Living Donor

I donated an organ! My kidney is inside another person! Holy emotions! The questions . . . What did I do? Can I ask for it back? Do I need it back? What's next? How is my recipient feeling? How am I feeling? Is my kidney thriving in its new "home"? The roller coaster of emotions is real, and I wouldn't trade them for the world. I am a proud living kidney donor who is tuned into my feelings, and the overall needs of the organ transplant community, more than ever before. Honestly, I knew nothing about "living" organ donation prior to learning about my recipient's hereditary illness and need for this life-saving organ. I have always wanted to be an end-of-life organ donor and thought that was the only option. Now, 20+ years after putting the "donate life" sticker on my license, I am honored to share that because of organ donation

- Friendships have blossomed and deepened,
- Moments and memories have happened,
- Purpose and practice have sparked opportunity and life . . .

I have my reasons for saying "yes" to donating my kidney! They are special and personal, and as I have learned through this donation experience are embedded in the fabric of my being. At the core of my decision is my love and admiration for my father! I absolutely cherish the family he and my mother have built. My earliest memories of my dad are filled with countless laughs of the experiences he created and ensured for our family. These moments are built on his "true north." He taught me the importance of hard work, giving back, and never giving up. He is a kind soul who cared for and loved his family, including his beautiful wife (my mom!) with all his heart. Now, as a mom of two strong and kind daughters, I love watching him share his lessons and build those same experiences with my girls. I couldn't imagine life without him. The endless smiles on his granddaughters' faces are rooted in my organ donation story.

When I think of that moment when I said "Yes. Let me go learn more about living organ donation," it was because of the deep connection I have with one of my best friends and my recipient's daughter, Sarah. Like many, our friendship has a backstory, blossoming when big hair and hair bands were cool. I am so thankful that our friendship has turned into a forever story, and a part of that is because of organ donation. She too has a bond and love for her "pops" that gave me no pause to learn more about how I could help. When I learned of her father's need for a life-saving organ, the first person who popped into my mind was my own father. I couldn't imagine Sarah and her daughters not having their pops/gramps in their lives. At this time, my recipient, Mr. H (as I called him back in high school) was given only two years to live and those weren't going to be the healthiest of times for him. I had a life-saving decision to make and was committed to learn if I could help change his course, potentially allowing for more memorable moments with his family. Sarah was a champion storyteller for her father! Her plan was to walk to the ends of the earth until she found someone willing and able to donate their kidney. Who knew that a traffic jam on our way to a Bon Jovi concert would be so life-saving! While waiting patiently to see one of our favorite bands, she shared her continued plans to search for a kidney, and in the moment, I was moved and our road to saving her pop's life began. . .

My evaluation was a short two months as the stars, antibodies, and tissue matching from the various tests were lining up. It was looking really good that I was going to be a solid, non-relative match to Mr. H. The process with my transplant center gave me the desired time to ask my questions, understand the risks, evaluate my family's future health needs, and realize why this donation was so important to me. This life-saving decision, while physically taking a piece of me, was giving me the chance to feel whole again. I felt grounded in my decision, ultimately this calm connection, knowing this was right for me. The benefits outweighed the present and future risks, and I knew I wanted to say "yes" to organ donation and save my best friend's dad's life!

Today, already six years after donating my kidney, I remain grounded in my decision; I wouldn't change it for anything. I am committed to a lifestyle that maintains my kidney health, which is filled with lots of water and an annual wellness check. I have new connections within the transplant and health care community that bring sustained determination and positivity to my life. Sarah and I have solidified our plans to attend as many Bon Jovi concerts possible to honor our new forever family! I am thankful for my amazing family and friends, especially my parents for their endless love and support. To my husband, Bob, and our daughters, Emily and Kayla, this life-saving gift was only possible because you believed in me! I will always remember and honor your courage, strength, curiosity, and love . . . Finally, to the man who is rocking his new kidney, and I can now call by his first name, there are not enough words to describe the emotions of our journey, but I appreciate how a simple picture connects us. I cherish every text you send with pictures of your travels highlighting where my kidney has been and how great you feel. With every photo, I see the continued importance of organ donation... a gift of healthier tomorrows and the opportunity to create more memorable moments. And for that, Dick, I smile endlessly.

About Michelle

Michelle Schuerman has devoted her career to strengthening the operations of health and human service organizations, particularly those supporting children and families. She is an active volunteer for the National Kidney Foundation of Wisconsin and co-leads a social support group, Living Donors Together of Wisconsin. Together with her husband, Bob, and two daughters, she loves traveling, spending time outdoors, and going to live concerts.

You can connect with Michelle on Facebook: https://www. facebook.com/groups/livingdonorstogether

Discovery of My Hereditary Disease

by Richard Hanusa, Recipient

I was born on September 12, 1948, to Roger and Evelyn Hanusa. Dad was a WWII veteran and Mom a homemaker, and they had a little farm just outside Loganville, Wisconsin. Little did any of us know I was born with a gene that predisposed me to the potential for kidney disease, which came from my mother's side of the family. We moved to Oshkosh when I was a toddler, and a very significant thing occurred when we lived there: my sister, Eunice, became ill with some type of kidney disease that resulted in her missing a year of elementary school. During this same time, my grandfather, Herman Hamburg, passed away. I did not know it at the time, but his passing was from issues related to kidney failure.

Fast forward to 1966, I graduated from Oshkosh High School, met the love of my life, Rita, and had no known health issues. I received my draft notice in the spring or early summer of 1967 and enlisted in the US Army. A friend of mine from high school received his letter about the same time, so we went to the recruiter together, where I saw a pamphlet with a helicopter on it. It looked interesting, so I signed up to go to the Warrant Officer Candidate Rotary Wing Aviator Course. The Army had very stringent physical standards for flight school candidates: no glasses, no hearing loss, or any other medical issues. I passed all the flight physicals with no problems.

During the next 15 years, I served in Vietnam, in the 1st Air Calvary Division in '68-'69, and the 128th Radio Research Company in '72-'73. I married Rita on January 3, 1970, and started planning our life together. We lived in Alabama, Georgia, Arizona, Maryland, and Germany, and started having our children: Matt, Erick, and Sarah. I continued my military service in a variety of roles and had yearly flight physicals with no sign of any kidney-related issues. It was 1975 when the first signs of abnormalities appeared. During a military physical, my urine sample contained microscopic hematuria and protein. One year later, with the same physical results, I went to Walter Reed Army Hospital for testing, in hopes of determining the cause. The doctors could not diagnosis anything significant from the tests.

I left active military duty in 1981, took a job flying for the Department of Defense in Pennsylvania, and remained in the US Army Reserve. My annual flight physicals showed hematuria and protein in my urine samples, but it wasn't in amounts that would take me off of fly status, especially as I still had no other symptoms. In 1985, with a desire to return to our home state, I took a job with the FAA at the Flight Standards District Office at Mitchell Field in Milwaukee. Rita found us a house in New Berlin, which she chose primarily because of the schools. When our daughter, Sarah, went to middle school, she became friends with Michelle Sweeney; little did any of us know the significance of this friendship.

Over the next few years, the abnormalities of my kidneys were increasing. I went to our local Clement Zablocki VA Hospital to get further testing. In 1993, they diagnosed me with polycystic kidney disease. They assigned me to Samuel Blumenthal, MD, a very talented nephrologist, and he explained that there was no treatment or cure for this hereditary disease. Eventually my kidneys would no longer function properly, and I would be ready for dialysis or transplant. Finally, we had a diagnosis for what was going on with my kidneys!

Life continued in New Berlin with the kids finishing school and going to college. Rita started working at Landmark Credit Union and became a Branch Manager and Vice-President. I continued my job with the FAA and retired from the US Army in 1996. I continued to take annual flight physicals and visits to Dr. Blumenthal to monitor my kidney function. We had a big scare in 1999 when Rita was diagnosed with stage four colon cancer. We focused our next few years on her health which included cancer surgery and chemo, a liver resection, and lung surgery; she fought through it all and survived. After Rita's cancer scare, we decided it was time to put our retirement plans into action, giving us time to continue to enjoy life together. Over the next five years, we both retired and moved back to Oshkosh into our lake home, and I continued my doctor visits to monitor my kidney function.

We stayed very active! I came out of retirement and started an aviation consulting business, which allowed me to travel extensively throughout the world. Rita joined me for the interesting destinations! In 2010, my creatine level rose into the 6.0 to 7.0 range, which showed my kidney function was getting worse. Dr. Blumenthal and the nephrology staff at the VA hospital started talking about dialysis and getting a fistula in my arm. This is where I met Dr. Johnson (remember this name) who, besides the dialysis/fistula conversations, also started discussing the process for getting on a kidney transplant list with two options: the VA hospital in Iowa City and another hospital.

Because of Dr. Blumenthal's connection with Froedtert Hospital, and the location being not too far from Oshkosh, we started the process in 2012 to get on the transplant waiting list. This is a very detailed step-by-step process that involved several meetings: general transplant educational meetings, medical insurance meetings, physiological evaluation, financial evaluation, evaluation of general overall health, and determining if I had a caregiver. I had to take several medical tests to determine if I was fit for the surgery or had any other medical issues. They approved me and placed me on the kidney waiting list at Froedtert! I could still continue all my normal activities as in the past. The only symptom I felt and others noticed, especially Rita, was that I would tire easily. I really didn't notice it, but Rita would comment that once I got home and sat down, I would fall asleep within minutes.

Once placed on the kidney waiting list, we started looking for potential living donors. Matt, Erick, and Sarah weren't suitable candidates because of symptoms of potential kidney disease. Rita wasn't eligible because she has a different blood type and because of her cancer history. Sarah got on Facebook, trying to find a donor and checking with all her friends and acquaintances. In 2013, I continued my checkups with the doctors at Froedtert as my creatinine level continued to rise to the 8.0 to 9.0 level.

In late 2013, Sarah and her friends had a get-together for a Thanksgiving feast, and Michelle (remember New Berlin middle school) asked Sarah for the paperwork to start the process to donate a kidney. Based on their previous conversations of Michelle's interest to learn more, Sarah gave her the application and the process began to see if she could donate one of her precious kidneys to me. Fortunately, Michelle was a great match for me—same blood type and everything tested out very well. My kidney function was down to 9%; the most telling sign for me was getting tired quickly. We had Christmas and New Year's as usual, and then we headed down to Florida for some warm weather.

What happened next may be hard to believe, but it really is how it happened. As the Safety Program Manager for the EAA Aviation Center, we flew back to Wisconsin for training commitments earlier than expected. During our visit, we agreed to babysit Sarah's daughters, Alexis, Natalie, and Rebecca, and pick them up at Michelle's house. We had never been there and when we arrived, Michelle was on the telephone with someone. Michelle's husband, Bob, and their girls, Emily and Kayla, and Sarah and her girls were all there. When Michelle got off the phone, she had a big smile on her face; her call was with the kidney transplant coordinator at Froedtert. They had approved her as a living donor for me! It's hard to describe the emotions you feel when you hear something like that. Everyone in the house was very excited, and I was too, but to be honest, I felt a calmness and relief.

Based on our family and work commitments, we confirmed a surgery date of August 6, 2014. Time moved quickly and before we knew it, we were up early at Froedtert Hospital at 0500. When we arrived, Michelle and Bob greeted us, and we checked into the transplant center. They scheduled surgery for 0800. In pre-op, thankfully, our beds were side-by-side! Sarah and Michelle look similar and the way we were all talking and goofing off, the nurses thought Michelle was our daughter. We explained our connection and our care team was amazed! Michelle went into surgery first, and I followed shortly after. Michelle's surgeon was Dr. Johnson, who was my doctor from earlier at the VA—the same skilled doctor with a great personality. I had Dr. Rosa, and I asked upon arrival in the operation room if I could watch, but, unfortunately, he said no, and then I was out.

Rita was with me in recovery. I remember little of the rest of the day as I was still groggy from the anesthetic. Rita, Matt, and Erick were always by my side, and Sarah was going between my room and Michelle's. When I was awake, I felt good, and they had me taking hallway walks. I was still groggy the next day, but started eating and walking more. I remember visiting Michelle's room to see how she was doing. The nurses would come in every hour to check on me, plus the pharmacy and nutritionist personnel, to explain my medications and diet. One thing I remember was having to memorize all the medications I needed to take and when. The doctors said I couldn't go home until all my bodily functions were back to normal. My kidney was functioning very well and had produced urine shortly after Dr. Rosa hooked up the plumbing during surgery! On Friday, I was feeling good and had no pain unless I sneezed, laughed, or coughed. Michelle and I visited several times, and things progressed nicely. Michelle went home on Saturday and I followed on Sunday.

It was a little interesting once we got back home. Our house was being remodeled, and we had very limited use of space for my initial recovery. Rita took amazing care of me, and was spoiling me, of course. I had to get blood tests every day at the Aurora Hospital in Oshkosh. I was lucky because I didn't have any pain from the surgery, and the kidney was working great. My recovery went smoothly, and I returned to doing my normal functions about a month to six weeks after surgery. I was on two of the typical anti-rejection medications, Cellcept and Prednisone, and a newer medication called Balatacept, which I received intravenously once a month. All my checkups continued, including blood work and monthly visits to my post-transplant doctor at Froedtert, Dr. Bresnahan, who I continue to see today.

And then a scare. We went to Florida after New Year's in 2015, and I visited a doctor to set up my monthly intravenous treatments and blood work. Everything was great until late February. I had been taking an anti-viral medication, and the protocol was to stop the medication about six months after surgery. In early March, I came down with flu-like symptoms, achy all over, tired, and a fever. We worked to figure out what was going on, and after several doctor visits and consultations with the doctors at Froedtert, they determined I had Cytomegalovirus (CMV). They prescribed medication that finally got me though the Illness; it lasted a month.

It thrilled me to be living my life while feeling absolutely great! I was flying, working at EAA, and traveling doing audits, plus all the fun times with our family and friends. In August of that year, after going for a checkup and tests, I got a call from Froedtert that there were indications in my blood work that my body was trying to reject the kidney. It was something we did not want to hear, and I was concerned that I would "waste" Michelle's kidney. We asked what the options were and found out that I could have a treatment called Plasmapheresis. I had four treatments in the fall of 2015, and a chemo-type drug to help destroy the antibodies trying to attack the kidney. The greatest news of all was that the treatment worked, and my body stopped trying to attack Michelle's beautiful kidney.

So, how am I doing now? Well, for a late middle-aged guy, I'm doing exceptionally well. I'm healthy and have been able to do everything I want with Rita and our family. My new kidney and I have traveled all over the world and have had wonderful experiences. The biggest question for me as a kidney transplant recipient is how to thank everyone involved, and the best way I know of is to live my best life with all of them. I think of Michelle every day and thank her when I put my kidney transplant medic alert necklace on after a shower. The best things of all have been seeing our grandchildren grow up, including our new granddaughter, Morgan, and seeing Matt and Linn and Sarah and Luke get married.

Because of organ donation, I appreciate every single day to the fullest and enjoy my wonderful life with my family!

About Richard

Richard, "Dick," married the love of his life, Rita, in 1970 and is the father to Matt, Erick, and Sarah, and grandfather to Sean, Alexis, Ella, Natalie, Rebecca, Morgan, Cody, and Carson. He enjoyed a fulfilling career as Chief Warrant Officer 5/Master Army Aviator, US Army (retired), and FAA Supervisory Aviation Safety Inspector (retired). Dick is the President of DH Aviation Safety Consulting. He is an inductee in the Wisconsin Aviation Hall of Fame and has received the FAA Wright Brothers Master Pilot Award. He started flying in 1968, and is still actively flying out of Oshkosh, Wisconsin, and loves every flight.

Dick and Rita have the most
beautiful love story.
Photo: 1968.

Dick's love for flying began way before
they detected his hereditary illness.
Photo: 1969.

A life-saving friendship between Sarah and
Michelle began in middle school.

Schuerman family leaving the transplant center after donation.

They met in their hometown. Their kidneys connect them for life.

Dick and his kidney at the Great Wall of China

Dick and Michelle celebrate their kidneyversary!

The kids have been a special part of the kidney journey and love to raise awareness to support donate life efforts!

Dick and Rita celebrating life and "positive mojo"!

Dick's reason for living!

Tony and Victoria Schmalstig

A Second Chance at Life and Love

Tony's Story

I was born in 1961, and my infancy was normal until around my ninth month. My behavior and moods changed from being a happy, carefree baby to one of crying and being miserable most of the time. Alarmed, my parents took me to their doctor, who sent them to their local hospital for a better evaluation. After many tests and procedures, they determined one of my kidneys was destroyed and the other severely damaged. The cause was never determined, but they could only say it was a birth defect of some sort. Before my first birthday, I had countless surgeries and procedures to remove the bad kidney and repair the damaged kidney as best as they could. However, the doctors cautioned that I may not live past my fifth year.

My childhood was normal, although I got sick easily, but I passed the dreaded five-year mark and then some. I played sports throughout grade school, mostly baseball and basketball, and looked forward to competing in high school. However, my parents had other thoughts and wouldn't allow me to play baseball anymore, saying it was too dangerous for me. I didn't understand their reasoning, but I let it go and concentrated on my studies. I graduated high school and entered college, and things seemed to go in the right direction.

After two years in college, I wasn't doing as well as I had hoped and I dropped out for a while to rejuvenate myself. After a year of working, I gave a lot of thought to joining the Army and making something of myself. When I went to the recruiting station, I found that the only service who would take me with one kidney was the Navy. I gave it a shot and began the process. I did very well on the ASVAB test, a 97, and was told I could have my pick of career choice once I passed the physical. However, during the physical, they discovered I was in renal failure. It devastated me, but I tried to get past this roadblock. I continued to play softball for my church team, that I had played with the previous three years, but I found it increasingly difficult to maintain my strength.

They determined I would begin peritoneal dialysis in the fall of 1983. My nephrologist also suggested that my family think about a kidney transplant for me . . . something that wasn't very common. Without me knowing, many a heated argument ensued because my mother wanted to be the only one tested and didn't want my brother or sister to go through the testing process. My father has a rare blood type and wasn't considered. My brother-in-law also objected to my sister being tested, but she and my brother ignored all the arguments and were tested, anyway. After they completed the testing, my mom was a fair match, my sister was a suitable match, but my brother was a perfect match! He said later that he felt he was destined to give me a kidney and that no one else would do it. He was right.

We decided March 16, 1984, would be the date of the transplant. It was the beginning of his school break and it would give him enough time to recover to get back to his studies. On the morning of the transplant, the hospital staff forgot to give me a dialysis treatment. They didn't figure this out until they had already begun my brother's surgery. My potassium levels were too high to put me under normal anesthesia, so they gave me a spinal block instead. Therefore, I was awake throughout the entire surgery! I watched the surgery through a mirror on the surgeon's forehead. It was fascinating and didn't gross me out at all! My brother's kidney began working as soon as they removed the clamps, turning a bright pink and producing urine right away. And it has worked perfectly ever since.

My recovery was quick, and I was able to get back to a normal life without difficulty. My brother, however, had a long and difficult recovery. His incision was from his sternum to his belly button and he was in extreme pain for many days after the transplant. With rest and help from his fiancé, he made a full recovery within a few months. To this day, he says every bit of pain was worth it.

A few months later, I fulfilled a lifelong dream of attending a tryout camp for the Cincinnati Reds. It was an amazing experience which I will never forget. Although they didn't sign me, it was just the beginning of a new life for me, one of new goals and accomplishments. I met my first wife and began dating her in the fall of 1984. We married in 1988 and welcomed a son into the world in 1992. In 1991, I began my career with the Montgomery County Sheriff's Office as a Corrections Officer where I remained for 15 years until knee injuries forced me to take an early medical retirement. I took up bowling as a hobby and have excelled at it. I now have three 300 games and three 299 games to my name. This inspired me to compete in the Transplant Games of America, where I have won seven gold medals, and one silver medal. The Transplant Games are a week of competition featuring organ, eye, and tissue transplant recipients competing against each other in their respective age groups. They hold these games every two years in different places around the United States. Some of the sporting events are bowling, corn hole, tennis, swimming, basketball, volleyball, darts, and many others. I also began volunteering for Life Connection of Ohio, an organ, eye, and tissue procurement organization in Dayton, Ohio. I have accomplished and seen so many things because of our transplant, and I can never thank my brother enough for his selfless Gift of Life. To this day, he will tell you it was no big deal, that anyone would do it, but I know otherwise. He is and always will be my hero.

My first marriage ended in divorce after twenty-four years, but that turned into a blessing and a second chance at love.

Victoria's Story

I was born with Reflux Nephropathy. I was not diagnosed with Kidney Disease until I was three years old. As a baby, I would get a lot of urinary tract infections, and the doctors told my mom she was not changing my diapers enough. However, my mom knew that was not true and continued to look for answers. Eventually, they referred me to a nephrologist who diagnosed my problem and put me on a medicine regimen that maintained my kidney function through my grade school years. I will always thank my mom for advocating for me instead of just accepting continual UTIs.

As I neared my high school graduation, my kidney function began declining, and talks of dialysis and an eventual kidney transplant became a topic. My parents did not want me to endure dialysis and asked about the possibility of being living kidney donors. They ruled my mom out as a candidate because diabetes ran in her family, but my dad tested and was a suitable match. On July 16, 1993, my dad gave me his kidney, and it worked well from the start. Six months later, however, I began having problems, and the doctors started treating me for rejection. It was not the correct diagnosis. Before the transplant, there was an infection in my native kidneys which the doctors were unaware of, and the infection spread into my dad's kidney. By the time my problem was correctly diagnosed, it was too late to save my dad's kidney. I was on a roller coaster of emotions. I was angry because of the original misdiagnosis, sad because I felt my dad gave up a kidney for nothing, and scared because I didn't know if I would ever get another transplant. My native kidneys were removed, but it was too late in my mind.

In 1994, I married for the first and only time, I thought, to someone I had been dating for three years. He had seen me in the best of times and the worst of times, but it still surprised me when he offered to be a living donor to me. I didn't know, at the time, that a non-family member could donate. He tested and was a suitable match. This surprised the doctors very much. The transplant took place on April 9, 1996, but it wasn't meant to be. An artery was tied off incorrectly and produced a blood clot in the kidney. Three surgeries later, the kidney could not be saved, and I woke up on life support ten days later. The kidney only lasted six hours.

Not wanting to see another family member unsuccessfully donate to me, I started peritoneal dialysis and would continue this treatment for six years. It was during this time when I felt depressed about my journey. I was scared that I would never receive a transplant from a deceased donor and I also had anxiety about letting a living donor donate to me, considering what had happened the two previous times. My nephrologist suggested I look into the Transplant Games of America so I would see success stories and understand that a transplant could work for me. I went to the Orlando Games in June 2002, and it changed my way of thinking and my life. I saw kidney transplant recipients competing and living normal lives. It got my head straight, and I felt positive again. But, while at the Games, I contracted peritonitis and had to switch to hemodialysis. I did not do well on hemodialysis, and my health declined fast. The doctors suggested that I ask friends and family to donate to me, but I was still reluctant. I had only gotten a call once for a deceased donor kidney in six years, and that one was not viable. It was at this time we were told I had four to six months to live if I didn't receive a transplant. My younger brother told me he couldn't imagine me not being around to be an aunt to his children, so he got tested. He turned out to be a perfect match for me, and on March 4, 2003, he donated his kidney to me. To this day, I still have the absolute best kidney function I have ever had, and I am forever thankful to him for his gift of life.

I am forever blessed to have three living donors. I still have my father's kidney in me, and that means even more to me since he passed away in June 2020. Part of him will always be with me. Even though my first husband and I separated in 2010 and divorced in 2011, I am grateful he tried to donate to me. With my brother's kidney, I have been able to do and see so many things. I've seen my nieces and nephews grow and have children of their own. Because of this amazing gift of life, I have made so many memories that might not have been and continue to create more every day with my second chance of life. I competed in the Transplant Games of America in 2006 and something happened there that changed my life, although I didn't know it at the time.

Our Story, as Told by Tony

We first met in Louisville, Kentucky, at the 2006 Transplant Games of America. It wasn't love at first sight, and fireworks didn't go off. I was married and so was Victoria, and we just knew each other as teammates for Team Ohio. We didn't compete in any sports together, but we attended team functions. Over the next few years, we saw each other sporadically at Team Ohio's events. Because of financial constraints, I didn't compete in the 2008 or 2010 Games, whereas Victoria did. A few days after Thanksgiving of 2010, we were both invited to a Team Ohio bowling get-together in Cleveland. It was a great time for both of us, but before we knew it, it was time to go home. It was a long drive home for both of us. Since she lived in Columbus and I lived in Dayton, our friends invited us to spend the night at their house. We agreed, and it was the beginning of something special.

As everyone relaxed and sat down for the evening, we started talking and just couldn't stop. We discovered we were both going through divorces for the same reason, and there were so many other things we had in common; our love for baseball, political views, bowling, our transplant experiences . . . and the list went on and on. Our conversation was so effortless, it seemed as if we had known each other forever. We talked until 2:30 in the morning! The next morning, our conversation was just as easy, and it scared us both. We didn't know what to think of it. Neither of us was looking for a relationship at the time because our divorces hurt us deeply, and we didn't want to get into another relationship again right away. Victoria invited me to accompany her to her friends' wedding reception the following weekend, and I accepted. The rest is history, so to speak. When you find the right person, the perfect person for you, you hang on for dear life. It didn't take long for us to fall in love, although we tried to talk ourselves out of it many times. We thought our relationship was the perfect setup since we lived two hours from each other, but God had other plans when he brought us together. Weekdays became very long before we got to see each other on the weekends. Soon, we missed each other so much when we were apart that we knew we were in trouble.

We danced around the subject of marriage for quite a while before I proposed to her, and she accepted on February 11, 2013. It had been a rough day for us, as it was the birthday of a dear friend, a heart recipient, who had passed away. We had been talking about him all day, reminiscing about the good times. I was going to the kitchen for a snack and I asked Victoria if she wanted something as well. She answered in a joking tone that a house, a new car, and a ring would be nice. I went to where I had been hiding the ring and retrieved it. I gave it to her and asked if one of the three would work. It may not have been the most romantic proposal, but it was perfect for us. Our families and friends were thrilled and wondered why it took us so long!

Our intention was to have a long engagement, but that went out the window when my sister heard of our nuptial plans. She had contracted ALS in 2006 and was starting the last stage of her illness, although we didn't know it. When she learned of her illness, she set some goals; to see her boys graduate from college and get married, and to see her first grandchild; and she wanted to see me happy, which meant my getting married to Victoria. She hounded us all the time about setting the date. Kidding a little, we told her a date two years into the future. It satisfied her, and she didn't ask anymore. Sadly, two weeks later she passed away, and we knew we would honor her request. On September 19, 2015, a little over two years after my sister's death, we stood in front of our family, friends, and transplant family at home plate at Babe Ruth Baseball Park and said our vows. Our donor brothers stood by us through it all, and it wouldn't have been right without them being there. After all, they gave us a second chance of life, which gave us a second chance at love. It was a baseball-themed wedding, as you might suspect, with everyone sporting their favorite baseball team attire. Hamburgers, hot dogs, and Cracker Jacks was our menu at the reception. It was a perfect day, and we had an amazing time!

Since then, we have seen and done so many things together, including our medical issues. It is so much easier going through medical difficulties when you know your spouse has gone through the same things. We know with our issues, marriage isn't always going to be 50/50. Sometimes it's 60/40 or even 80/20. But we know that we'll get through it together, no matter what. Together, we have competed in two Transplant Games and won gold medals twice in mixed doubles bowling. It was during the Transplant Games in 2016 that people started calling us "The Kidney Couple," which we loved! We never tire of telling our transplant story. Traveling is our passion, and we have gone to so many wonderful places and made many more memories because of organ donation. Our goal is to see a baseball game in every major league ballpark. Seven down, twenty-three to go! Another goal is to see Australia, Germany, and Hawaii. One day we'll get there.

Memories that may not have happened . . . this has been our recurring theme throughout our transplant journey together. Without our brothers' heroic and selfless acts, we have no idea where we would be now. Although neither of our brothers likes to hear it, they are our heroes. We thank them every day for their gifts of life.

Tony & Victoria at the 2016 Transplant Games of America in Cleveland, OH with her brother Mike, his wife Raechelle and their boys Aaiden and Tatum.

Tony with his brother Dennis at his home in Florida, March 2019; Holding gifts made to commemorate their 35th Transplant Anniversary.

Victoria with her dad Larry awarding him the gold medal she won at the 2018 Transplant Games of America in bowling mixed doubles.

295

Tony and Victoria with their brothers—kidney heroes—on their wedding day, September 19, 2015.

Tony and Victoria at the 2016 Transplant Games of America before they bowled for gold.

Tony and Victoria with donor mom Kathi Flew after she presented them with their gold medal in mixed doubles bowling.

Tony and Victoria during Opening Ceremonies at the 2018 Transplant Games of America in Salt Lake City, UT.

Tony and Victoria while participating in the Guinness Book of World Records for most recipients gathered in one place during the 2018 Transplant Games of America.

Tony and Victoria posing with their gold medals in mixed doubles bowling at the 2018 Transplant Games of America.

Tony and Victoria stopping to pose on the podium at the 2018 Transplant Games of America.

About Tony & Victoria

Tony and Victoria Schmalstig are both kidney transplant recipients who received from their brothers. Tony received the gift of life from his brother, Dennis, in 1984, and Victoria received the gift of life from her brother, Michael, in 2003. They met in Louisville, Kentucky, in 2006 as part of Team Ohio while competing in the Transplant Games. They began dating in 2010 and married in 2015.

Tony and Victoria have competed in two Transplant Games as a married couple and have won gold medals twice in mixed doubles bowling. Because it is rare to find a married couple where both the husband and wife are transplant recipients, they have been dubbed Tony and Victoria "The Kidney Couple" by many of their friends in the transplant community.

In their spare time, they travel, go to baseball games to root for the Reds and Indians, bowl, babysit their great nephew, and volunteer for Lifeline of Ohio, their local organ procurement organization, and the YNOTT Foundation.

Tony and Victoria live in Newark, Ohio, where he is a retired Corrections Officer with the Montgomery County Sheriff's Office in Dayton, Ohio, and Victoria is retired from State of Ohio certified child care.

You can connect with Tony Schmalstig and Victoria Schmalstig on Facebook.

Trisha Phillips

Being Part of a Miracle

Never did I imagine being part of a miracle in giving the gift of life. Let me start with why I am in awe of how my journey to donate my kidney is so unexpected to me. I was born and raised in a small two-traffic-light town, on the Gulf of Mexico in the Florida Panhandle, named Port St. Joe. In my town, you knew everyone, and the Piggly Wiggly was the most exciting attraction. In a town of less than seven thousand people, there weren't any malls, movie theaters, spas, etc. The first, and only, McDonald's did not come to the town until the mid-1990s, and I had already moved away by that time. I grew up with strict, old-fashioned parents, and organ donation wasn't anything I was even aware of.

Once I moved away for college, my life opened up to a lot of new ideas and possibilities of what the world offered. I was only 19 when I moved from my country town to what I considered the big city, Fort Lauderdale, FL. After I graduated from Broadcasting School in 1994, I continued life in South Florida. After settling into city life, I was hooked.

Five years later, the universe started lining up the cards for me to become a living kidney donor to one of my closest friends. Kimberly and I met one Saturday afternoon at a family-owned hair salon where she was a hairstylist. The owner was my hairstylist, but over the many years of getting my hair done at this salon, I formed a fond friendship with Kimberly. I got to know her two adolescent daughters and I became their pretend Godmother. As the years went on, my stylist, who also owned the salon, decided she was going to retire and closed down the salon. I was in a frenzy as to the future of my hair, but then my nerves calmed when Kimberly shared with me that she was buying a salon just up the road from there. It was a simple decision to follow her to the new salon and have her as my hairstylist. Over the years, I spent a lot of time in Kimberly's chair, and we became fast friends. In our heads, we coined ourselves "The Modern Day Thelma and Louise Adventures Together."

The stresses of owning a salon and working long hours as the lead hairstylist affected her general health, and Kimberly was starting to not feel so well. Years passed by with her health being managed with the help of doctors, but then one day she discovered she had kidney disease running in her family, and in 2013 they diagnosed her with IgA Nephropathy. This is a kidney disease that occurs when antibodies build up in the kidneys. She then began dialysis, knowing that a transplant would be in her future.

Have you ever felt a Higher Power at work in your life? I feel this and I know these unexplainable things are the work of my Higher Power, the one I know as God. When my recipient first started her battle and suffered on dialysis three days a week for three and a half hours each time, my parents were aging and battling different illnesses. So by the time they gave Kimberly her diagnosis in 2013, I was on the road every two weeks driving back and forth to the Panhandle helping with my parents' care since I was their Power of Attorney. For two years, I drove back-and-forth to Port St. Joe to help my family and wasn't able to spend much time with my friend Kimberly. My parents' health took a turn for the worse, and devastation hit on October 18, 2014, when my mother died. The pain continued as, only a short eighty-six days later, my dad gave up the will to live and died on January 12, 2015. Many refer to this as "dying of a broken heart." I believe this happened with him because my mom and dad were married for fifty-nine years.

With all the commuting back and forth, nine hours each way, I ate a lot of fast food; grieving the loss of my parents and dealing with the stress of being appointed the Trustee over their estate, I soon found myself overweight and unhealthy. I realized that my parents wouldn't want an unhealthy lifestyle for me, so I pulled my life together as much as I could.

I also realized God had a hand in all of this, and the pieces of the puzzle were fitting together for my organ donation journey. For instance, how would my strict parents understand me wanting to give up an organ to someone that was not a blood relative? I also believe it was divine intervention since I had been struggling to lose those extra pounds I had packed on. Because of my will and determination to donate, I could finally lose weight.

After the death of my parents, Kim would often console me, even though she was still going through her own trying time. However, one particular phone call stood out because I could hear the desperation in her voice. Dialysis had drained her, and she was not feeling well. She also had some frustrations with other potential living donors that didn't pan out. I knew from my medical field experience what the process of dialysis entailed, and it was at that moment I asked her, "How can I find out if I am a match to donate my kidney to you?"

I admit, I knew little about organ donation and didn't have any knowledge of this process. I assumed you had to be a blood relative to donate to someone. Kimberly appreciated that I even inquired and offered to get tested. Once she gave me the information, I reached out to her transplant center at Tampa General Hospital which was three and a half hours away from where I lived in Fort Lauderdale.

Tampa General is one of the top-rated transplant centers in the country. I must be honest, before I even dialed their number; a weird feeling came over me. It wasn't nerves, but was more like excitement and butterflies rolled into one. This was from determination of my wanting to be a match for my friend!

My first step in this Living Donor process was to speak with one of the Transplant Coordinators at the hospital. The meeting lasted almost an hour as she explained to me what testing included and asked if I was willing to start this process. I, of course, said "yes" with excitement! Because of the distance, she mailed me a blood draw kit to take to a local lab to have my blood drawn. It surprised me to see so many vials in the box; but, little did I know, I hadn't seen anything yet with having my blood drawn.

A couple weeks later, I heard from the hospital that they had approved us to move on to the next phase! YAY, I passed the first step! With tears in my eyes, I called my friend to let her know the good news. Moving on to step two is where my determination kicked in. Step two for me was the 24-hour urine collection process, which I thought would be a piece of cake. Boy, was I mistaken. This 24-hour process is normally one-and-done, but it took FIVE times for me. This intense urine collection not only tests your overall kidney function, it also measures your creatinine levels and everything in your urine. Remember, I was also trying to lose weight. I worked out six days a week, and two of those days ended up being twice a day because of time restraints. It was easier to do strength training with weights and a personal trainer in the mornings and then go back in the evenings to do my 30-45 minutes of cardiovascular. I also switched to a low carbohydrate/high protein diet, without realizing these items could make my creatinine levels higher. After turning in two 24-hour urine collection jugs, my Tampa General Nurse Coordinator and I tried taking the next one with no exercise or high proteins for 10 days prior. That worked, and it lowered the creatinine drastically; so we gave it another try for a fourth test with cutting everything out for a full two weeks prior to urine collection.

By this time, it was my fourth round with this now-familiar orange urine collection jug; I became a regular at my particular lab location, and by now I felt sad for my friend that this kept happening. It worried me I was giving her false hope. I turned in my fourth jug with the hope I would get the green light call from my Nurse Coordinator. The two-week break brought my levels to where they needed to be, but I had to do a FIFTH round because my menstrual cycle was an issue. I had no idea I should have waited to do that fourth urine collection; but I didn't give up, and the fifth time was a charm! I had the green light to move on to the last phase of the process . . . step three.

The last phase required me to go to Tampa General Transplant Center to take part in a three-day series of tests. These tests would be to figure out if I'm a good crossmatch for my friend and to make sure I'm healthy enough, mentally and physically, to become her Living Kidney Donor. I had kept this entire journey a secret from all of my friends, family members, and coworkers. I didn't want to take the chance of anyone giving me negative remarks about wanting to do this. I confided in my boss, to explain to him what I was trying to do and why I needed time off for this testing. He and I discussed what would happen if this was a go, and what would happen with my job if I need to temporarily move away to another city and be off work. I had positive feedback from him, and he said, "Go. Don't worry about it now, we will figure it out and make it happen if it's supposed to happen. But save your vacation and sick days, just in case. So only use what's needed for this testing." When I heard that, a heavy burden was lifted off my shoulders. I had been at my job for 22 years and loved it, so I didn't want to put it in jeopardy. A feeling of serenity came over me once I hung up the phone. I felt his mother's presence. She was deceased, but he had told me that his mother and I shared the same birthday. I know what you are thinking, *this isn't a supernatural book,* but these are all events that made me realize this organ donation was all predestined to take place.

Let's go back to my trip for testing at the hospital in Tampa. I told Kimberly she couldn't come with me on this trip. I couldn't have handled the nerves that would have come if she had been next to me, waiting to see if I was going to pass each test. She agreed, and I kept her posted and sent pictures of the three-day adventure. It was an endless process with many tests, evaluations, tons of blood work, and with so many doctors and nurses. I never knew they could draw so many vials of my blood. Hands down, the entire staff at the hospital was AMAZING. Testing took place in the middle of September that year. Once back home in Fort Lauderdale, it was time to play the waiting game and continue to lose weight. Once it was determined if I passed the testing and I was a match, my case to donate to my friend would go before the Transplant Medical Review Board in order to receive their permission to donate my kidney.

I got the call at the end of October letting me know it was a green light! I was having lunch with a client when I took that call. It overjoyed me; I started screaming and celebrating! During the waiting period, I discussed with Kimberly and my boss when would be the best time to have the transplant, and we agreed the Christmas holiday would be best. That time frame would give me more time to get my job tasks organized and handled, and provide me with extra days off besides my personal days. I had mentally prepared to tell my friend the wonderful news with a big grand surprise, but that all went out the window when the excitement and tears of joy overcame me. I called her right away, and we cried together and settled on December 15, 2016, as our date that our miracle kidney transplant would happen.

The move to Tampa went as planned, and the transplant outcome was a positive one as well. I had a full Five Star experience that I would remember for the rest of my life. To this day, I am grateful they performed our transplant at Tampa General Hospital in Tampa, Florida. From what I have read, not all transplant centers offer the royal experience like I experienced.

It brings me joy to share that my recipient and I are both doing well and we're still as close as can be, with an even stronger bond now. We've had a few minor hiccups since our donation, but we both remain in good health. Since being part of this miracle, I've made it my mission to bring awareness to Organ Donation, especially in the African American communities. We represent the highest percentage of kidney patients on dialysis, but the lowest percent to become living or deceased donors. My goal is to work with foundations and educate this community, and all others, that you can donate as a living donor and still live a normal life. I also hope to change the thoughts about organ donation myths regarding living and deceased organ donors. I started a local weekly radio show, sponsored by one of the largest African American family owned and operated roofing companies in Florida, Darcy Jackson Roofing and Waterproofing LLC. I'm grateful for this company believing in my platform. I have also become an Ambassador and a Volunteer for several foundations to help spread awareness.

I leave you with these thoughts: Would you want to help someone have a better quality of life, or even save their life, if you could? Would you want someone to do the same for you or your loved one? We need your organs on earth, not with you when you leave this earth, so please, if you haven't already, register to become an organ donor. Because of organ donation, I experienced a miracle and became a living kidney donor. Giving the gift of life was the most rewarding feeling I've ever felt. I have absolutely not regrets and would do it again if I could.

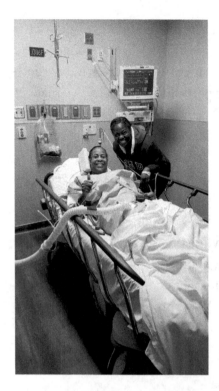

Transplant 12/15/16 at Tampa General Hospital. Before, with Kimberly (left), and after.

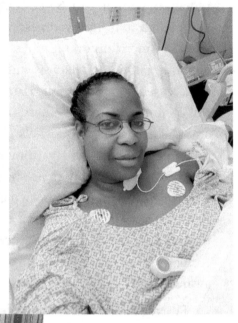

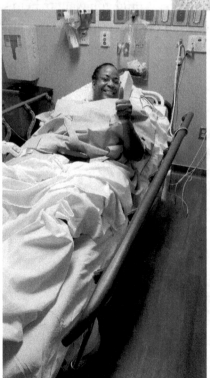

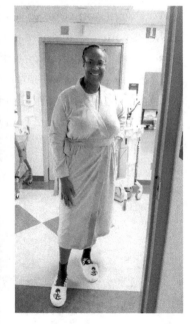

Trish and Kimberly photo for the 2020 The Faces of Transplantion LifeLink Foundation Calendar for the month of January.
Photo Credit: Barbara Banks Photos

LifeLink Foundation 2020 Rookie of the Year recipient.

About Trisha

Trisha Phillips, was born and raised in Port St. Joe, Florida, and moved away to South Florida, and currently resides in Fort Lauderdale. She has worked over two decades in the field of Broadcasting at a local radio station there, right after receiving a Degree in Broadcasting in the year 1994. Trish decided to become a Living Kidney Donor for one of her best friends of twenty-plus years. This decision was made after witnessing her friend battle dialysis for over two years, Trish went on a journey to provide her friend with a better quality of life. Since their successful transplant that took place on December 15, 2016, Trish has been on a mission to inform others that you can live a healthy lifestyle with just one kidney, and to also sign up to be a Living or Deceased Organ Donor. She has become active in this mission several ways, such as starting her own weekly Kidney Awareness Radio Show, signed up to volunteer with Donate Life's Foundations: LifeLink Florida and Life Alliance. Volunteered and received a Top Fundraisers Club membership from The National Kidney Foundation Walk, along with partcipating in many of their campaigns. She is a current Ambassador for "Howl the Owl on the Prowl", along with "Worldwide Kidney Donors" Banner Ambassador, and has become more involved with African American Outreach Health Informing. If you would like more information on becoming a Living Donor or registering to become an Organ Donor, please go to registerme.org

Shannon Andreas

Because of Case

How blessed I feel to contribute to this book, *Because of Organ Donation*. My journey with eye, organ, and tissue donation has been fast and furious, starting only a few months ago after the passing of my son, Case Michael Andreas, on December 16, 2019. We are a donor family. I am the mother of a four-month-old tissue donor and a baby hero.

In this chapter I will refer to "organ donation," but regarding my family's experiences, this includes tissue donation. My son, Case, donated his heart valves. I will also refer to my son, Case, as Baby Case, Case Michael and Turkey Boy. Baby Case is what my daughter, Aria, calls her baby brother. Case Michael is his first and middle name, after his daddy, Christopher Michael. Turkey boy, is my pet name for my baby boy, Case.

Baby Case

Our family's hero entered this world at 11:00 pm, on August 16, 2019. Case Michael Andreas, 8 pounds 1 ounce, and 21 inches long, was the perfect addition to our family. Case made his arrival at thirty-seven weeks. He was healthy, happy, handsome, and absolutely perfect. Case was quite big for an early baby, had thin brown hair (although it was announced that he had blonde hair at birth), dark brown eyes, and the most charming little smile.

As Case grew, he showed a great deal of physical strength, and his characteristics were in alignment with the "big dreams" that we had for him since finding out that Aria was going to have a baby brother. We imagined Case was going to receive scholarships and play baseball in college, and then he would get drafted to play professionally, just like his daddy.

Over the next few months, Case continuously impressed us with his size, strength, intelligence and easy temperament. Reflecting on the short time we had with Case, we underestimated just how amazing he would be. We never considered that Case would be a blessing for so many others at such a young age, or that he would quite literally save someone's life. Little did we know that Case would exceed every dream that we had for him but not without us experiencing indescribable pain and heartbreak. On December 16, 2019, Case Michael Andreas would go to sleep and drift off to Heaven. I'm sure there is some curiosity that comes with learning about Case's passing at the young age of four months old, especially when he's been described as a healthy and happy baby. The night before Case went to Heaven, we kissed him goodnight, he went to sleep, and he passed from what was called "failure to wake."

Know Better, Do Better

I want so badly to share the events from the night that Case passed away in order to educate others, but that's for another time and another book. For now, I'll focus on how Case became a hero, and the day I started on a path to becoming a better person. A few hours after we kissed our baby boy goodbye and left the hospital, Life Gift called. Life Gift is an organ procurement organization in Texas that gives hope to those in need of organ and tissue transplants, and allows bereaved family members, like my husband and I, to consent to give the gift of life after to another after the passing of a loved one.

I honestly don't even know why I answered the phone the day Case passed, but I'm so thankful that I did. I'm thankful that my husband and I could give permission for them to take Case's heart valves, and anything else they could, to help save the life of another.

After being asked to become a contributing author for a book focusing on personal stories, *Because of Organ Donation*, I knew there was a reason Brenda and I connected a few months prior. I started reflecting on my own journey because of organ donation, and this riddle came to mind, *Which came first, the chicken or the egg?* Obviously organ donation came first, but it's only because of Case that I did anything "more" with organ donation. Aside from becoming a registered donor, before December 16, 2019, I wouldn't know anything more than the heart on my driver's license. It is because of Case that my family, friends, acquaintances, and even strangers have been introduced to organ donation and have become registered donors.

Recently, I have been described as strong, inspiring, and encouraging. I don't agree with those words or anything similar. I am just a grieving mother trying to survive the death of my child. I am a bereaved mother trying to honor my son. I am also the mother of a living child, and I'm doing my best to teach her how to be a good person and ignite a passion in her to help other people before there's a "reason" . . . before she feels she "need" to be a better person, and Christian, like myself, her mom, did. I'm regretful that it took the loss of my sweet boy Case to take on the challenge of helping a stranger, but I'm here and that's what counts.

Don't make the mistakes I did. Don't skim over another person's efforts to bring awareness to you about organ donation. These generous people take part in selfless acts of kindness, whether they're living donors, donor recipients, or donor families involved with, or apart from, Donate Life. Either way, they were doing something far greater than I. How did I miss the pain, appreciation, and hope from so many people touched by organ donation? Maybe it takes direct relation to the cause, working with the cause (like Case's aunt and my sister, a paramedic), or working for the cause, to truly understand how meaningful organ donation is. Well, now I see it. Now I know about it. And now I'm helping.

I pray you don't wait until you HAVE to see the importance with organ donation until you get involved. Take a moment right now and think about what real involvement might look like for yourself. Will you register as an organ donor? Will you start a conversation about organ donation, or tell someone you meet about Baby Case? Will you consider becoming an advocate for organ donation and joining Life Gift? Whatever choice you make, I hope it involves action. It is my hope that in reading my son's story, and the story of others, that you will find a meaningful way to get involved with organ donation. Do it BeCAUSE of Case.

Let Me Count the Ways

As a mother, my biggest fear was losing one of my children. As a bereaved mother, my biggest fear is that my son's name will be forgotten. But people will know his name, and they will know his story, because I'll make sure of that. People will know how beautiful, sweet, and loving Case was, and they'll know that because of organ donation.

There are so many ways that eye, organ, and tissue donation has made me a better person, and that is ultimately because of Case. For starters, it made me smile. Can you imagine that, smiling the same day your child has passed away? But it did. My husband and I were given the opportunity to help Case become a hero and give the gift of life. How could I not smile at that? I could then see the light of a new dream for our baby boy, Case, and a new role as a mother, a bereaved mother. Three days after Case went to Heaven, I became involved with organ donation.

Humble Beginnings

My husband and I returned to work three weeks after Case passed away (one week absent from work and two weeks for winter break), and, as you can imagine, I didn't feel like working on anything unless it involved Case. So, that's all I did. I got on the Donate Life Texas and Donate Life America websites. I wrote any important dates and events I could find in my calendar. I printed literature about organ donation. I visited any site asking for donor stories, and I submitted my turkey boy's story on every single one I could find. I created a flyer with Donate Life events listed using one of Case's pictures as the background. I created an email address where inquiries about organ donation could be made, and I'd be sending out any future information about a cause for Case. I also designed at least twenty different yard signs about registering to become an organ donor and a hero like Baby Case. I had fifty signs printed and shipped with stakes and then ordered another fifty (thanks mom and dad for purchasing them). I delivered them to friends and family to put in their yards (HOAs be damned). I wanted strangers passing by to know that Case Michael was a hero and they too could be generous if they registered to become an organ donor.

As a newly bereaved mom, I needed to find anything I could to surround myself with things related to Case. This led me to make a large purchase from the Donate Life store so that I could look almost anywhere and be reminded of the gift of life that our Baby Case shared. These tangible items show other people just how proud we are of our baby boy and help us recall, in the deep waves of grief, that

Case Michael had a bigger purpose on this Earth. I ordered donor family shirts, car decals, car magnets (the big ones), candles, picture frames, garden stones, key chains, a badge reel, and honestly, there's probably more, but I've gotten rid of the receipt. No, none of this is necessary or meaningful, but all of this Donate Life donor family merchandise symbolizes the hero we have in Case and is something tangible that other people can see and talk about.

Ambassador of Hope

Surely someone more accomplished than I am should be writing about organ donation, but here I am. I've been blessed with the opportunity to write about my experiences with organ donation, and I attribute that to a couple of things: because I'm a "doer" and because of Case.

Before Case passed away, I didn't really understand how I, or anyone else, could be a doer regarding organ donation unless they themselves had donated or received a transplant. But when a mother needs to keep her baby's memory alive, she finds something to do. Three days after Case went to Heaven, I registered to become an Ambassador of Hope with Life Gift.

It was three weeks after Case had passed that I returned to work and attended my Ambassador of Hope training. I remember everything about that meeting. I was given a certificate with Case's name on it as a donor, an ornament, and some Donate Life swag items for myself, my husband, our daughter Aria, and family. I took a handful of pins because they all had "Donor Family" printed on them. I was proud, I am proud, and I wanted to show off that I'm the mother of an organ donor. When the meeting began, they asked us to share our "story." I volunteered first because I was a proud mama and wanted to talk about Case. Plus, anyone that knows me well, knows I'm not shy.

I connected with another bereaved mother, a living donor (to a complete stranger; so amazing), and the husband of a recipient. This educated me on facts of organ donation. I am happy to say I was able to answer some questions posed about organ donation, and I even knew all the significant dates for Donate Life (I'm a former classroom teacher, so the studying and responding for a Q & A came naturally). The next evening, I signed up to work multiple Donate Life events, and my first event would be that Saturday, just four weeks shy of Case joining Jesus in Heaven.

My first event was for the Smilin' Rylen Foundation at a brewery in Katy, Texas, close to where I grew up and just down the road from where we live. I felt so much strength from Case on that afternoon, and I held it together (as in, I didn't curl up on the ground in the fetal position crying uncontrollably because that was another new normal for me) throughout the event. I should also mention that I have an amazing support system, and that's another reason I kept it together that day. My husband, daughter, sister, and brother-in-law came out, and their friends were even sweet enough to make the drive out to be there to support me, Case, and organ donation. My mom had cookies made with Case's name and Donate Life on them, which made perfect conversation pieces. I even helped three people register to become organ donors that day: a stranger, my brother-in-law (thank you, Uncle Anthony), and one of his friends. One of the nicest things about that day was being able to talk about Case to another bereaved family, and to hear all about the angel baby, Rylen. Bereaved families have to stick together, and no one understands more than grieving parents how important it is to say your child's name.

I continue to volunteer as an Ambassador of Hope, trying to build connections with other donor families and share Case's story. I've been told several times as an ambassador that sharing your story is the best way to get people to register. I'm glad it does, but honestly I'll do anything that allows me to talk about my angel baby, Case.

BeCAUSE of Case

BeCAUSE of Case was born out of all the love and energy we still had to give to our sweet boy. This cause gave me, my husband, our family, and close friends a way to honor Case's life, and find a way for us to give selflessly, just as he did. Following the creation of BeCAUSE of Case, a nonprofit organization, I wrote a mission statement and tried to include everything that was weighing on our grieving hearts. When I started BeCAUSE of Case, I knew this would be our opportunity to create new dreams for our baby boy, so I needed to include everything in my grieving mama heart. We obviously chose to highlight educating people involved with or benefitting from BeCAUSE of Case on organ, eye and tissue donation.

BeCAUSE of Case Mission Statement

BeCAUSE of Case was created in honor of "Baby Case," our little angel in the outfield, and the positive impact he had on others in his four short months of life. We wish to inspire other people to live and give selflessly. We are committed to educating others about giving the gift of life through organ, eye, and tissue donation, supporting bereaved family members affected by infant loss, and helping high school baseball players realize their potential for greatness on and off the field.

I decided if we were going to award a scholarship in the Spring of 2020, a few months after Case had passed, then five hundred dollars would be a good starting point. I began working on a t-shirt fundraiser, securing company donations, creating a scholarship application, and outlining the recipient criteria. My husband worked hard advertising the scholarship to prospective applicants in his hometown of Brenham, Texas, and the high school where he coaches in Cypress, Texas. Our love and nurturing for BeCAUSE of Case paid off, literally, and I am proud to say that my tiny initial goal for Case's scholarship in year one was exceeded and then so much more. After the 2020 school year, we awarded six thousand dollars. Eight seniors, with plans to pursue higher education after high school graduation, applied for the BeCAUSE of Case Angel in the Outfield scholarship during the 2020 school year. Each applicant pledged to share Case's donor story and registered as an organ donor, if they weren't already.

Right after Case passed away, I began searching for understanding (which I don't think I'll ever find) and hope that I'll be reunited with my perfect boy again one day, and the only place that I've been able to find peace and comfort has been in God. I pray daily. I'm on pace to have read the bible in one year, which I will finish shortly after the one-year anniversary of Case's journey to Heaven. I've also finished six books about grief and child loss. One of the first books I read was titled *Safe in the Arms of God*, by John MacArthur. This book brought me an immense amount of comfort and hope as I sat reading it each night in the recliner where I used to rock Case to sleep. I knew if Case couldn't be in my arms, then who better to be holding him than Jesus himself. Although this doesn't take away the pain and grief of losing my turkey boy, it sparked some healing knowing my boy was safe in Heaven. It gave me hope that there's a greater purpose in Case's life than we could have ever imagined.

Since the foundation of BeCAUSE of Case in February 2020, I have delivered eighteen *Safe in the Arms of God* books to grieving mothers who have experienced miscarriage, stillbirth, or infant loss. Many of the mamas I've delivered books to I don't know personally. I've heard about their losses first hand, and also through friends or family members. I've also connected with grieving mothers through social media with the help of various hashtags like #grievingmother, #infantloss and #bereavedmothers. As everyone says, it's a club that no one wants to be a part of, but no one understands grief like that of bereaved parents. It's because Chris, Aria, and I have been blessed with continued love and support from God, friends, and family that I wanted to offer support to other families and mamas trying to survive such an unimaginable pain. So, each time I hear of a mother that has lost her child, I send her a book and pray that she finds peace and comfort knowing her baby is "safe in the arms of God", even if organ donation wasn't directly part of their journey.

Big Sister, Aria

Aria Kelm Andreas; my anchor baby. Because of Case, I'm intentionally trying to become a better person and a better Christian. But it's because of Aria that I'm able to get out of bed each day and keep going. I wouldn't be able to physically or mentally do anything following the passing of Case if it weren't for his big sister, Aria. Aria was two and a half when her brother went to Heaven, and if you think losing your child to be unimaginable, think of adding a bereaved sister that is toddler age to the grieving process. Trying to tend to her curiosity, her grief and her toddler energy in general. Aria has made each day since Case's passing bearable. She is the reason I can function. She is the reason I have survived these past seven months without Case and how I know I will continue to survive each and every day.

I may not know or understand God's plans for us, but I can't question the God that has blessed me with these two perfect babies. I know in my heart that God gave us Aria to help anchor me when the waves of grief from Case's passing come crashing over me. I've made it a priority to know Jesus better, and to make sure Aria knows just how much Jesus loves her and her brother. Every day, when I'm crying and sad, Aria tells me that everything is going to be okay, because her brother is in "Heaven with Jesus." The love this girl has, for her family, her baby brother, and God, is so pure. My, oh my, does Aria love her "baby Case." It is because of Aria and because of Case that I will continue to share the goodness of God and advocate for organ donation, so that they may know how good God is through the hope that organ donation offers so many people.

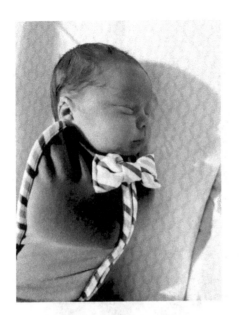

About Shannon

Chris and Shannon are the parents of an angel baby and tissue donor. Shannon and her husband Chris live in Cypress, Texas, with their daughter Aria, and are expecting Case's baby sister, Faith, to make her presence in March 2021. Shannon works as an educator supporting students and staff in the areas of classroom and behavior management in her hometown of Cypress. Chris is a special education teacher and high school baseball coach in Cypress. Case's scholarships are currently awarded to high school baseball players from Chris' hometown of Brenham, Texas, and the school he currently coaches at in Cypress.

Shannon became involved with organ donation when her four-month-old son, Case Michael Andreas, went peacefully to sleep and drifted off to Heaven. Case then became an angel organ donor and baby hero. We hope to one day contact the little girl who Case helped by giving the gift of life. Shannon and Chris are now Ambassadors of Hope with Life Gift and volunteer their time educating others about organ donation in memory of baby Case.

Because of organ donation, Shannon, with the support of her family and close friends, has created the BeCAUSE of Case Foundation. BeCAUSE of Case's mission includes educating people about eye, organ, and tissue donation; providing high school baseball players with scholarship money for continuing education; and lending support to bereaved families affected by miscarriage, stillbirth, and infant loss.

In her free time Shannon enjoys spending time with her husband, daughter, family, and friends, sharing memories of "baby Case," watching sports, and eating Tex-Mex. Shannon is a renewed Christian, having been baptized again with her husband two months after Case's passing. Shannon is an avid reader, choosing books that primarily share the word of God, hoping to provide continued peace and comfort that her son is in the safest place possible, in the arms of Jesus.

It thrills Shannon to collaborate with so many people that have been touched by organ donation. She has a passion for sharing Case's story and hopes that she is blessed with more opportunities to write about her son, God, her grief, and organ donation in the future. You may contact Shannon Andreas via email at becauseofcase@gmail.com.

Shannon would love to have you follow her family's journey about grief, love, organ donation, family, and Case. You can follow along on Instagram @srandreas. I've chosen to share all things BeCAUSE of Case on my personal accounts, so I can maintain that personal connection as his mama and keep him a part of our daily lives just as if he were here living with us Earth-side. If you would like to make a donation to BeCAUSE of Case in honor of our sweet boy, you can send funds via PayPal to becauseofcase@gmail.com. All donations received go directly to senior high school baseball players that commit to becoming registered organ donors and wish to pursue higher education upon graduation.

Sponsors

We would like to thank all the amazing supporters who helped make this book a reality for us. Your generosity means more than you all know! It is an honor to include you in this book.

If you can, please learn more about the organizations listed below, and support them if possible. They are all doing amazing work to Help Others With Love!

TRANSPLANT SUPPORT ORGANIZATION (TSO) SENDS ITS
THANKS TO EVERYONE WHO SUPPORTS ORGAN, EYE,
AND TISSUE REGISTRATION AND DONATION.

THIS LIFE SAVING AND LIFE AFFIRMING ACTIVITY
DEMONSTRATES THE HIGHEST REGARD OF PEOPLE
FOR EACH OTHER.

FOR MORE THAN 20 YEARS, TSO HAS SERVED THE NEEDS
OF THE TRANSPLANT PATIENT COMMUNITY

WITH PATIENT OUTREACH, EDUCATION,
MENTORING, AND SUPPORT.

TSO IS COMMITTED TO ALL EFFORTS TO ELIMINATE
THE TRANSPLANT WAITING LIST.

Ryan Robert Viator

Pasadena Rose Parade
Journeys of the Heart
Class of 2012-13

August 30, 1979
April 7, 2000

**Transplant Games
of America 2014**

Louisiana Organ Donor #3

Forever In Our Hearts and Will Love You Always

RYAN ROBERT VIATOR was a loving and tenderhearted young man with a great spirit of adventure and belief in staying healthly. At the age of 20, he was the proud owner of a local health club that inspired others to live healthy lifestyles. On April 7, 2000, Ryan's life ended, but three others were able to live thanks to the donation of Ryan's liver and kidneys. Ryan was never able to realize two of his dreams; flying in a fighter jet and visiting California. Donation made both possible, as one of his recipients is a retired Air Force pilot, and his image adorned the Donate Life float as a floragraph in the 2013 Rose Parade, representing Louisiana.

NKDO

National Kidney Donation Organization

National Kidney Donation Organization (NKDO) is the leading organization devoted to protecting the interests of the living donors and advocating for living kidney donation.

NKDO is a nationwide team of living donors and transplant recipients who advise and counsel prospective donors, and help patients in need of a transplant to find a living donor.

http://www.nkdo.org

http://www.facebook.com/TheNKDO

LiveOnNY
Foundation

LiveOnNY serves a population of 13 million people in the greater New York City area and its neighboring counties. But we don't do it alone. We are proud to partner with 11 transplant centers and nearly 100 hospitals to ensure that an individual's wishes to donate are honored and lives are saved

Facebook: https://www.facebook.com/
LiveOnNewYork

Twitter: https://twitter.com/LiveOnNewYork

Instagram: http://instagram.com/LiveOnNewYork

LinkedIn: https://www.linkedin.com/
company/76663/

Organ and Tissue Donation Saves Lives

Learn more at LiveOnNY.org

HEATHER MILLER MEMORIAL GOLF CLASSIC

"Here Comes The Sun"

Always the last
Friday in July
Heather Nicole Miller,
Donor, 8/7/86-3/31/08

Facebook
"Heather Miller Memorial"

Website:
heathermm.shutterfly.com

Jim Brien is celebrating 39 years with his kidney from his living donor brother, Jerry Brien. Jerry selflessly donated his kidney to Jim on June 23, 1982. Jim has been living life to the fullest ever since, with his gift of life. He competes in the Transplant Games of America, the World Transplant Games, and many other competitions. Running, biking and skiing are some of his favorites. Jim heads up Team Wisconsin for the Transplant Games of America, he is a member of the Quarter Century Club, he is a recipient of the Bounce Back Award in 2017 from the Chris Klug Foundation, and is a tireless advocate for organ donation awareness.

Glenda Daggert and Ira Copperman express their gratitude for everyone who supports the cause of organ, eye, and tissue donation and transplantation.

We applaud the efforts of the transplant community and all its professionals, for their commitment to donation.

We especially honor donors, living and deceased, as we celebrate the re-birthday miracle of 21 years.

Diane

Caitlin

Diane Kavanaugh received her Kidney Transplant on June 10, 2004, Living Donation from her Daughter Deb.

Caitlin Rosenbaum was a big advocate for Organ Donation and volunteered at many of the events for The National Kidney Foundation serving the Dakotas, Iowa and Nebraska.

THE TRANSPLANT JOURNEY, INC.

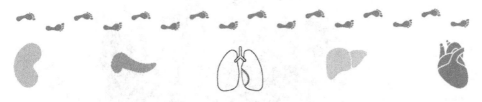

To provide compassionate "one-on-one" support to transplant mentees and their families rooted in the personal experience of transplant patients who have lived *The Journey*. The group works to turn patient and family frustrations, confusions, emotions and stress into strength through increased knowledge and access to credible and timely information with support throughout the complex journey.

Jen Benson, Founder/CEO   1-203-682-5890 (M)
Jbenson@transplantjourney.org / www.transplantjourney.org

One Breath Foundation is a 501(c)(3) non-profit organization.

Our mission is to assist patients who are diagnosed with a lung and/or other organ disease. Usually, these patients face financial hardships. One Breath Foundation assists those living with lung and/or other diseases, those waiting for a life-saving organ transplant, and post-transplant patients who are struggling with their recovery with restricted incomes.

In addition, we assist patients, caregivers, and their families overcome difficult times, by holding a monthly support group meeting, to educate and provide resources to prepare them for their journey.

CEO/President Terri Pilawa, 310.948.5397
terri@onebreathfoundation.org
onebreathfoundation.org
P.O. Box 1101, Covina, CA 91722
Secretary: Tish Trevino
Treasurer: Elissa Casper.

"Because every breath matters"

I'd like to dedicate my chapter to my Bloom Besties Tana, Bianca (holding Miss Avery Cade) Lindsey, and Holly!
Thank you for supporting me throughout my Donation Journey!!
~Kate Griggs

My son and best friend, Andrew, who helped take care of me after I donated.

This is David, the man I originally tested for who received a kidney from another donor. Had it not been for reading David's story on the news, I probably wouldn't have donated my kidney at that point in my life.

Because Of Organ Donation David was blessed to marry his beautiful wife, Taryn. Their son, Caleb Charles, was born on March 1, 2021, five years after his father's kidney transplant.

My husband, Allen, was, and will always be, my biggest supporter of donating my kidney.

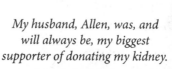

My heroes didn't wear capes,
they simply went by mom and dad.
My mom, Debra A. Petrie was the most caring and
compassionate person. For the first part of my life it was
her and I against the world. She would do anything to
help her little girl out! Unfortunately, I lost my best friend
to lung cancer back in 2008.

When my dad passed away on 9/17/2012, I found out that
he had signed up to be a hero. He was able to help over
75 people with his generous donation. Frank J. Rydzik Jr.
would give the shirt off his back! He thrived at teaching
people new things and loved his family unconditionally!
To say I'm lost without them is an understatement.

I will always be Daddy's little girl and Mama's world!
Love- Kasey Nicole Schmitz

Thank you to all the donors and donor families out there,
and a special thank you to our kidney donor,
Mary Kay "Auntie KK" Diderrich.
Thanks for Leftski!
With all our love to you, Rick, Emmy, and Elly
- Mike, Angela, Liam Timothy MK, and Shaydon MK Nicloy

Thanks to Brenda Cortez for your organ gift,
and for bringing all of these people together
to make this book happen.
Be like Brenda: SHARE YOUR SPARE!

The "One Kidney Club of the Dakotas, Iowa and Nebraska" provides support to other Living Kidney Donors, Advocates for Living Kidney Donation, Encourages Potential Donors to Take the Leap, as well as, Assistance/Support to The National Kidney Foundation Serving the Dakotas, and Iowa-Nebraska.

The National Kidney Foundation - Fueled by passion and urgency, NKF is a lifeline for all people affected by kidney disease. As pioneers of scientific research and innovation, NKF focuses on the whole patient through the lens of kidney health. Relentless in our work, we enhance lives through action, education, and accelerating change.

<u>**Living Donors of the "One Kidney Club of the Dakotas, Iowa and Nebraska"**</u>

(SD): Deb Kavanaugh – Direct Donated, June 10, 2004 to my mom Diane.

"I encourage anyone thinking about becoming a living donor to do it."

Marian Redlin-Reitt – Direct Donated, October 22, 2002 to my nephew.

Samantha Jensen – Non-Directed Donation, June 20, 2019.

"If I could do it again I would."

Lorna Hofer – Direct Donated, May 13, 2019 to Ashley Heinz.

Jeaneen McLaren – Donated, August 1, 2018, a 14-person chain to Mitchell McLaren.

Pam Gutzler Coffman – Donated, May 28, 2020 through the Donor Exchange Program so that her Intended Recipient, Jack Alexander, could receive his kidney.

"Jack is doing terrific and thinking about all the people we helped makes me feel great."

Stacy Krall – Direct Donated, April 12, 2017 to Jeff Spain.

(ND): Jeff Botnen – Non-Directed Donation, January 26, 2007 to Paul Berrisford.

"One of the Greatest Experiences of My Life."

Danielle Scherr – Direct Donated, May 18, 2020 to her dad, Bruce Scheie.

(IA): Colleen Hjort – Direct Donated, March 25, 2014 to her cousin Debbie.

Leslie Day – Direct Donated, September 14, 2016 to Katherine Dostart-Drahos.

Meredith Davies-Vogt – Non-Directed Donation, June 2020 through a chain.

"I am happy that my recipient is living his new life to the fullest."

"Tough Times Don't Last but Tough People Do"

My family knows Paul Osterholm is an angel sent
from God. He has forever changed my
sister Nicole's life by being her kidney donor.
We can never thank him enough.
~April Bousqet

A **HERO** is someone who has given his or her life to something bigger than oneself.
-Joseph Campbell

Honoring the legacy of a hero.....Always be kind....
#EMSTRONG....Donation saves lives and spirits!
~Dan Sauer

Rich Warns, husband, father,
best friend, and donor hero -
Helped others by leaving his
precious eyes, bone, tissue,
and muscle to improve
the lives of thousands –
5/12/2017.
Always and forever my
soulmate.

In honor and loving memory of Emily Christine Lyons. Thank you to the "tribe," the family and friends that make up team #emstrong. We are forever blessed.

CENTRAL WISCONSIN
GIFT OF LIFE DONATE

"Supporting Organ and Tissue Donors, Recipients and Donor Families throughout Central Wisconsin and beyond"

#DonateLife

"Be A Hero, Be An Organ Donor

Grateful Transplant Recipient

How do you thank someone who gave you your life back? After pondering this question for 16 years I have come to the conclusion...you can't. There are not enough words in the English dictionary to properly express the depth of my appreciation. You see, I was waiting on a liver transplant when I got the call. A young woman had died in an accident and I was chosen to receive her liver. I never met the lady who made the biggest difference in my life, but I will be forever thankful to this angel, Andrea Rea Dominguz, and her family, Ricardo & Ophelia Dominguz, for the gift of life!!! Andrea saved 8 people and helped countless others....

~ Pam Westbrook

Transplant
Families

Are you the parent of a transplant child? So are we! Our mission is to unite families like ours by providing support, resources, and education. Join us today *https://transplantfamilies.org* or *contact@transplantfamilies.org*

Live. L♥ove. D♥nate.

Live.Love.Donate. Inc. is a Wisconsin family-run nonprofit saving lives through organ donation education and advocacy efforts. Our dad experienced two life-saving gifts; one from a deceased kidney donor, and one from our mom, Amy, as a living kidney donor. We are passionate about the cause and work tirelessly to share our family story, reduce the number of patients on the waiting list, and register more organ donors. In honor, and loving memory, of our dad, Steve. We love you and miss you. *livelovedonate.com*

Briar, organ donor, February 14, 2014
Briar's family and friends,
thank you for sharing your memories
with us and allowing us to know,
through you, the very special boy that
gave Hailey the Gift of Life.
Hailey may share Briar's heart, but it
is evident to us that he lives on in the
many lives that he touched.
Love,
The Steimel Family

Dedicated in loving memory of Vivian Meitzler, sister and best friend of Jean Sime who received her life-saving kidney transplant from her selfless living donor Patricia Milford on 06/25/2019.
We all love you Viv and miss you so much.

Love, your loving husband Timothy, your son Steven, and your kitty Becker…

Forever in our hearts♥

For my wife Jean Sime. I am so very proud of you for handling all of life's challenges you have faced. Through it all you have stayed kind, caring, generous and inspiring to so many including me.

Thank you to Pat Milford for saving my wife's life with your selfless gift of life on 06/25/2019. Thank you for giving us our life back!

Jeanie, I will love you forever, always, and a day.
Love, your husband Eric W. Sime

Inlovingmemory19 is a safe caring community for those who have lost loved ones to COVID. The support group is about knowing you are not alone.
Inlovingmemory19.com
We are in this together.

Bari Himes, Founder

LONG ISLAND TRIO
TRANSPLANT
RECIPIENTS
INTERNATIONAL
ORGANIZATION

LI TRIO is a non-profit all volunteer organization committed to improving the quality of lives touched by the miracle of transplantation through education, support, advocacy, and organ donation and transplantation awareness.
Read more at: https://litrio.org/

TRIO – Long Island Chapter PO Box 81 Garden City, NY 11530
litrio.org Hotline 516-620-5900

Thank you to all the selfless and incredibly heroic donors for giving miracles to these recipients. Your kindness and generosity are great examples to all of us.
Good health is wished to all! - DJV

STEVE BELCHER – Author of *How to Survive Outpatient Hemodialysis: A Guide for Patients with Kidney Failure*
Websites: https://stevenlbelcher.com, www.urbankidneyalliance.org
Facebook Page: Steve The Kidney Nurse; Instagram: @stevethekidneynurse

You have made us all proud with joy Trisha Phillips! Love; Canesia, Tia, Tonya, and Caprisha. And smiling down from Heaven; Columbus (Dad), Ruth (Mom), Charlotte (Sister), and Elmeaty (Grandmother).

A proud supporter of Organ Donation and Sponsor of the "Kidney Awareness Show" Hosted by Trish Phillips. All the best, Darcy Jackson Roofing and Waterproofing, staff, management, and family.

This is dedicated to Jean Sime, kidney recipient, and all the amazing kidney warriors. Love, Donna Tissot – Kidney Advocate.

BeCAUSE of Case was created in honor of "Baby Case," our little angel in the outfield, and the positive impact he had on others in his four short months of life. We wish to inspire other people to live and give selflessly. ~Shannon & Chris Andreas

Love Life – Family | Live Life – Flying | Donate Life – Friends Our Kidney Transplant Story Cheers from the Hanusa/W and Sweeney/Schuerman Family

Mary Pat DiPippa, kidney donor, 08/22/2016. Much love to my kidney family: Lenny, Tony, Nicole, Kari and Denise; and to my biggest donation supporters my hubby Rob, my daughter Holly, and my late sister Deb... I Love You!

Pamela Locke - Atlanta, GA, kidney recipient, 1/31/2011, from living kidney donor, Laurie Collins - Brooklyn, NY. Thank you to my amazing friend, Cindy Shultz Comstock, for helping make the gift of life possible!

Every donor is a life saver...Will Borenius, living kidney donor to Victor Cirrigione, recipient on 08/22/2019, a perfect match. Our family is blessed forever and grateful...JUST BREATHE...

Jerry Ray Jr. - received a double lung and a kidney transplant at St. Luke's on 12/2/16, and pancreas transplant on 10/1/19 at Methodist Hospital in Houston, Texas. Forever grateful.

Pauline Ames, Liver Transplant Recipient, January 16, 2016.

Valerie Wood. Dedicated mom and my best friend. Radiant smile
and generous soul. Donor hero who saved many.

Bill Simmons, Heart Transplant Recipient, February 12, 2013.

To our Dad-Michael Breese (Recipient).
with Love-Jennifer, Sarah, Benjamin & Samuel

Mary Trizila/Shared Her Spare & Ryan Renfro/Forever Grateful, 11/14/2018.

Congratulations Nick Sauter on your gift of life. Love, Donna

Love, Respect & Gratitude to the Respiratory Care Profession
& all Organ Donors. -Sarah Schroeder, RRT

The best person I never knew, Courtney, who gave her HEART ~ Tony Triola

Patricia Milford, kidney donor, 06/25/19.
Wishing good health to all donors and recipients

Nick Sauter, Kidney Recipient, Rob Connizzo, Donor, February 12, 2019.

In loving memory of my mom Maria Da Gloria Branco.
- Love, your son Jose Branco

Lin family- supporting Jean Sime and Brenda E. Cortez.

In memory of David Lyons, known to many as "Uncle Dave", the dearest
friend to whomever he met, our donor hero. Forever loved and missed.

Briggs Elliser, our miracle and blessing! Love you Briggs, Aunt Susan Kolb.

Blessed by donors who chose to say yes to organ donation, Briggs Elliser, our three time liver recipient and blessing! Love you Briggs, MawMawMawMaw.

Marian Redlin-Reit - Living Kidney Donor - October 22nd, 2002.

In memory of my donor ~ liver and kidney recipient, Amy Whitney, September 29, 2019.

In honor of my caregiver ~ Fran Allen ~ my mother always by my side.

Laura Allton, living kidney donor, July 23, 2014.

"A son's first hero." Andrew and Bryce Mullett, 8/7/2018.

Verna Johnson, Kidney Transplant Recipient, Date October 24, 2019.

Karma Inc Apparel- We donate a portion of every purchase.
- karmaincapparel.org

Maria Teresa Pilawa double lung transplant recipient 6/24/2015 and tissue recipient 11/18/2020.

Kidney Donor, Trish Phillips; Recipient, Kimberly Bennett, December 15, 2016.

Congratulations Ms. Trish Phillips! Thanks for being a great General Manager. The Radio Station DJs of WEXY

Etta McDonald, Living Kidney Donor to Jim McDonald on 02/28/2008.

Anne Runkle, Non-Direct Kidney Donor, 10/30/2019.

Jocelynn James Edmonds, living kidney donor
to Terelle Potter on July 21, 2020.

Thankful for my friend Jean Sime's kidney transplant on 06/25/2019.
- Love Jean Sadek

Joyce Johnson supporting her BFF Jean Sime, Kidney Recipient, 06/25/19.

In loving memory of Carmelina Cabanillas- your family misses you.

Nicholas J. Best, Dover Fire Fighter for 28 years-Organ Donor July 2010- RIP
- Judy Campione.

Dedicated to my friend and coworker Jean Sime, kidney recipient.
- Love, Nadia Post

Forever grateful to Mindy for my kidney Zoe-Love Jill 07/12/2019.

Dawn Cerruto-Kirkowski, Kidney transplant recipient 09/06/2000.
Thank you to my donor family!

Honoring Steve Hill and our transplant sisters, Pat and Jean 06/25/2019.
- Melissa Hancsin

Judy and Don Zimmerman, in loving memory of granddaughter of
Emily Christine Lyons.

Joanne Lyons, proud grandparent of Emily C Lyons.

Ned and Donna Wood, donor grandparents of Emily Lyons.

Cori McBride, deceased teen organ donor, July 12, 2017.

Brody "B" Austin – Lived as Superman and left a superhero's legacy,
05/06/95-04/26/15.

Jill and Katie Schmidt-Hahn, Aunts of donor Emily C Lyons, #emstrong.

Lisa Goodrich, Angel on earth promoting Emily Lyons'
legacy of kindness daily.

Elle, Doug, and Lexi Callies, in memory of Emily C Lyons,
forever is she who brings love.

Cheryl Stedman, kidney recipient, amazing human being,
and beautiful spirit.

Donna Endres and Denise Jumes, loving donor aunts of
Emily Christine Lyons.

Curt and Marcy Jackson, aunt and uncle of Emily Lyons.

Jim and Chris Braemer, in honor of our beloved Emily C Lyons,
who continues to lead by shining example forever.

Proud Lyons Family Aunts and Uncles of Emily C Lyons,
Go to it with Confidence Fightingly Relaxed.

CPSIA information can be obtained
at www.ICGtesting.com
Printed in the USA
JSHW021753160421
13600JS00003B/8